Credit Portfolio Management

Global Financial Markets series

Global Financial Markets is a series of practical guides to the latest financial market tools, techniques and strategies. Written for practitioners across a range of disciplines it provides comprehensive but practical coverage of key topics in finance covering strategy, markets, financial products, tools and techniques and their implementation. This series will appeal to a broad readership, from new entrants to experienced practitioners across the financial services industry, including areas such as institutional investment; financial derivatives; investment strategy; private banking; risk management; corporate finance and M&A, financial accounting and governance, and many more.

Titles include:

Daniel Capocci
THE COMPLETE GUIDE TO HEDGE FUNDS AND HEDGE FUND STRATEGIES

Guy Fraser-Sampson
INTELLIGENT INVESTING
A Guide to the Practical and Behavioural Aspects of Investment Strategy

Michael Hünseler
CREDIT PORTFOLIO MANAGEMENT
A Practitioner's Guide to the Active Management of Credit Risks

Ross K. McGill
US WITHHOLDING TAX
Practical Implications of QI and FATCA

David Murphy
OTC DERIVATIVES, BILATERAL TRADING AND CENTRAL CLEARING
An Introduction to Regulatory Policy, Trading Impact and Systemic Risk

Gianluca Oricchio
PRIVATE COMPANY VALUATION
How Credit Risk Reshaped Equity Markets and Corporate Finance Valuation Tools

Andrew Sutherland and Jason Court
THE FRONT OFFICE MANUAL
The Definitive Guide to Trading, Structuring and Sales

Michael C. S. Wong and Wilson F. C. Chan (*editors*)
INVESTING IN ASIAN OFFSHORE CURRENCY MARKETS
The Shift from Dollars to Renminbi

Global Financial Markets series
Series Standing Order ISBN: 978–1137–32734–5

You can receive future titles in this series as they are published by placing a standing order. Please contact your bookseller or, in case of difficulty, write to us at the address below with your name and address, the title of the series and the ISBN quoted above.

Customer Services Department, Macmillan Distribution Ltd, Houndmills, Basingstoke, Hampshire RG21 6XS, England

---

Credit Portfolio Management

A Practitioner's Guide to the Active Management of Credit Risks

Michael Hünseler
Managing Director, Assenagon Asset Management S.A.

palgrave
macmillan

First published 2013 by
PALGRAVE MACMILLAN

Palgrave Macmillan in the UK is an imprint of Macmillan Publishers Limited, registered in England, company number 785998, of Houndmills, Basingstoke, Hampshire RG21 6XS.

Palgrave Macmillan in the US is a division of St Martin's Press LLC, 175 Fifth Avenue, New York, NY 10010.

Palgrave Macmillan is the global academic imprint of the above companies and has companies and representatives throughout the world.

Palgrave® and Macmillan® are registered trademarks in the United States, the United Kingdom, Europe and other countries

ISBN: 978–0–230–39149–9

This book is printed on paper suitable for recycling and made from fully managed and sustained forest sources. Logging, pulping and manufacturing processes are expected to conform to the environmental regulations of the country of origin.

A catalogue record for this book is available from the British Library.

A catalog record for this book is available from the Library of Congress.

To my family, Susi and Emmi, who are an inspiration beyond and above any words to me. With their patience, encouragement and trust, nothing seems impossible.

Contents

List of Tables

List of Figures

Foreword

The sound management of credit portfolios should be a core competency of banks. Even with the growth in complexity of financial services and instruments in recent years, providing credit through lending remains one of the essential functions of banks. Over the years, we have seen great examples of banks that do this well. Unfortunately, we have also seen the opposite.

Just in the course of my own career, there have been a number of crises, all linked to credit risk and credit portfolios, that have threatened or ended the existence of many an institution. As I write this, the world's financial institutions are grappling with European countries that are having trouble repaying their debts. This current crisis began to grow even as the previous one, which had U.S. subprime lending at its core, was still resolving. About a decade ago, we had a credit crisis centred on accounting irregularities at large corporate borrowers (Enron, Worldcom, Parmalat). Before that, there were crises driven by Russian debt, U.S. commercial real estate, Latin American debt – the list goes on. Credit portfolio losses remain the primary reason banks get into trouble, so we must strive to get better at this discipline. Fortunately, many practitioners have been doing just that.

The modern approach to managing credit portfolios is a relatively new field. During most of the history of banking, banks managed credit in a straightforward but old-fashioned way. They assessed individual borrowers and decided whether or not to grant a loan, and if they did, they held the loan until the borrower either repaid it or defaulted.

A new approach developed when credit practitioners began to understand that there are really two distinct businesses underlying credit. There's the business of creating loans (origination), and there's the business of holding a portfolio of credit assets. Different competencies drive the success of each.

Consider what would make a firm excel at the business of origination. It would need expertise in the industries in which it wanted to lend. It would need specialized knowledge and relationships with firms in that sector. For example, if a firm wanted to be a major lender to the telecommunications sector, it would need to understand that business and its financing needs, and it would need to have and cultivate relationships with the CFOs and treasurers of the companies in that sector. Bankers would have an incentive to originate larger loans, as loan size is a stronger driver of revenue than of non-interest expense.

If a firm were successful at the business of origination, consider the type of credit portfolio that would result from its achievements: one that was concentrated in the names and industries where it had the most success. This is exactly the type of portfolio that a firm doesn't want if it wants to be successful at the business of owning credit portfolios, because in the portfolio business, you want credit assets that are diversified across industries and geographies and that minimize single name concentrations.

More active approaches to managing credit portfolios evolved to reconcile these two businesses, so that the business of holding a portfolio wasn't just passively driven by the business of origination. This practice began with the largest banks but was quickly adopted by others that needed to manage concentrations. It shouldn't be a surprise, for example, that Canadian and Australian banks, which have naturally concentrated customer bases in a limited number of industries, were some of the earliest adopters of more active approaches to credit portfolio management. In recent years, these practices have spread around the globe.

The modern credit portfolio management approach is challenging in that it is a multidisciplinary endeavour. To do it well, you need many skills and tools.

To start with, you need a good foundation in traditional credit analysis – the fundamental quantitative and qualitative assessment of individual borrowers that is at the base of lending decisions. However, the nature of portfolios of credit risk, with their asymmetric distributions and 'fat tails', requires a deeper understanding beyond that of individual credits. You need the analytical knowledge and tools, developed in the last several decades, that focus on identifying and measuring diversification, concentration, risk and return in credit portfolios.

Once you have measured and understood the risk that you hold, you must also have the ability to take action to manage it. When originating the credit, you have to apply credit limits, which emerge from strategic decisions about a firm's risk appetite. Portfolio perspectives, either qualitative or quantitative, can also be incorporated into the origination process to complement the individual credit decision. Loan transfer pricing is one of several ways to approach this. Once a credit is in the portfolio, you must also have an understanding of the capital markets tools used to adjust and manage that exposure dynamically as the world changes. These range from guarantees and loan participations to credit default swaps, structured credit and securitizations, and other modern instruments for risk transfer and mitigation.

The list of requirements doesn't end there, however. You need to have practical knowledge of the organizational structures and processes that allow a firm to implement credit portfolio management and the ability to manage the very human activity of changing business tactics. Then there are the rules imposed by accounting and regulation; they must be understood and accommodated as well.

There is a lot to master in order to implement credit portfolio management well. Perhaps as a result, there are very few books on the totality of the subject. Certainly, there are many works that cover one or more subtopics effectively and in detail, but few that cover the entire scope of knowledge that you need for credit portfolio management in an integrated way.

I am grateful to Michael Hünseler for writing such a book (the one you are now reading); it is a good one, covering the breadth of topics one needs to understand as a credit portfolio manager. Michael is well positioned to provide a standard reference book on the subject. Since I have known him, he has demonstrated that he is a thoughtful implementer of these strategies and has developed practical and creative solutions to difficult problems in the field. I have been very happy to have him contribute to the industry association for credit portfolio practitioners that I lead.

I hope that this book will be a useful reference for practitioners in our field, so that they are effective in their day-to-day work. Good credit portfolio management is the foundation for good banks, and as we have seen, the world can certainly use more of these.

Som-lok Leung
Executive Director
International Association of Credit Portfolio Managers
New York

Preface

Several years ago, the concept of active credit portfolio management (ACPM) was introduced at a large European financial institution with the aim of improving both origination pricing discipline and the risk metrics of a portfolio of multinational corporate loans. Shortly after a methodology was established for pricing loans consistent with credit spreads observable in capital markets, a senior commercial banker raised the question of why the transfer price for an undrawn backup facility was so negative. The banker argued that such lines are inherently risk-free in nature because (a) they have never been drawn in the past, (b) their only purpose is to please the rating agencies, (c) if the company did draw under the line, this would be perceived by markets as a very negative signal, thus preventing the company from doing so even if it felt tempted, and – most importantly – (d) if the company got into trouble, he, the banker, would be the first to know because of his closeness to the company. On the other hand, the relationship manager concluded, there was some income from the commitment fee, which allowed a few salaries to be paid even though the bank did not take any risk. In any case, the gap between market spreads and loan income, evidenced by the transfer price, had no relevance, and there would be no way to cover it through revenues from ancillary business. He did not have to wait for the financial crisis to prove him wrong. When credit spreads started to increase in 2008, one of his corporate clients broke the taboo and fully drew the committed line, only to invest the proceeds in higher-yielding assets. This might have been seen as exceptional and inappropriate behaviour by the customer. But then came the financial crisis, bringing to an end the discussion about whether committed but undrawn lines are risk-free or not. In addition to the erosion of capital by losses from credit and market risks, a major threat to banks when the crisis hit was exactly the liquidity drain caused by the banks' customers drawing on their granted lines. As the crisis unfolded, corporates were quick to react to the looming credit crunch, either as a precautionary measure or because of a drop in their own liquidity. Unfortunately, the crisis did no favours to many credit portfolio managers either. Although portfolio management aims at protecting the bank from serious threats such as tail risks, it often did not live up to expectations. Portfolio managers suddenly had to deal with a variety of problems which, at least partly, were known in advance but seen as acceptable given the high-level objective of making the bank a better place. Overconfidence in model results, basis risks from derivative hedges versus bond investments, failed securitizations, the introduction of significant mark-to-market volatility through hedges and an isolated view of credit which missed the connectivity of risks, to name but a few, did not help to provide comfort at the top management level of any financial institution. The underestimated market volatility, the massive economic downturn and the substantially reduced liquidity in financial markets came together in a perfect storm to shake the financial industry in an unprecedented manner, with the fallout still weighing on corporates, banks and sovereigns alike. However, while all portfolio managers had to cope with extreme credit market conditions, there were some which did better and managed to hold the course. Others, especially those with a lower level of management support, are struggling to find their new place. The hostile environment, developing from a subprime to a financial to a sovereign debt crisis, clearly forces financial institutions to find appropriate solutions to manage risks, as do regulators, stakeholders, rating agencies and, of course, the public. The social costs imposed by those banks that failed are immense and have led to a significant loss of faith in banks. However, the fundamental technical expertise required has increased significantly in recent years. Numerous mathematicians and physicians have opened the field to scientific research. Enough historical time series are available, with the significantly improved data quality and quantity essential for credit risk quantification and model validation. Mass data storage and computational power have become much more affordable. Portfolio models are ever more sophisticated. Notwithstanding the growing emphasis on models, we are now much more aware of the fact that there are limits to our ability to anticipate the future. Even if we manage to accurately forecast the data which are input into our models – and that was never the case – there is still a level of uncertainty in correctly assessing the implications of those events. Models help in making educated decisions, but judgement and experience are not substitutable and should be the drivers of a conscious strategy that considers risk, return and capital.

The objective of this book is to provide practical guidance on the management of credit risk in a holistic way, based on experience gained before and during the years of financial turmoil. It is structured along the lines of the credit value chain. Part I deals with the definition of the credit risk strategy that serves as a map, a frame and a filter for business flow. Derived from the available capital, the strategy is expressed in terms of risk limits and targets, thereby addressing concentration risks, which are a major source of concern for financial institutions. Stress tests aim at raising awareness of the potential consequences of adverse developments in those markets in which the institution operates. In Part II, conceptual aspects of ACPM are discussed. This discussion ranges from the description of the value proposition to a full credit cycle approach to portfolio management. Since in most organizations a loan transfer pricing scheme underpins the internal role of ACPM to optimize the risk *and* the return side of the credit portfolio, it is given some consideration. Acknowledging that there is no one-size-fits-all model, we review practical aspects of the implementation of ACPM. A chapter on the accounting symmetry of credit derivative hedges and loans outlines solutions to an issue which creates major headaches for many portfolio managers. More often than not, a key objective of portfolio management is regulatory capital relief, which is discussed in detail. Part III focuses on the back-end management of a credit portfolio. Corrective actions are usually carried out using credit default swaps. However, the devil is in the detail, and the near accident of the Greek sovereign debt credit event raised serious concerns about this instrument's effectiveness. The text therefore provides a non-technical, in-depth description of the main features of this product of choice for credit risk transfer. A chapter on complementary hedging instruments such as loan CDSs and subparticipations adds to the discussion of the toolbox of a portfolio manager. Finally, hedge strategies, linear and non-linear, are considered. Many case studies are provided to illustrate these topics, using real-life examples to highlight the issues and make the text livelier.

Acknowledgements

My very special thanks go to Erik Banks and Dr Dirk Schubert for invaluable advice and support. I also thank Palgrave Macmillan for the patience and guidance offered to me. A big thank you goes to Rüdiger Rohner for sharing his enthusiasm and expertise.

During the past decades, I have had the privilege of working with some of the best practitioners in credit portfolio management, risk management and financial research. Friends and colleagues at Assenagon, the IACPM, HVB/UniCredit, Deka Investment and elsewhere were tireless in their efforts to teach me the essentials of credit risk. I am grateful for their friendship and the deep knowledge they made available to me.

List of Abbreviations

ABS	asset backed security
ACPM	active credit portfolio management
ATM	at-the-money
BCBS	Basel Committee on Banking Supervision
BIS	Bank for International Settlements
bps	basis points
BRIC	Brazil, Russia, India and China
CAC	collective action clause
CAD	Canadian dollar
CBOE	Chicago Board Options Exchange
CDO	collateralized debt obligation
CDS	credit default swap
CEBS	Committee of European Banking Supervisors
CEEMEA	Central & Eastern Europe, Middle East, Africa
CEO	chief executive officer
CFO	chief financial officer
CHF	Swiss franc
CLN	credit linked notes
CLO	collateralized loan obligation
CPM	credit portfolio management
CRD	capital requirements directive
CRM	credit risk mitigation
CRO	chief risk officer
CSO	collateralized synthetic debt obligation
CVA	credit valuation adjustment
DC	Determinations Committee
DCF	discounted cash flow
DKK	Danish krone
DTCC	Depository Trust & Clearing Corporation
EAD	exposure at default
EBA	European Banking Authority
EC	economic capital
ECB	European Central Bank
EL	expected loss
EST	eastern standard time
EUR	euro
EWS	early warning system

FASB	Financial Accounting Standards Board
FG	financial guarantee
FtD	first-to-default
FVO	fair value option
FX	foreign exchange
GBP	British pound
GSE	government-sponsored enterprise
HACR	hedge accounting for credit risk
HHI	Herfindahl-Hirschmann Index
HY	high yield
ICAAP	internal capital adequacy assessment process
IFRS	international financial reporting standards
IG	investment grade
IMF	International Monetary Fund
IMM	inside market midpoint
IR	interest rate
IRB	internal ratings-based approach
IRS	interest rate swap
ISDA	International Swaps and Derivatives Association
ITM	in-the-money
JPY	Japanese yen
M&A	mergers and acquisitions
MIR	market implied rating
MtM	mark-to-market
NIG	non-investment grade
NOPS	notice of physical settlement
LBO	leveraged buyout
LCDS	loan credit default swap
LDN	London
LGD	loss given default
LLP	loan loss provision
LTRO	long-term refinancing operations
OECD	Organisation for Economic Co-operation and Development
OTC	over the counter
OTM	out-of-the-money
P&L	profit and loss
PD	probability of default
PSE	public sector entity
PSI	private sector initiative
RCF	revolving credit facilities
RWA	risk weighted asset
SNAC	Standard North American Contract

STEC	Standard European Contract
TRS	total return swap
UL	unexpected loss
VaR	value at risk
WACC	weighted average cost of capital

Part I

Charting the Course – Credit Risk Strategies

The intense challenges for financial institutions arising from the ongoing difficult market conditions call for a systematic, proactive, and sustainable approach to credit risk management. Public perception of the value that banks contribute to society has been shaken, and the community needs to restore confidence. Ever more demanding regulators push banks to measure, manage, and monitor their risks in a prudent and consistent way, with the objective being to safeguard a firm's capital adequacy. A comprehensive framework for taking acceptable risks, risk appetite and derived credit risk strategies aims at a coordinated and stringent approach to risks. Since the transformation of traditional banking into a credit risk structuring and distribution approach has been effectively reversed, emphasis is again put on sound credit risk origination, management, and control processes in order to meet stakeholder expectations and to guarantee the bank's future. Part I of this book describes the framework in which credit risk is originated and managed. It is composed of three chapters: the first provides a brief description of the role that credit risk played in the financial crisis and thereafter; the second deals with the credit risk strategies which aim at optimizing the risk/return profile of the portfolio under the condition of adequate capital; and the third provides an introduction to stress tests, targeting a proactive and forward-looking approach to portfolio management by letting the improbable become quantifiable.

1
The Case for Credit Portfolio Management

The unprecedented dynamics of credit markets, as well as reinforced regulatory and shareholder pressure, have required banks to reassess their conventional methods of transacting business, often leaving them in protracted transition phase. With investors again in search of yield enhancements and portfolio managers in need of hedging and return on capital improvement, a new equilibrium with generally lower liquidity but improved transparency and counterparty risk management seems to have been found. Additionally, the formerly distinct loan, corporate bond and credit derivative markets increasingly have merged as alternative sources for acquiring credit risk and for refinancing, serving the needs of both investors and borrowers. A record-setting new issuance of corporate bonds in 2010, 2011, and again in 2012 bears witness to the decision of corporate treasurers to prefer reliability of available funds to flexibility in terms and conditions that only loans offer. As a Bloomberg article[1] noted, the amount that firms borrowed in the form of syndicated loans and credit lines fell by a hefty 13 per cent for the U.S. and 25 per cent for Europe in 2012 compared with same period in 2011, while corporate bond issues in Europe now account for 52 per cent of the €467 bn total new funding volume, overtaking loans for the first time in history. This is certainly also due to the increased reluctance of banks to provide sufficient liquidity to corporates when they needed it the most during the financial crisis. On the other hand, with some banks having to turn to central banks for last-resort lending, the traditional monetary supply transmission mechanism appears to have been disturbed. Consequently, an integrated approach to credit and liquidity risk management has become one of the major objectives of portfolio management at financial

[1] See Bloomberg, 'Libor Scandal Threatening to Turn Companies Off Syndicated Loans', July 10, 2012.

institutions. While the details of Basel III and Solvency II were still under development, banks started to anticipate the rules, with effects already being felt. Standard and Poor's predicts that Eurozone corporates will bear the brunt of additional debt costs when borrowing from banks, with estimates ranging from €30 bn to €50 bn per year, when the new regulations are fully implemented in 2018.[2] Regardless of how accurate Standard and Poor's prediction of the rise of the cost of debt is, the cornerstones of Basel III will very likely lead to more restrictive lending and in particular will make certain credit products economically less attractive. For instance, banks, will have to put in place capital and liquidity to back up credit commitments, even when those loans remain undrawn, and are likely to pass on the extra costs to their clients wherever possible. Corporate treasurers will have no choice but to pay the price. In turn, they will be expected to increasingly tap financial markets for funding. Banks may find a new niche in advising those clients that are seeking alternative sources of funds, thereby leveraging their role as the borrower's 'agent', with the lending relationship serving as a kind of certification of creditworthiness for other capital market investors.[3]

While the prospects for the debt capital markets business appear to be rosier, those for proprietary and non-proprietary trading are not as bright. Significant additional capital charges for over-the-counter derivatives will eat up a reasonable chunk of the return on equity for trading, with possibly pronounced negative implications for the liquidity of secondary markets for debt securities and derivatives. The round trip of investor-initiated trades, which usually ends up in one of the bulge bracket investment banks before finally being passed on to another investor at a later point, may have seen its best time. All these have changed the landscape in which portfolio managers operate. They may respond by reviving credit risk mitigation techniques other than credit derivatives; i.e. guarantees or subparticipations, to fine-tune their credit portfolios. At the same time, European corporate debt pricing will probably soar when Europe's market catches up with its U.S. counterpart, which still accounts for a dominant share of the global corporate bond market. In addition, the concerns about European sovereign indebtedness currently contribute to a hefty increase in risk premiums. As a consequence, if the gap between loan margins and hedge costs widens further, it is increasingly unlikely to be closed by client revenues generated from cross-selling. However, not

[2] Standard and Poor's (2011a).

[3] The concept of a loan as an implicit creditworthiness certificate for corporates issuing debt at public debt markets is described in Chapter 4.3, 'Bridging distinct worlds: Loans, bonds and credit derivatives'.

only will the convergence of bank loans and debt capital market instruments create feedback loops for the pricing of loans; the connectivity of credit risk prices will also enhance the ability to value credit instruments based on markets' risk premiums, even though client-relationship managers, for obvious reasons, tend to dismiss profitability measures based on shadow prices derived from financial markets. A cross-debt-asset-classes strategy permits dynamic credit portfolio management by adopting an asset manager–like approach. Determining relative value and deriving the optimal portfolio composition even for less liquid credit risks may sound challenging, but it is a unique advantage that integrated credit markets offer – and implicitly underpins the role of active credit portfolio management for a bank.

1.1 Evolution and innovation: Ups and downs of credit

Credit risks remain the dominant challenge for both regulators and risk managers. The regulatory framework for credit risk has been in continuous revision mode since it was introduced in 1988. According to the Financial Times, financial services companies were confronted with an average of 60 regulatory changes every working day in 2011.[4] The Dodd-Frank Reform Act and Basel III contain numerous initiatives, but international and domestic responses to these do not appear to be coordinated. After decades of spectacular growth, the new Basel III rules will require the banks to tighten their belts. Banks worldwide have until 2015 to raise an estimated additional core Tier 1 capital of $1.3 trn to comply with the standards. If no new capital is available or if capital is available but too expensive, lenders will have to shed assets. Cutting risk-weighted assets – or optimizing the balance sheet, as banks prefer to call it – is often is done by adjusting models and parameters rather than by squeezing the asset base or raising equity when share prices are battered. Consequently, the process receives close scrutiny from regulators because it represents a cheaper way of improving the capital ratio while not necessarily enhancing the ability to absorb losses. However, even within models and ratings there is (economically justifiable) room for discretion. The complexity of measuring credit risks to determine appropriate amounts of capital to hold for losses and to manage portfolios of credit risks still attracts a great deal of scientific research. Although the activities of credit portfolio managers who are engaged in selling, hedging, structuring, securitizing, and repackaging became a highly

[4] See Financial Times, December 9, 2011: 'Financial sector "drowning" in regulation flood'.

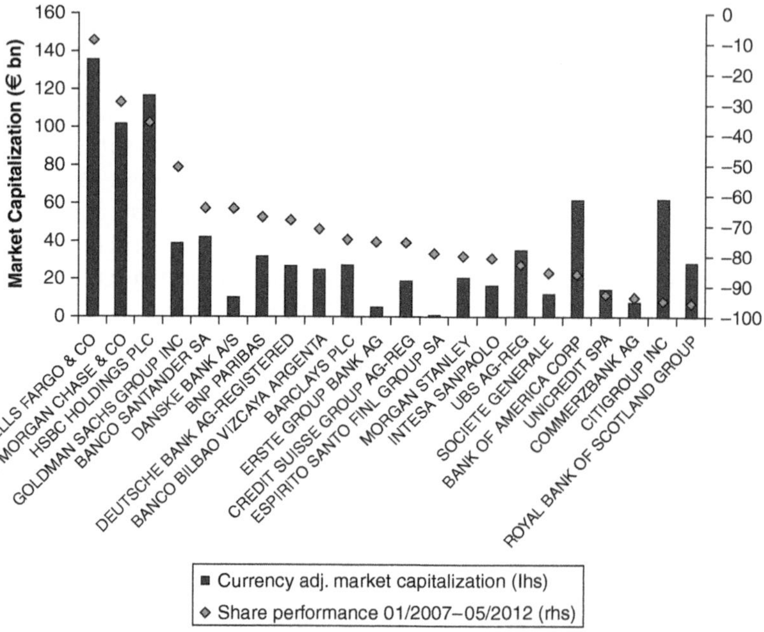

Figure 1.1 Performance of bank shares and market capitalization[5]
Data source: Bloomberg.

profitable business for investment banks, the post–Lehman default era will see a back-to-basics reversal of the practices financial institutions employ to manage their credit risks. Prevailing and unsettling uncertainties over the future and role of banking and finance and the corresponding implications for the global economy make it paramount for both business and the risk managers of financial institutions to assume responsibility for making changes. That might require a change in the mental attitude towards models, fundamental assumptions, and risk in general. The sophisticated quantification of risk by means of probability distributions and correlations more than ever needs to be complemented by experience, intuition, and expert judgement. The regular questioning of risk and return must become a habit if the lessons taught by the financial crisis are to have any effect. The often disappointing performance of bank shares over the last couple of years confirms that the financial industry faces challenging times.

[5] * Share Price Performance: May 25, 2012 versus January 3, 2007. ** Market Capitalization Currency adjusted at EUR/USD 1.2515; EUR/GBP 0.7999; EUR/CHF 1.2011; EUR/DKK 7.4306.

1.2 The age of credit crises

These days, one of the most commonly heard terms in Wall Street trading rooms is the 'black swan' event, depicted in Nassim Taleb's 2007 best-seller, *The Black Swan: The Impact of the Highly Improbable.* The former option trader got the timing right. Only shortly after publication of the book in May 2007, the subprime crisis devastated the global financial landscape, with banks being forced to take at least $188 bn of write-downs and shockwaves still roiling markets many years later. It seemed to some as if a flock of black swans had found a new home in global financial markets. A black swan event is rare by definition, meant to happen but once or twice in a lifetime, like an eclipse of the sun. Low probability of occurrence combined with a potentially high impact is the definition of tail risk. However, large-impact events became more frequent during the last decade, with the subprime crisis, the Lehman default and the Greek tragedy being the most prominent. Statistically, there is a 2.5 per cent chance that tail risk will materilize under the standard normal distribution. And not all these once-in-40-years events will have a high impact. The scope of high-impact rare events – known as *fat tails* in quantspeak, because this is what the bell curve resembles when plotted – undermines the self-confidence of risk managers. It basically raises the question whether there is a way to accurately predict risk or whether stress tests – designed

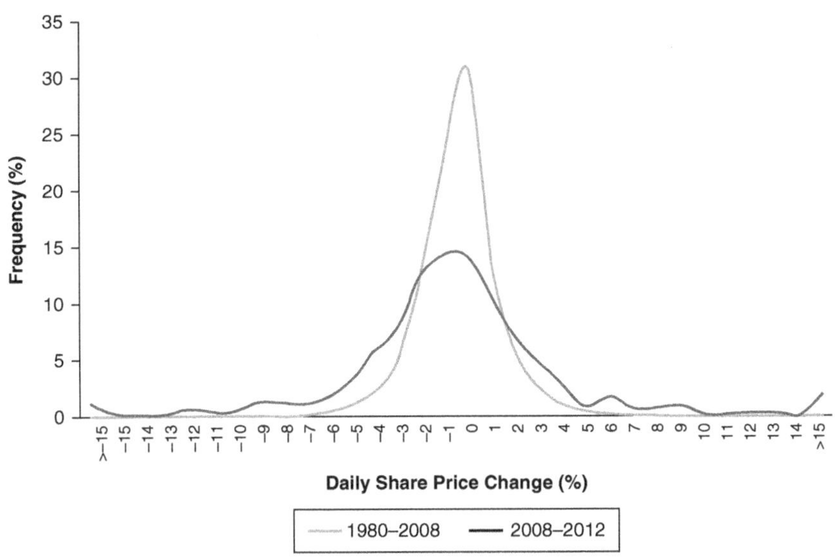

Figure 1.2 Distribution of daily share price changes of Bank of America
Data source: Bloomberg.

to describe and forecast risks – and models are inherently flawed, utterly useless, and consistently underestimate risks which might eventually break financial institutions. As a senior executive at a European bank puts it: *'Normal distribution is man made. Life is negatively skewed.'* That we have seen a permanent change from the low-volatility environment to more unstable and uncertain conditions seems to be confirmed by the distribution of daily price moves of the larger banks and brokers. For decades, the majority of daily stock price moves were small, with the bulk of them concentrated at ±1 per cent. Since 2008, when the subprime crisis fully unfolded, the distribution of changes in equity value shifted significantly to larger moves, reflecting the increased volatility and risk in the financial industry.

One of the reasons for this paradigm shift was the overwhelming growth of difficult-to-value assets and investments during the last decade, which turned into unprecedented losses during the financial crisis. Many financial experts and highly skilled professionals were forced to realize that they knew little about something they took for granted: their ability to assess and correctly price risks. The crisis has shaken the confidence of markets and the foundations of commonly used models alike. A prominent example is the capital asset pricing model (CAPM) which serves as the basis for modern finance theory and is widely accepted by portfolio managers around the world. The model helps to determine the required return for an asset given its contribution to the diversification of a portfolio. Input factors are the expected return on a risk free-asset, the asset's correlation to systemic (non-diversifiable) risk, and the expected market return. However, the risk-free rate is defined as an investment that carries no risk of financial losses, usually the yield of short-dated U.S. government bonds. Unfortunately, government securities are no longer considered to be risk free and barely earn an AAA rating. These days, corporates can be less risky than governments, and government default risk can be largely determined by external factors like bank rescues or bailouts of other sovereigns.[6]

In response, regulators are increasing their efforts to keep in step with the volatile, changing financial environment. But many of the problems which led to the formation of the Basel Committee on Banking Supervision (BCBS) are still prevalent and growing. Neither early warning systems nor resolution regimes for international banks have stood the test of time so far. To be sure, while Basel set the standard for the capital

[6] The vicious circle of government struggling to cope with bank bailouts became evident again when Spain sought as much as €100 bn to recapitalize its larger banks in June 2012, followed by another €40 bn in December 2012.

that banks should hold to withstand unfavourable operating conditions, the ratio has been revised and newly defined by politicians as part of their efforts to resolve the threat of the Greek default. The increasing politicization of financial regulation – the Basel Committee is answerable to the G10 group of central bank governors, who in turn are accountable to their parliaments – is not new but will make a big difference going forward. In the early stages of Basel, and to the surprise of the supervisors, banks were keen to implement Basel I[7]–as its credibility was a convincing and motivating factor. However, the U.S. actually never implemented Basel II,[8] whose rules are suspected to have contributed to the crisis due to the pro-cyclical effects caused by the methodology of calculating risk-weighted assets and the determination of the capital ratio, as well as the loopholes which have led to systematic capital arbitrage. As Basel III[9] awaits implementation, not only banks but also nations are wrangling with the potential distorting effects on global competitiveness. There are ongoing concerns that uneven playing fields may be created. Jamie Dimon, CEO of JPMorgan Chase, goes so far as to call Basel III 'blatantly anti-American'.[10] All in all, significant steps have been taken to make financial institutions a safer place. To some extent, they have required or contributed to speeding up improvements in risk management in various ways. Moreover, Basel II Pillar 2's internal capital adequacy assessment process (ICAAP) has become a lucrative field of activity for consultancy firms advising banks on the complex issues attached to it. But these steps cannot replace efforts by financial institutions to strengthen their risk management capabilities to cope with the demanding and difficult operating environment.

No doubt, the consequences of the market turmoil, be they the costs of continued regulatory tightening or the uncertainty-driven difficult market environment which continuously makes dents in the operating profit of banks, will prove to have a greater detrimental effect on the financial industry. Tighter regulations call into question the sustainability of the pre-crisis business models of many investment and commercial banks. The easy profits of the boom years are gone and are unlikely to return. But the continued declines in banks' and brokers' earnings also reflects

---

[7] See BCBS (2000).

[8] See BCBS (2006).

[9] See BCBS (2011).

[10] Interview with the Financial Times, September 12, 2011: New international bank capital rules are 'anti-American' and the U.S. should consider pulling out of the Basel group of global regulators, Jamie Dimon, chief executive of JPMorgan Chase, has said. 'I'm very close to thinking the United States shouldn't be in Basel any more. I would not have agreed to rules that are blatantly anti-American,' he said. 'Our regulators should go there and say: "If it's not in the interests of the United States, we're not doing it."'

how slow the process of adapting to the new world is. In addition, the practice of some banks of marking down their own debt to market values, while making earnings look less poor, nevertheless does not reflect the economic truth. Increased costs of funding, a result of the growing concerns of markets about the creditworthiness of financial institutions, and one significantly damaging to their bread-and-butter business of granting loans to clients, is turned into a positive for the profit and loss statement – in line with or even driven by prevalent accounting rules. Imagine having this applied by heavily indebted nations like Greece and Italy. The public debt surplus would be stunning. This is just one example where accounting, regulatory, and economic realities significantly differ. And large parts of new banking regulations are yet to become effective. Combined with a looming recession or potential stagnation in Europe and the U.S., there is reason to worry. The need for banks to stay profitable (and the challenges of doing so), at least to attract investors for capital and liquidity, receives little attention in current discussions of what the new role of financial institutions should be. The call for altruistic financial intermediation, serving only the public need, can be realized only by public banks which are non-profit. The devastation from the financial crisis – particularly observed in Germany, where public sector banks

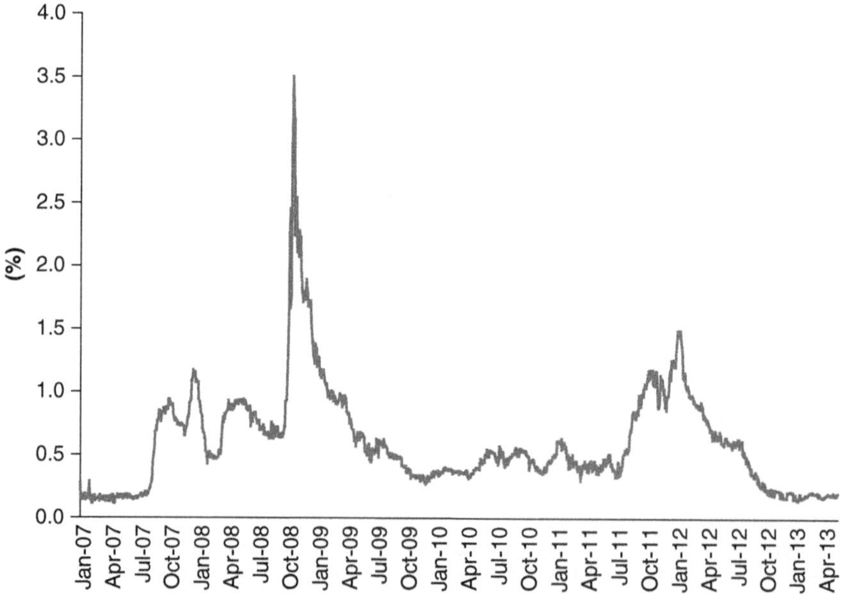

Figure 1.3 TED spread, Europe
Data source: Bloomberg.

were among these hardest hit – is confirmation that the social costs when banks lack a sustainable business model can be way in excess of zero or slightly negative profit.

All this – increasing risks, their eroding impact on banks' capital and strained profitability – weighs heavily on banks. There are various measures for these kinds of stress, and the financial crisis barely left any one of them unnoticed. Additionally, credit problems do not happen on their own. Distress within funding gauges is observed with great attention, because for banks, a squeeze of liquidity is fairly equal to a sudden death. One of these measures is the TED spread, the gap between three-month LIBOR interbank rates and U.S. Treasury bill yields in the U.S. and Bund yields versus Euribor in Europe. When banks start to mistrust each other, meaning that there are concerns about each other's ability to repay loans, the TED spread begins to rise, as banks are then perceived to be riskier, compared with riskless government debt.

Clearly, the pain being felt in Europe is linked to the sovereign crisis of late. European sovereign debt is widely distributed and concentrated among European banks and other financial institutions, but outside Europe significant holdings have also been noted, with approximately €359 bn of Italian government bonds dwarfing the €81 bn of Greek debt. Even though the European Central Bank (ECB) did its best to inject liquidity into the system by substantially increasing the long-term refinancing operations (LTRO) and the theoretically unlimited bond-buying program outright monetary transaction (OMT), easing the problem of interbank liquidity, the concerns about sovereign debt remain. Indeed, MF Global, the U.S. futures broker, has become the first financial institution outside Europe to fall victim to the Eurozone debt crisis. The firm failed at the end of October 2011, after placing a $6.3 bn bet on securities of highly indebted European sovereigns that went sour. Given the far-reaching implications when a European country defaults on financial stability and the world economy, the nervousness of capital markets – expressed by volatility of stock markets and the spreads for credit risks – seems understandable. Ensuring the orderly functioning of financial markets and the stability of the financial system in the EU as a whole is part of the responsibility of the European Banking Authority (EBA).[11] Stress tests are carried out regularly for an early identification of trends, potential risks, and vulnerabilities. However, when its predecessor, the Committee of European Banking Supervisors (CEBS), conducted a stress test on 91 banks in July 2010, the stress scenario did incorporate an adverse

[11] Articles 21 and 32 of the EBA regulation give the EBA powers to initiate and coordinate the EU-wide stress tests, in cooperation with the European Systemic Risk Board (ESRB); www.eba.europa.eu/EU-wide-stress-testing.aspx.

economic development, including a macroeconomic and a sovereign risk shock, but did not assume a sovereign default. That was in line with the establishment of the EFSF and EFSM, which were set up to support struggling member state governments. At that time, 51 of the participating 91 banks would still have had a Tier 1 capital ratio of more than 8 per cent under the severe adverse scenario, which was double the then regulatory minimum requirement.[12] Only 7 banks would have had a capital ratio below 6 per cent,[13] which was the stress test benchmark set by the EBA, none of which were the Bank of Ireland and Allied Irish Bank. While the two Irish banks passed the exam, only months later AIB needed a government bailout. Anglo Irish Bank Corp. which was not tested, suffered a similar fate. The EU and IMF rescue package for the two troubled banks amounted to a whopping €85 bn. To counter the widespread criticism of the reliability of the tests, the 2011 stress tests were designed to build in harsher macroeconomic conditions and a larger degree of transparency, in particular regarding banks' exposures and capital composition. This allowed analysts to perform their own assessments based on individual stress assumptions. This time, 8 banks did not surpass the threshold of 5 per cent core Tier 1 ratio, while another 16 banks settled in the danger zone between 5 and 6 per cent core Tier 1. Since the impact from the sovereign crisis had in the meantime moved on from losses related only to credit to restricted access to funding, the stress test again was argued to not reveal the full picture of potential risks and vulnerability. Dexia, the troubled French-Belgian-Luxembourgian lender, did have sufficient capital, according to the stress test results, to withstand the assumed write-downs on its sovereign debt holdings. But as the sovereign debt crisis unfolded, lenders became more wary of each other, and Dexia's heavy reliance on rolling short-term funding became a problem, one eventually solved by another government-sponsored bailout. Two issues related to the EBA stress tests became apparent. The first was the ability of the tests to adequately identify hidden vulnerabilities given the interconnectedness of risks, and to appropriately determine the stressed capital position, thereby identifying potential gaps. The other concern was related to the perception that the modelled test results failed to correctly

[12] Directive EC/2006/48 – Capital Requirements Directive (CRD). The CRD regulatory minimum Tier 1 capital adequacy ratio amounts to 4%, while the minimum for the overall capital adequacy ratio is set at 8%.

[13] For results of EBA 2010 stress tests, see http://stress-test.c-ebs.org/documents/Summaryreport.pdf.

[14] For the EBA-published 'Recommendation and Final Results of Bank Recapitalisation Plan as Part of Co-ordinated Measures to Restore Confidence in the Banking Sector', see www.eba.europa.eu.

predict bank failures. In December 2011, the EBA finally published a formal recommendation for European banks' recapitalization[14] as part of a broader European package previously agreed by the European Council on 26 October and confirmed during the ECOFIN Council on 30 November. The objective of the plan was to restore stability and confidence in the markets. A total capital shortfall of almost €115 bn across Europe was identified after banks required to meet by end of June 2012 an exceptional and temporary buffer, such as the core Tier 1 capital ratio level of 9 per cent. Measures to comply with the new capital threshold include retained earnings, scrapped dividends, capital increases by means of the new issuance of common equity, and qualifying contingent capital, as well as other liability measures and restricted bonus payments.

Although it is of great importance that banks have sufficient capital in place to absorb major losses and thereby avoid the economic implications of a failure, the willingness and ability of international investors to provide additional equity is limited. At the same time, government buy-ins not only distort the functioning of the markets; they also create knock-on effects which potentially undermine the credit standing of the country. While it is understandable that adequate bank capital remains the prime source of concerns for regulators, they have to strike a balance to avoid discouraging banks from performing their roles as financial intermediaries for credit. Financial institutions in turn may defuse the situation by strengthening the first and last line of defence: their credit risk strategy and credit portfolio management.

1.3 Credit risk management at the forefront

In many banks, investments in skilled and qualified personnel and technology and IT infrastructure, methodologies, and processes have been substantial, not only to satisfy regulatory demands, but also to retain a competitive edge in an increasingly difficult and uncertain environment. Measuring, modelling, managing, and monitoring credit risk have become the '4M' mantra of modern banking. Although banks have been encouraged by regulators to step up their efforts to comply with Basel II and the upcoming Basel III rules, sound credit risk management practices are not just a formal requirement; they enable management decision, thereby improving business performance overall. Of course, the introduction of Basel II supported a harmonization of the risk language, where probability of default (PD), loss given default (LGD), exposure at default (EAD), and expected loss (EL) have become standard, allowing all parties to communicate efficiently and for increased comparability of risk assessments between various business segments and even whole financial institutions. Unfortunately, there is no unique way to measure risks as evidenced by differing, sometimes contradicting, views of regulators and accounting standard setters. Integrating the different methodologies to the extent possible ensures cost-efficient and consistent risk management and reporting. In some cases, conceptual differences, for instance in the case of determining loan loss provisions, highlight the diverging purposes of Basel II and international financial reporting standards (IFRS). While the regulatory objective is to safeguard the stability of the financial system as a whole, accounting rules aim at transparency and precision with respect to financial statements. Consequently, Basel II emphasizes expected loss and unexpected loss, whereas IFRS focuses on incurred losses.[15] At the same time, IFRS explicitly acknowledges changes in economic conditions as a reason for adjustments on loan loss provisions (LLPs), provided that a deterioration of those conditions results in a measurable decrease in

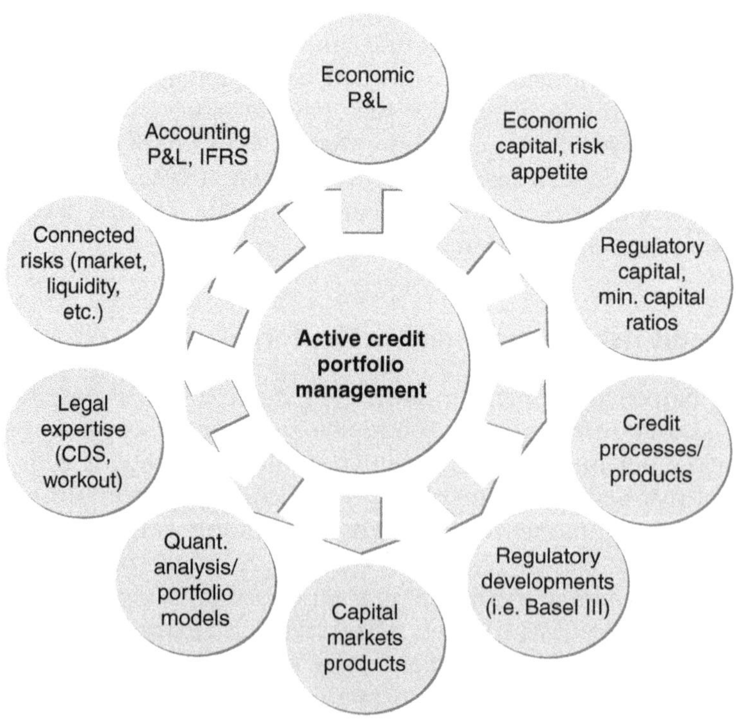

Figure 1.4 Dimensions of credit portfolio management

[15] IAS 39 distinguishes three loan loss provision (LLP) categories under the IFRS methodology: (1) Specific LLPs, which are individual; (2) General LLPs; and (3) Portfolio LLPs.

the estimated cash flows of certain assets, while Basel II prefers more stable capital ratios and thus capital requirements through the credit cycle. The diverging approaches have considerable ramifications on credit portfolio management objectives and decisions. For example, some credit risk mitigations will be recognized for capital relief, but not from an accounting perspective when it comes to offsetting LLPs. So while portfolio managers have access to extended and improved data, the regulatory and accounting implications of their activities of course have a notable influence on their decisions. Hence, a credit portfolio manager must take a multidimensional view which connects the dots of accounting, regulatory, and economic dimensions, while developing an integrated risk-management approach. Doing so requires having skills in a range of different dimensions to develop optimal solutions for defined objectives.

Notwithstanding the increase in risk-management sophistication, which will ultimately add value for all stakeholders, a prime incentive for banks to adopt Basel II relates to the prospects of lower regulatory capital requirements. Banks are reluctant to increase capital when their stocks are trading at or close to historic lows, and balance sheet optimization is seen as a suitable alternative. Part of that effort is taking a more active approach to portfolio management. Advanced risk management usually becomes visible only when risks are apparent. Even before the financial crisis spurred further efforts to improve risk management at financial institutions, the CEBS set out the regulatory requirements on risk management:

> Risk management includes ongoing identification, measurement and assessment of all material risks that could adversely affect the achievement of the institution's goals. The procedures for risk monitoring and assessment need to be updated regularly. The management body (both supervisory and management functions) should set the risk strategy, the risk policy, and accordingly the riskbearing capacity of the institution.[16]

In order to facilitate internal discussions and debates about portfolio risks, with some pushing for short-term volumes and revenue generation while others take a more conservative stance towards risks, adequate risk measurement, and reporting technologies are a necessity and a prerequisite for balanced and prudent risk taking. Especially within larger, multinationally or internationally operating and consequently more complex organizations, there is a strong need for effective risk-management

[16] See CEBS (2006a).

functions which address, in a coordinated and consistent way, the risks taken across the various levels and subentities. According to a report from the European Commission, the *European Financial Stability and Integration Report 2010*,[17] large cross-border banks categorized as coordinated or centralized adopt an integrated risk-management approach defined by a common strategy, standards, and practices that ultimately allow them to balance complexity and achieve efficiency. Moreover, effective risk management is vital to sound and sustainable business activities characterized by regionally, culturally, and attitude- and product-specific diverse business practices:

> Integrated risk management requires a bank-wide approach that addresses risks across all levels and entities in the organisation, bank-wide risk policies and standardised concepts to facilitate effective implementation across the bank. It presumes that risks across the bank are aggregated, monitored and managed on a comprehensive basis. In an integrated approach, risk management is incorporated into the overall business planning and decision-making process. This is achieved through a risk management framework, based on economic capital, measured using risk-adjusted performance metrics. It is then executed through operational limits that control the level of risks run by the group, business lines and regions.[18]

Setting a suitable risk strategy in line with the capital position of a financial institution is at the heart of the credit risk strategies. It should be noted that the connectivity of risks does not allow for an isolated view of credit risk only. Any credit portfolio strategy has its foundations in the risk-appetite setting, which allocates capital and liquidity to all sources of risks. The challenge here is also very much about translating high-level targets into day-to-day operating goals to achieve the objectives expressed in the risk strategy. Risk- and capital-adjusted decision making are the connective tissues in a top-to-bottom system, with portfolio management at the centre of the risk, capital, and liquidity process and execution.[19]

However, what seemed to be the right balance for taking risks at the time of decision making might be seen as too risky later, as there is a tight borderline separating reasonable from excessive risk taking. Sound risk and portfolio management therefore is very much also about taking appropriate and sometimes corrective measures, based on rational and educated

---

[17] See European Commission (2011).
[18] See European Commission (2011).
[19] See Bain and Company (2012).

decisions and using reliable internal control systems. Nonetheless, the next phase of active credit portfolio management (ACPM) will move beyond micro risk management by hedging single-obligor credit risks. Four main drivers for reviewing ACPM can be identified: (a) achieving adequate regulatory and economic capital when capital is scarce; (b) overhaul of business models of financial institutions in face of tightened restrictions; (c) the necessity to improve liquidity ratios; and (d) constantly changing and demanding regulatory requirements. The far-reaching implications of hostile market conditions, coupled with the efforts of regulators to prevent bank runs when banks become troubled, call for strategic solutions. In fact, the reluctance of financial institutions to sell down or exchange assets in sufficient amounts to improve capital ratios and liquidity to the level set by regulators or governments may be ultimately brushed off by sovereigns not willing or no longer able to absorb further potential losses from banks. In this new environment, dedicated credit portfolio management is no longer just a competitive advantage, as it heralded to be in the early days of ACPM. It is a prerequisite for attracting new shareholder money, and is very often pointed to in this context. It is a must-have to cope with the new paradigm of fast-changing business models and the new holistic approach that companies need to stay on track.

2
Credit Risk Strategies

Basel II regulations, incorporated into national law by many countries, require banks to develop and implement effective risk-management strategies and processes. But besides these regulatory requirements, banks have a vital interest in the proactive management of risk and return that encompasses all sources of risk. Continuous and purposeful asset allocation supports the competitiveness of a bank and creates value, thereby satisfying the stakeholders. Profound risk-management operations; a suitable risk culture spread throughout the firm; adequate methods, processes, and instruments; and organizational structures, which are all part of risk governance, enable a bank to successfully respond to a dynamic and volatile operating environment. The increasing complexity of the banking business – but also the tremendous opportunities arising from a fast-changing and globally interconnected business environment – calls for a comprehensive and integrated approach to the management of risks. The formulation of consistent strategies and the implementation of efficient controll processes are ultimately part of the a bank's management responsibility. Consequently, management must be in a position to assess holistically the prevailing risks and take informed decisions on the management of those risks and, in some cases, on counterbalancing efforts which aim at improving the overall situation.

2.1 The risk appetite framework

The challenging operating conditions for financial institutions make the sound understanding and management of risks on an aggregated basis necessary for finding a sustainable balance between risk and return. This is the key objective of a comprehensive risk appetite framework. "Risk appetite" is defined as the risks that an organization is willing to take to achieve its strategic objectives and meet its obligations to stakeholders.[1] Since risk is an expression of volatility, the risk appetite implicitly addresses the variability of returns accepted by senior management to accomplish a corporate strategy. The importance of a clear formulation of a bank's risk appetite and related disclosure[2] cannot be overstated and is subject to the ever-increasing scrutiny of regulators, rating agencies, investors, market participants in general, and other stakeholders. For instance, rating agencies carefully assess a bank's risk appetite, which in turn factors into their judgement of the bank's credit riskiness. According to Standard and Poor's, a strategy could lead to a weaker business position if 'Management's risk appetite, strategies, financial targets... are more aggressive than average for the industry.'[3] A well-defined and focused risk appetite contributes to the of comfort level of investors. The interests of bondholders, who are in favour of low risk given their limited participation in the upside and the significant downside potential of their corporate bond investments, conflict to a certain extent with the mantra of shareholders calling for a higher return on equity and dividend payments, but both bondholders and shareholders actually prefer predictable, stable, and solid growth. The focus of regulators on financial strength and capital adequacy makes them prime addressees of the risk appetite settings. Moreover, stakeholder expectations such as customer satisfaction and reliability of services to local communities, as well as corporate identification of employees, are necessarily to be considered.

The cornerstone of any assessment of risk appetite is capital adequacy, both regulatory required capital and internal or risk capital, which is measured using complex models that recognize correlation structures within the portfolio. While the composition of regulatory capital is clearly defined, the layers of risk capital have to be set out.[4] The level of risk capital that covers and limits unexpected losses serves as a constraint

[1] Towers Perrin (2010).

[2] An adequately transparent governance of a bank to its shareholders, depositors, other relevant stakeholders and market participants demands the disclosure of the risk appetite: 'The bank should also disclose key points concerning its risk tolerance/ appetite (without breaching necessary confidentiality), with a description of the process for defining it and information concerning the board involvement in such process.' BCBS (2010), III. Sound corporate governance principle, F. Disclosure and transparency, Principle 14, Article 130.

[3] Standard and Poor's (2011b).

[4] Approaches to harmonize risk and regulatory capital differ in that, for example, some firms include forecasted profit, goodwill or the net present value of capitalized tax while others do not. Moreover, internal capital is derived from confidence levels and risk horizons, which in turn is indicative of the target credit quality an institution wants to achieve.

which should not be exceeded in order to guarantee the survival of the firm. It is usually referred to as risk-taking capacity or risk-bearing capacity. Since risk-taking capacity is defined as the maximum risk that the institution can stand, it usually provides a buffer to the target risk profile. It further serves as a basis for setting risk limits, such as concentration limits for credit risk or value-at-risk limits for market risk. The capital cushion, or difference between the risk-taking capacity and the capital to be deployed to execute the business strategy, is derived from the risk appetite, ensuring that the bank's capital position remains sufficient at all times, even under sustained negative conditions. Hence, risk appetite is integrated into the business strategy, which details the bank's targets in respect to markets, clients, product offerings, and the like, and a general assessment of its positioning. The alignment of the risk appetite with the business strategy allows for a coherent, risk/return optimized capital allocation and target portfolio, taking into account the operating conditions and competitiveness of the firm.

Articulated in terms of qualitative as well as selected quantitative targets, triggers, and limits, the risk appetite elaborates on the strategic objectives and sets the boundaries within which the organization must operate. For financial institutions, relevant risk appetite measures may consist of

- credit quality;
- capital ratios;
- liquidity ratios;
- balance sheet composition;
- profitability;
- shareholder value metrics.

These measures define in a forward-looking, flexible, and stringent manner the risk a financial institution is prepared to take when executing the corresponding business strategy. If effective and underpinned by robust risk data, they help to improve the firm's strategic and tactical decision-making capabilities and communication. Key pillars of an effective risk appetite framework are accountability, incentive, and constraint. Business ambitions, capital, and risk allocations must be translated into operational metrics to be applied in day-to-day business.

Risk management generally encompasses the process of monitoring and assessing decisions to accept particular risks and determining appropriate risk mitigation measures, and whether risk decisions are in line with the board-approved risk tolerance/appetite and risk policy.[5]

[5] BCBS (2010), III. Sound corporate governance principle, C. Risk management and internal controls, Principle 6, Article 69.

In a broader sense, a risk mission statement, which defines the risk tolerance levels or risk thresholds, helps to ensure that the risks the firm takes stay within boundaries set by the risk appetite. Risk tolerance and risk thresholds are defined by key risk indicators that are specific and measurable.[6] Inter-risk correlations and feedback loops among different types of risk, such as credit risk, market risk, liquidity, and operational risk as the main risk sources, are addressed by the risk appetite framework in a comprehensive way. Risk strategies identify the optimal risk profile given the risk appetite, thereby making high-level strategic objectives actionable at the business unit front desks. It should be noted that risk limits are derived from capital; they do not incorporate profitability or return aspects. However, the objective of risk strategies is to specify the optimal portfolio composition that is within the limits, based on risk/return attributes exhibited by the existing stock and by the revenue and capital allocation for new business. Risk strategies elaborate on how an organization deals with specific risks, considering both quantitative and qualitative aspects. Moreover, they provide the basis for reporting and monitoring procedures, allowing management to verify or review the risk appetite and derived strategies. Risk appetite triggers serve as an early warning system to develop or implement mitigating activities to reverse the trend. When risk appetite limits are breached, predefined contingency plans become activated to ultimately prevent failure of the firm.

2.2 Risk culture

Full transparency and a common understanding of the firm's strategic plan and the associated target risk profile, facilitated by a shared risk appetite language throughout the organization, help to foster the acceptance and execution discipline. The BCBS pointed out that

> Senior management contributes substantially to a bank's sound corporate governance through personal conduct (e.g. by helping to set the 'tone at the top' along with the board) by providing adequate oversight

[6] In the BCBS (2010) document, the terms 'risk appetite' and 'risk tolerance' are mostly used in combination. This is due to the fact that there is no consensus among supervisors or banks as to how to clearly distinguish between the two terms. In this book and following a suggestion of the BCBS (2010), risk appetite describes an overarching and forward-looking approach to risks which are in principle and a priori acceptable to a bank in the sense of a risk mission statement. In contrast, risk tolerance is a more immediate definition of the risk appetite and thus allows the monitoring and reporting of the risk appetite.

of those they manage, and by ensuring that the bank's activities are consistent with the business strategy, risk tolerance/appetite and policies approved by the bank's board.[7]

Due to their importance, supervisors will critically assess risk governance processes, risk-management standards, and discipline, all of which contribute to the risk culture of an institution. A powerful risk culture has its origins in shared values and goals and the commitment by top management to execute the firm's strategy within the defined risk appetite. However, having a risk appetite framework is effective only when it is communicated in a transparent and straightforward manner. Although the risk culture is a soft concept as it refers to behaviour of individuals, there are more precise measures which gauge the level of a common purpose, understanding, and attitude. Four areas representing the risk culture of a firm can be identified:[8]

Transparency: An unclear or imprecise formulation of risk appetite and risk strategy may create confusion or lead to purposeful interpretation in favour of the risk taker. The allocation of responsibility to individuals within the firm not only gives them the authority to conduct a task but also supports accountability. Internal competition, overlaps, and redundancies are not just inefficient; they also create improper incentives such as the first come, first served principle, thereby potentially putting the interests of the people concerned over those of the firm. Communicating sound risk appetite statement enables managers to explicitly determine whether operations comply with the mission. As markets and conditions change constantly, regular communication of the risk appetite is helpful – even if no adjustments are made.

Acknowledgement: Overconfidence can undermine awareness of risk taking. When a business unit is very successful or a market performs extraordinarily well, adequate care and attention to risk may be replaced by a sense of superiority. Openly challenging each other – for instance, regarding the quality of results underlying assumptions used for strate-

[7] BCBS (2010), III. Sound corporate governance principle, B. Senior Management, Principle 5, Article 66.

[8] See also Banks (2002), McKinsey (2010) and Institute of International Finance (2009). Banks provides an excellent and comprehensive text of various aspects of the risk governance chain. It discusses the essentials of risk management, including concepts such as the risk appetite – well before other literature or even regulators picked up on it after the financial shocks from 2008. No doubt, a thorough read would have helped to avoid many of the failures of the recent years.

gies and actions, and even the approach taken to run certain businesses – should become a norm rather than an exception, encouraged by the management at various hierarchy levels.

Responsiveness: Silo thinking – where people care only about issues in their area of responsibility but not about those of others – ignores the interconnectedness of risks. More often than not, banks are organized along the main sources of risks – credit risk, market risk, liquidity, and operational risk – not taking account of the increasing complexity of banking. An integrated approach towards risk requires a high level of experience, specialization, and expertise but also a broader, overarching view and understanding of risks, as well as a shared sense of responsibility for the firm. Passivity or slow responsiveness may develop in an overly hierarchical organization in which people do not feel valued or recognized for their contributions. Especially during times of cost cutting, headcount reduction, and uncertainty, people may not be prepared to go the extra mile. In order to counter dangerous complacency, managers should foster team spirit.

Recognition: Purposeful disregard for risk, either because of personal convictions that are incompatible with the risk appetite or because of a desire to beat the system when it has no serious consequences, renders any risk strategy meaningless. If limits are not taken seriously as a matter of principle or if they are occasionally relaxed giving revenues and budgets priority, the consequences can be disastrous throughout the organization. Near misses or near failures can substantially contribute to improving the standards or eliminating the sources of errors if the corrections are encouraged with appreciation rather than blame.

Shaping a risk culture throughout an organization starts at the top. It is not just the decisions taken and executed that matter. Equally important is the way senior management arrives at decisions. There are various examples that indicate weaknesses in the risk culture of some firms, from trading scandals and rogue traders to poor decisions resulting from unsound analysis. The lack of challenge to the quality of management's actions has been cited as a key factor in the demise of the Royal Bank of Scotland (RBS).

However, RBS is not a unique case. The failures of Enron, WorldCom and Long-Term Capital Management (LTCM), to name but a few, also clearly exhibit shortcomings in the risk culture. Similarly, trading scandals at Société Générale and UBS bear witness to deficiencies in the risk culture. While the conclusion that those firms which weathered

Case Study 1. The Failure of the Royal Bank of Scotland

In October 2008, after incurring substantial losses, the former UK banking champion RBS had to be nationalized by the UK government by receiving a capital injection and emergency liquidity assistance from the Bank of England. As of December 2011, the government still owned an economic total of 82 per cent of the RBS Group.[9] In the years prior to the failure, RBS grew significantly in terms of profit and balance sheet, becoming the fifth largest bank worldwide by market capitalization.

Base on a request by the Treasury Select Committee, the UK Financial Services Authority (FSA) conducted an investigation into the reasons for RBS failure with the explicit purpose of finding grounds for enforcement action; that is, charges that FSA rules were breached. On December 12, 2011, the FSA published its board's report, 'The Failure of the Royal Bank of Scotland'.[10] The FSA report identified several factors that caused the RBS collapse, among which were a weak capital position resulting from the ABN Amro acquisition, overreliance on short-term funding, and concern about RBS's asset quality and substantial losses from credit trading, which eroded the market confidence. Although the financial crisis swept away a number of financial institutions, in RBS's case a flawed risk culture in an already extremely vulnerable firm made the demise inevitable. Particularly, the FSA report notes 'the poor decisions made by RBS management and Board which made RBS highly vulnerable to failure, and the underlying aspects of RBS's management style, governance and culture which may have contributed to those poor decisions'. The FSA noted that RBS had taken; that important decisions without a sufficient understanding of the risks involved, based on inadequate monitoring and risk mitigation; knowingly accepted high levels of risk, and expanded into markets where there were already signs of deterioration. However, some practices and decisions were not dissimilar to those observed at other banks, including the remuneration practices which incentivized the management to prioritize revenues over risks. After having analysed the CEO's leadership capability and management style, the FSA concluded that these factors ultimately contributed to RBS's weak position. That view confirmed an observation made by the FSA prior to the review carried out for the report that the challenging management culture led by the RBS CEO raised particular risks that had to be addressed, although it remained open if any kind of action followed. Anecdotal evidence of the UK government's displeasure with the former CEO, Frederick Goodwin, was shown when the Queen annulled his knighthood in 2012 because of allegations that he had brought the honours system into disrepute.

---

[9] See www.investors.rbs.com/equity_statistics.

[10] See FSA (2011).

the storm may have benefitted from a superior risk culture could be misleading, there are some institutions which are frequently praised for their attitude to managing risks. The regular rotation of managers between risk management and business operations, indicating a level playing field between the two, has often been cited as a success factor at Goldman Sachs. Indeed, although Goldman has not always met ethical standards expectations,[11] the firm appears to have a solid track record in managing risks.

2.3 Credit risk strategies

While risk appetite can be seen as a mission statement, a more detailed road map of specific long-term risk and business strategies, addressing the business lines or regional locations, ensures a coherent approach throughout the organization. Embedded in a holistic risk strategy and risk-management approach, credit risk strategies are the concrete deployment of the high-level targets of the institution's risk appetite. They specify where and how the risk capital should be allocated in order to maximize the risk-adjusted portfolio return. Credit risk encompasses all risks arising from an obligor that fails to meet its obligations when due, including issuer, counterparty, and settlement risk, both on and off the balance sheet.

In general, risk is a commodity that any financial institution deals with. The objective of the risk strategies, therefore, must be to optimize

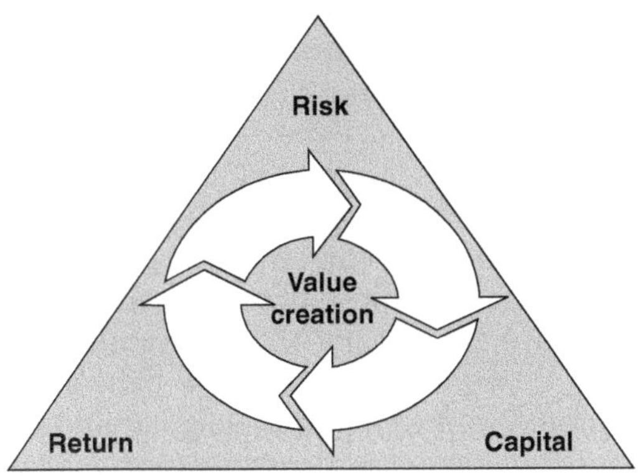

Figure 2.1 Credit risk strategy triangle

[11] In 2010, the CEO of Goldman, Lloyd Blankfein, had to defend at a U.S. Senate hearing why the firm sold investments to clients that were dismissed by the bank's own staff as junk. It should be noted that Goldman Sachs, too, had to receive a capital injection in 2008.

rather than minimize risks. At the same time, risk is very often seen as an outcome of business operations rather than a conscious decision that contributes to determining business budgets. A portfolio optimization reveals all the possible combinations that are within the risk limits while maximizing the risk/return, connecting the business and risk strategy while recognizing capital constraints.

2.3.1 Key requirements for an effective credit risk strategy

A successful execution of credit risk strategies relies on three prerequisites:

1. An intense and permanent communication and alignment of the intention of the strategy – horizontal between top management and vertical from top to bottom to ensure the buy-in of the units involved, founded on knowledge and understanding;
2. Targets and limits based on observable and manageable measures, since high-level measures are often dismissed as non-operational and therefore irrelevant;
3. The timely and frequent monitoring of portfolio trends and developments, verifying that business operations adhere to the approved credit risk strategies – and in case they do not, followed by an adjustment of the risk strategy or corrective actions.

The formulation of a risk strategy is a balancing act. A very granular and strictly defined strategy supports the applicability but reduces the managerial discretion and flexibility to adjust to a changing operating environment and taking on business opportunities. In addition, the efforts to monitor the implementation of a granular risk strategy may become intense, although it may provide useful information on the state of credit operations on a micro level. On the other hand, a generic strategy will probably fail to find acceptance and may create confusion if not sufficiently specified. A credit risk strategy that succeeds in making risk appetite transparent and enforceable therefore needs to have the agreement of top management on the overall targets and on the measures which appropriately represent the bank's ambitions, hence diminishing the room for interpretation. Regular and ad hoc reviews of the credit risk strategy enable the firm's decision makers to keep track of portfolio development and to react in a timely way to undesired deviations from the approved strategy. Such monitoring may further stimulate the exchange of views and expectations between top managers and may finally encourage them to critically assess the situation the bank is in.

2.3.2 Credit risk strategy measures

Ensuring consistency between the Basel II metrics of Pillar 1 and Pillar 2 – that is, to align business goals with risk and capital measures as required by ICAAP – represents a challenge given the involved and iterative nature of the process. The objective of credit risk strategies is to translate a strategic mission into applicable, manageable, and measurable daily operating rules and restrictions and match top-down ambitions with bottom-up reality. This can be done by setting targets and limits, both on a portfolio and segment level. Sub-level strategies for products or business lines additionally improve the applicability of the strategy. Measures relevant for formulating a credit risk strategy are, among others, growth rates of loan exposure and exposure at default (EAD), profitability thresholds, regulatory and economic capital, as well as the relative and absolute expected loss (EL). Portfolio migrations, the ratio of impaired to performing loans and the share and evolution of the portfolio subject to early warning signals are further criteria completing a risk strategy. Although the focus of this book is on credit risk, an integrated risk strategy must consider all elements of risk as well as their interconnectedness. Moreover, concentration risk limits on portfolio, single name, sector, and country-level support the allocation and usage of internal or risk capital. Qualitative lending standards are suitable to fine-tune business operations in addition to targets and limits. For instance, financing principles which address the minimum borrower credit quality, eligible credit products, financing terms, and accepted collateral serve as a first line of defence since they provide an effective and timely at-the-gate selection mechanism even before a transaction enters the credit approval process.

The forward-looking nature of the credit risk strategy positions of a credit portfolio for an expected development of the macroeconomic environment and credit markets. An essential element of the risk strategy is to anticipate the changes in the portfolio credit quality due to economic and other developments. Any quantitative optimization of a business plan or portfolio must incorporate the feasibility and likelihood of execution. For instance, while the risk/return profile of the portfolio stock serves as a rough guide for potential new business, in most cases it cannot be replicated infinitely. Typically, business segments with very appealing risk/return profiles attract competitors or new market entries, which consequently decrease the future returns in what is known as the law of diminishing marginal return. In order to achieve a constant or higher return, disproportional risks have to be taken over time. The most obvious example is the tremendous growth of the structured credit business in the years prior to the financial crisis, in particular synthetic CDOs (CSO) and CDOs of asset-backed securities (ABS), which were designed to generate high margins for the structurer and superior returns for the investor. When credit spreads declined during the period of economic prosperity from 2005 to 2007, more complex and opaque structures, like the CDO^2, were developed, where increased leverage was used to compensate for the decreasing coupons of the bonds and CDSs that served as collateral. The complexity of the transactions allowed investment banks to charge significant upfront fees for the structuring of the deals while the risks taken by the investors were ever rising. These risks, sometimes masked by solid investment-grade ratings from the rating agencies that benefitted from the flood of sophisticated credit products by taking substantial charges for their rating services, clearly exceeded the risk-taking capacity (RTC) of many investors. The spectacular demise of the U.S. insurer AIG and of the German bank IKB are the most striking examples, confirming that the risk appetite was largely disconnected from strategic planning and prudent business decision-making.

2.4 Risk limits: Framing the credit risk strategy

Credit risks arise from systematic risk and idiosyncratic risk. Systematic risk is the impact that unexpected deteriorations of the macroeconomic environment have on all portfolio constituents. Since economic conditions affect all borrowers, although to varying degrees, systematic risk cannot be eliminated completely by diversification. In contrast, idiosyncratic risks are described as risks specific to an individual debtor, which, on a portfolio level, diminish with an increasing granularity. In other words, the smaller the share a particular borrower has in a portfolio, the less impact; that is, a borrower accounting for only 1 per cent has a smaller impact than another accounting for 2 per cent. Granular portfolios are typical for retail banks, while wholesale banks run credit portfolios with bulky exposures – reflecting the nature of their business, which is mostly serving large caps or multinational clients. But also smaller, usually specialized or regionally active banks exhibit concentration risks in their credit portfolios. Risk concentration is acknowledged as a primary reason for bank failures. By contrast, a well-diversified portfolio can withstand even adverse economic conditions, since the impact of certain factors will not be equally severe across the portfolio. Concentration risks arise from different kinds of imperfect diversification. In general, credit concentration-risks exist on the single name but also on the industry, country, and other levels. For instance, industry and country concentration-risk denotes the risk resulting from the sensitivity of the credit quality of borrowers to the economic conditions of a particular sector or country.

An extreme case of concentration-risk losses from a common cause surfaced when the U.S. housing bubble burst – one of the root causes for the financial crises in 2007. A combination of unsatisfactory credit standards and complex structured credit transactions collateralized by mortgages granted to low-credit-quality borrowers became known as the subprime crisis and caused a series of bank failures and bailouts. The common factor identified as the trigger of the subprime meltdown was a decrease of house prices which led to unsustainable indebtedness of many homeowners.

The subprime crisis also exposed another source of concentration risk: default contagion. Default contagion is the significantly negative, potentially default-triggering impact from the default of one borrower on another, even though they might belong to different industries and regions. Business or financial interconnections, between obligors such as when profits generated are predominantly from a single customer or when a critical share of funding is provided by only one creditor, create default dependency. Hence the survival of the borrower is conditional on the survival of the customer or the creditor.[12] In particular, the interconnectedness of financial institutions is a major concern for financial stability, with the potential for huge economic losses and social costs. Interbank contagion, where the failure of one financial institution leads to the failure of others, is the subject of various practical and empirical studies.[13] As one would intuitively assume, if the connectivity of banks is high, an unequal distribution of interbank claims increases the risk of second-round effects after the default of a financial institution. In the case of interconnected banks, equal distribution of claims is seen as the best shock absorber because of its superior diversification.[14] However, addressing contagion risk remains a challenge because banks' databases usually do not allow capture of business links between otherwise independent customers in a formal, quantitative way. Also, the exposure of the company that is conditional on the default of the banks' client would have to be added to the credit portfolio, which is especially difficult to do if no direct relationship to this company exists.

However, the financial crisis did reveal other material weaknesses of concentration-risk concepts which have since been intensively discussed by regulators and scientific research alike. In particular, regulators expect a holistic approach to concentration-risk management; it must cover concentration risks across risk sources, risk products, locations, and books. The CEBS[15] in 2010 issued comprehensive guidelines

[12] Contagion risk therefore describes a situation where the default probability of a borrower conditional on the default of another borrower is greater than the unconditional probability of default for the same borrower.

[13] For an overview of relevant literature, see Sachs (2010).

[14] See Sachs (2010).

[15] See CEBS (2006b).

on the management of concentration risks; they are rather exhaustive and also challenging from the perspective of supervisors and financial institutions. Concentration risks arise *intra-risk* – that is, concentration of risk within a single risk category – and *inter-risk*, or the links between different risk exposures across different risk categories. The decisive factor for inter-risk concentration is a common underlying risk driver or interacting risk drivers. The wider definition aims at overcoming silos, where concentration risks are assessed only in isolation and thus results in a conceptual underestimation of the full picture. Exposure to an entity or closely related groups of exposure across different products – that is, loans, bonds, stocks, derivatives, guarantees, or other collateral booked in different locations and books (i.e. trading and banking books) – must be aggregated to assess the full concentration risk. However, concentration risk does not relate solely to credit. A bank may also exhibit concentration within its funding structure or within sources of revenues and non-credit risk, such as market, liquidity, and operational risk.

Bulk risks reduce a bank's ability to absorb losses, not only because of the potential for serious loan losses in the event of default but also because substantial amounts of revenues from the defaulted borrowers will not materialize as planned. Nonetheless, diversifying away concentration risks should not come at the expense of taking assets for which there is no sufficient expertise. Concentration-risk limits have to ensure that a bank is not exposed to connected risks that exceed adequate capital. Mitigations for concentration risks are a combination[16] of

- **risk limits**, where comprehensive credit limit systems allow the monitoring of large individual exposures or connected counterparties and risk appetite for concentration risks, either in terms of credit limits on some kind of exposure or economic capital;
- **active portfolio management**, which is responsible for the monitoring and corrective measures of existing or anticipated concentration risks;
- **loan pricing**, which incorporates the marginal contribution to portfolio diversification, thus incentivizing transactions which add to diversification and penalizing those which decrease diversification;[17]

[16] See CEBS (2006b).

[17] According to a survey on credit risk concentration performed by the Concentration Risk Group of the Research Task Force of the BCBS, only a minority of banks used pricing tools that explicitly account for concentration risk. See BCBS (2006).

- **risk transfer and risk mitigation**, as a systematic approach by means of asset sales, hedging, securitizing, or using collateral, guarantees or subparticipations, among others;
- **capital buffers**, where capital above the minimum regulatory requirement is allocated to general risk rather than specific concentration-risk.

Risk limits are especially important when asset selection and risk mitigation are constrained by market conditions. Several times in the past, the execution of risk strategies, and in particular risk transfer, has been hampered by market liquidity, forcing portfolio managers to sell what they were able to sell rather than what they wanted to sell. As a result, fewer liquid assets than initially intended become larger portfolio components, skewing portfolio allocations. At times, banks were left with sticky assets; even the loan syndication market, which is less sensitive to short-term volatility in credit and stock markets, was effectively closed for a sustained period of time – for instance, in 2009 and, to a lesser degree, again in 2011. By then, larger tickets from M&A financing or backup facilities which were not syndicated into the market remained on the balance sheets of the originating banks longer, sometimes creating major headaches for both the bank and the regulators. Loan syndication and underwriting limits will not prevent assets from getting stuck on the balance sheet, but they can stop new deals piling up until the pipeline is successfully cleared.

Case Study 2. MF Global Holdings Ltd.

A more recent example of an investment manager getting into trouble because of unbalanced risks involves MF Global Holdings Ltd., which filed for bankruptcy protection on October 31, 2011. The New York–based company, run by former Goldman Sachs legend Jon Corzine, amassed $6.3 bn of bonds of some of the most heavily indebted European nations, which sparked regulatory concern and a credit rating downgrade. The default happened less than four months after the issuance of $325 mn notes, whose prospectus included a passus that in the event of the departure of Mr. Corzine as the company's full-time chief executive officer,[18] the notes' interest rate would be increased by 100 bps, highlighting the perceived value of Mr Corzine's

[18] The passus states: '...the departure of Mr. Corzine as our full-time chief executive officer due to his appointment to a federal position by the President of the United States and the confirmation of that appointment by the United States Senate...'. Source: Prospectus supplement to the $325,000,000, 6.250 per cent Senior Notes, due 2016, of MF Global Holdings Ltd., S-18.

managerial expertise to the futures broker. However, within a week the notes lost more than 65 per cent of their market value, as it became clear that managerial wisdom was no match for the sovereign debt–caused market turmoil. With hindsight, the investment strategy that was 'strongly advocated' by Mr. Corzine at least should have been flanked by appropriate risk limits to discipline the asset allocation and protect against major damage. It is said that the aggressive style of MF Global reminded market participants of Refco, another futures broker that went bust in 2005; some also blamed the corporate culture as a main driver of the risk attitude.

The broker's collapse once again called attention to the role of rating agencies, which did not change their ratings until the week prior to the default.[19] As it turned out, the rating agencies mistook the bulk risk of sovereign debt investments and only became alert when they were told about the regulatory requirement to increase the capital held against those bonds and because of a later drawing on revolving credit lines by the company.[20]

2.4.1 Forms of credit concentrations and regulatory view

The assessment of regulatory capital consistent with Basel II rules is based on portfolio invariant risk weights for assets, meaning that the capital charge of a loan or debt instrument is determined exclusively by borrower-specific risk measures such as exposure at default (EAD), probability of default (PD) and loss given default (LGD). As a result, the capital consumption of the credit portfolio can be calculated by the sum of the capital charges of the portfolio constituents. For portfolio invariance, it is necessary to assume that the risk contribution of any single obligor is vanishingly small, leaving the portfolio exposed to systematic risk only as idiosyncratic risk is diminished due to the level of portfolio diversification. Systematic risk is determined by a single factor. Hence, the single risk factor assumption of the asymptotic single risk factor (ASRF) model of Basel II therefore excludes effects from single obligor, sector, or other portfolio concentrations. The correlation of two obligors is derived by the

[19] On October 24, 2011, Moody's Investors Service downgraded the long-term ratings of MF Global Holdings Ltd. ("MF Global"), including its senior, unsecured debt rating, to Baa3 from Baa2. The rating was placed on review for possible further downgrade. Three days later, the rating was lowered to Ba2 and remained on review for further downgrade. On the day of bankruptcy, October 31, 2011, the rating was revised to Caa1 and still remained on review for further downgrade. Standard and Poor's Ratings Services placed its 'BBB–' counterparty credit rating on MF Global Holdings Ltd. on CreditWatch with negative implications on October 26, 2011. The rating was changed to 'D' and removed from CreditWatch negative after MF Global Holdings Ltd. filed for chapter 11 bankruptcy protection.

[20] Financial Times, January 29, 2012.

sensitivity of each obligor to the one systematic factor. These assumptions are, of course, an oversimplification accepted by the BCBS because of their preference for an easier-to-validate bottom-up approach where the risk of a credit portfolio can be assessed by each single obligor. Under Basel II, a portfolio consisting of exposure from one obligor or one sector only will result in the same regulatory capital charges as a portfolio which is equally distributed among a variety of single borrowers or sectors. Since credit portfolios are neither perfectly granular nor dependent on one systemic factor only, the portfolio risk attributable to concentration may be underestimated. As a result, the capital charges are set too low, which opens a gap between regulatory capital and economic capital that explicitly incorporates the correlation structures of a portfolio. However, banks are requested to hold sufficient capital to cover all kinds of risks. The assessment of capital adequacy under Basel II Pillar 2 has to explicitly consider the extent of credit risk concentrations. Consequently, supervisors expect banks to address concentration risks and to allocate additional capital where necessary, net of risk mitigation. Portfolio concentrations of financial institutions vary, depending on the nature of business, scale, and presence in countries, regions, and markets. The level of concentration risk which is adequate for a financial institution has to be assessed in relation to its capital, thus its capability to absorb losses from concentrations. Specialized lenders or regionally focused banks may have an advantage due to their expertise and market position, which may result in superior asset selection and, to a certain extent, may offset disadvantages from being exposed to risk concentrations. In the assessment of concentration risks within a portfolio it is important to analyse common sensitivities of exposures to key risk drivers. Wrong assumptions about correlations will badly affect the conclusion about adequate capital required for given concentration risks or the level of concentration within a credit portfolio constraint by the prevailing capital. Different forms of credit risk concentrations arise from[21]

- significant exposures to an individual counterparty or group of related counterparties;
- credit exposures to counterparties in the same economic sector or geographic region;
- credit exposures to counterparties whose financial performance is dependent on the same activity or commodity; and
- indirect credit exposures arising from a bank's credit risk mitigation activities (e.g. exposure to a single collateral type or to credit protection provided by a single counterparty).

[21] BCBS (2006), Article 773.

Banks have to develop effective internal policies, systems, and controls to identify, measure, monitor, and control their credit risk concentrations. Supervisors are asked to review the results of a bank's stress test and to take action if concentration risks are not managed appropriately or are not sufficiently considered in the assessment of the capital adequacy of the institution. The CEBS has provided high-level guidance for financial institutions and supervisors on the management of concentration risks,[22] setting out what the institutions should consider concerning concentration risk in their ICAAP,

> under which it is the institution's own responsibility to adequately manage (i.e. identify, measure, monitor and control) these risks and allocate internal capital, where considered necessary, in support of concentration risk in a structured manner.

Moreover, CEBS required national supervisors as part of the supervisory review and evaluation process (SREP) to enforce that institutions hold internal capital which is in line with the level of concentration risk, considering the nature, scale, and complexity of activities at the respective firm.

In 2010, the BCBS published its new regulatory framework, called Basel III.[23] Recommended by the G20, the directive is to be translated into national law by the end of 2012. A proposal made by the EU Commission, the CRD IV,[24] seeks to prevent unacceptable risk of loss due to excessive concentration of exposures to a single client or group of connected clients. In order to determine a group of connected clients and aggregating their exposures into a single risk, the risk arising from a common source of significant funding also has to be taken into account.

2.4.2 Measurement of concentration risk

Although there have been considerable efforts to measure such concentration risks as single name, industry, region or country risk, the challenge remains to put these risks into perspective to regulatory capital or economic capital as demanded by capital adequacy within Basel II. In the absence of a regulatory recommendation as to how concentration risks have to be quantitatively assessed, banks are left to find their own approach to meet the regulatory requirements. So how much more capital actually should be set aside, in addition to the regulatory capital, to cover

[22] CEBS (2010b).

[23] BCBS (2011).

[24] CRD IV consists of a) Capital Requirements Directive and b) Capital Requirements Regulation published in July 2011.

concentration risks? Surveyed in 2006,[25] selected best-practice banks indicated that they were using a combination of vendor and in-house models to assess concentration risk. Simple concentration indicators such as Simpson's Equitability Index, the Shannon-Wiener index, Pielou's evenness index, Moody's Diversity Score, and Gini coefficients are used for an ad hoc assessment of portfolio granularity. A popular indicator of portfolio concentration is the Herfindahl–Hirschmann Index (HHI),[26] defined as the sum of squared shares of each constituent of the total portfolio:

$$H = \sum_{i=1}^{N} b_i^2$$

or normalized as

$$\frac{\sum_{i=1}^{N} b_i^2}{\left(\sum_{i=1}^{N} b_i\right)^2}$$

where

b = portfolio share of borrower
N = number of borrowers in portfolio

The HHI displays the level of concentration on a continuous scale, from 0 for a fully granular portfolio to 1 for a portfolio consisting of only one asset. However, the HHI does not provide any information on changes in the riskiness of a portfolio because of risk concentration and is therefore of limited use for determining a capital surcharge. An increasing HHI value reflects a rising concentration and would in principle suggest a higher capital surcharge or a granularity adjustment to Basel II IRB capital. Preferably, concentration-risk indicators are based on risk-sensitive measures; that is, on the economic capital allocated to the borrowers concerned, risk weighted asset (RWA), or expected loss. Although the HHI can be applied on the economic capital consumption of an obligor, thereby introducing implicitly correlation aspects, portfolio models are clearly superior for measuring the effects from concentration risk as they specifically incorporate default dependencies, exposure distribution, and credit quality. Since the effect of single name bulk risks on economic capital is determined by correlations assumptions, the outcome of different portfolio

[25] CEBS (2006b).

[26] The Herfindahl or Herfindahl-Hirschman Index is widely used to measure the level of competition within certain markets in order to detect monopolies or antitrust practices. For those purposes, the HHI is in particular useful as it assesses the market concentration without the necessity to define an optimal market diversification.

models can vary significantly. An indicative calculation provided by the BCBS[27] of the contribution of idiosyncratic risk to economic capital, constrained by the maximum concentration resulting from application of the EU large-exposure rules, results in an estimated 13 to 21 per cent higher portfolio value-at-risk compared to a perfectly granular portfolio with otherwise the same characteristics. For larger portfolios, in excess of 4,000 exposures, which are more typical, the effect is less pronounced, with about a 1.5 to 4 per cent increase in value-at-risk. Smaller portfolios, with 1,000 to 4,000 exposures likely display a more significant increase, in the 4–8 per cent range.

2.4.3 Concentration-risk limits

Concentration risks arising from single exposures or groups of exposures have been stressed by Basel II[28] as the most important cause of major problems in banks because of their potential to produce losses which can threaten the bank's ability to continue its core operations. The BCBS requests that concentration-risk limits be set in relation to a bank's capital, its total assets, or, where adequate measures exist, its overall risk level. Please note that single name and industry concentration have to be looked at separately. A perfectly diversified portfolio as regards sector distribution can exhibit large single name concentrations within industries. Also, a very granular portfolio can be concentrated in a few industries, as is often the case with specialized lenders. CEBS explicitly noted that financial institutions which are highly dependent for profits on a single business sector and/or a single geographic area may be more affected by sectoral or regional business cycles.[29] While the competitive advantage of specialized lenders may to a certain extent counterbalance their vulnerability to adverse developments in the segments in which they are active, they will ultimately suffer disproportionately from a prolonged downturn due to the concentration. Banks have to take into account these dependencies along with the exposure to correctly assess their overall concentration risks. Since the purpose of a credit risk limit system is to ensure that the actual risk position complies with the stated risk appetite, a consistent set of risk measures needs to be implemented. The development of risk limits consists of four steps:

1. **Definition** of credit risk limits by
   a. Limit **object**
   b. Limit **measure**

[27] See BCBS (2006).
[28] See BCBS (2006), Articles 770–7.
[29] See CEBS (2010).

2. **Determination** of the limits
   a. **Quantitative** limit setting
   b. **Qualitative** limit setting
   c. **Consistency** check
3. Limit **controlling**, monitoring
4. **Management** of limit **breaches**, escalation procedure

Risk limits aim to protect the bank from excessive risk-taking; at the same time, they must leave sufficient room to execute the business plan, which is reflected in the risk appetite and the credit risk strategy. Hence, determining appropriate risk limits is not a purely formulaic process; it requires in-depth knowledge and understanding of a business and the attendant risks. Any periodic or ad hoc review of a business plan and risk strategy immediately affects the corresponding risk limits, potentially necessitating a limit revision.

2.4.3.1 Definition of risk limits

Credit risk limits are typically multidimensional and make use of a variety of risk measures to arrive at a limit framework which is sufficiently detailed to match the specific business and risk characteristics. Since no single risk metric fits all purposes of the limit setting, a combination of different metrics may achieve the objective.

2.4.3.1.1 Risk limit object. A coherent set of risk limits starts with a definition of the limit object or limit dimension. The most common are risk limits for single obligors, sectors, or industries and countries. Other dimensions include a limit for a predefined subset of borrowers, for instance the top five or top ten large-exposure groups, limits on products such as asset-based financing (i.e. leveraged finance, project finance, commodity finance, structured credit) and constraints for certain geopolitical risks; for instance assets or obligors with increased political influence or interest.[30]

2.4.3.1.2 Risk limit measures. Risk limit measures must be risk sensitive and directly manageable through active risk mitigation.

Gross EAD is an indicator of a worst-case loss, but it is not sensitive to changes in the credit risk of the obligor; nor do active risk mitigation measures impact gross EAD, except when the obligor makes an

[30] Examples of political influence or interest are the nationalization of YPF, owned by the Spanish utility firm Repsol, in Argentina in 2012 or the forced insolvency and subsequent distribution of the assets of the once dominant Russian oil conglomerate Yukos in 2004.

Table 2.1 Parameters for limit risk measures

<table>
<tr><th></th><th></th><th colspan="5">Measure</th></tr>
<tr><th></th><th></th><th>Gross Exposure</th><th>Net Exposure</th><th>Expected Loss, EL</th><th>Regulatory Capital</th><th>Economic Capital</th></tr>
<tr><td rowspan="5">Parameter</td><td>Exposure at Default, EAD</td><td></td><td></td><td></td><td></td><td></td></tr>
<tr><td colspan="2">Loss Given Default, LDG</td><td></td><td></td><td></td><td></td></tr>
<tr><td colspan="3">Probability of Default, PD</td><td></td><td></td><td></td></tr>
<tr><td colspan="4">Regulatory Capital Weights</td><td></td><td></td></tr>
<tr><td colspan="5">Correlation</td><td></td></tr>
</table>

outright sale or declines to refinance a maturing loan. Single name-specific risk mitigation such as collateral, CDSs, financial guarantees (FGs), and subparticipations decrease either the PD or the LGD, depending on instrument and respective Basel II rule, making the net EAD or EL a better risk limit measure, at least in combination with the gross EAD. It should be noted, though, that the introduction of risk-sensitive measures in connection with stepped risk limits (i.e. higher limits for better credit quality and lower limits for worse-rated borrowers) exposes the bank to passive limit breaches, which may occur due to a deterioration of the risk profile of an obligor that was hitherto limit-compliant. EAD limits furthermore contain a certain degree of volatility, since the EAD arising from revolving credit lines or backup facilities varies with the amount drawn.

While informative and in principle useful, operative limits on regulatory or economic capital consumption are subject to model risk, and are challenging to implement, as since loan originators have to assess potential limit breaches before requesting credit approval from the authorized credit officer. Thus, a real-time simulation of a new deal must be performed to evaluate ex ante the compliance of a transaction with the capital limit; this is difficult to do when whole portfolios have to be modelled. Alternatively, reasonable proxies based on the observed economic capital of comparable transactions may serve the purpose sufficiently well. In order to become operational, limits must be properly communicated and understood by relationship managers and credit risk managers, a state of affairs which argues for a more simplified set of measures for which timely data are available.

2.4.3.2 Determination of risk limits

The second step of the limit-setting process involves the determination of qualitative and quantitative limits, followed by a plausibility and feasibility check. When deriving risk limits, the perimeter subject to those limits has to be defined. For example, single-obligor concentration-risk limits based on economic capital may be applicable only for borrowers or groups of borrowers exceeding a predefined minimum EAD or economic capital threshold. The rationale for identifying a specific perimeter for each limit category is that limits should correspond to the portfolio characteristics. For example, single-obligor concentration-risk limits are less relevant for a granular credit portfolio consisting of private individuals; whereas the same portfolio may exhibit significant regional concentrations if the bank is only regionally active, hence requiring regional concentration-risk limits to reduce the bank's sensitivity to that region and to encourage increasing the portfolio diversification through active portfolio management.

2.4.3.2.1 Quantitative risk limits. Since limits are the expression of risk appetite and risk-taking capacity, they are derived from the bank's capital position. Economic capital, either actual or target, allows recognition of the correlation structure of the credit portfolio. This is particularly relevant for those limits where correlation is a predominant source of risk – for instance, for country risk limits, which deal with the correlation of sovereign default to transfer risk for companies domiciled in the defaulted country. A cushion between actual economic capital and available risk capital ensures that the risk-taking capacity will not be exceeded, even under stress. For example, the buffer of the German-based lender Commerzbank amounts to 20 per cent of its economic capital.[31] In other words, Commerzbank deployed only 80 per cent of its capital to absorb losses from risks taken so that it retains its ability to manoeuvre even under severe adverse circumstances. Specific stress tests provide insights into the development of economic capital under stress, allowing verification of the sustainability of a credit risk strategy, flanked by the various risk limits, under the stressed conditions. Determining limits for PD ranges, analogous to the rating scale of Standard and Poor's or Moody's, with the limits decreasing for increasing PDs, recognizes the higher correlation of weaker obligors, which are more sensitive to an adverse macroeconomic development. On the other hand, the economic capital of a very high-rated customer, even with a substantial exposure, is probably very low. A net EAD limit, along with an economic capital limit for a borrower, protects the bank from becoming vulnerable to single-obligor losses when the rating either underestimates the credit risk or rapidly deteriorates, and there are no measures available to reduce the exposure. Individual obligors subject to the concentration-risk monitoring often consist of subgroups

---

[31] See Becker (2008).

of firms which are economically or legally interconnected. The definition of connected clients provided by the CRD (Directive 2006/48/EC) encompasses the control one client has over another and the interconnectedness due to a common economic dependency.[32]

For setting sector limits, a segmentation where sectors show high asset correlation among borrowers in the same sector and low correlation to obligors in other sectors is necessary to achieve reasonable model results. However, in contrast to the more intuitive and clearer geographical segmentation, the definition of sectors is less straightforward. This is usually a limitation to industry concentration-risk assessment, since correlations are unstable and highly dependent on the availability of accurate data. A widely accepted official sector classification is the Global Industry Classification Standard (GICS®), developed by MSCI and Standard and Poor's. It consists of 10 sectors, 24 industry groups, 68 industries, and 154 subindustries; hence it is suitable for a levelled approach towards industry concentration-risk limiting.

2.4.3.2.2 Qualitative risk limits: Underwriting standards. Loan origination is the first line of defence when it comes to appropriate lending. Loan-officer surveys monitor the development of standards, best practices, and also restrictions, to gauge the increase in the risks banks are taking. When lending criteria become too strict, the liquidity position at corporates may be negatively affected. A prolonged credit crunch can have severe effects and ultimately drive an increase in insolvencies. A successful loan origination process incentivizes net revenues after risk costs rather than volumes and sheer balance sheet size. In the past, some leveraged loans have been issued with little protection for credit quality deterioration, dubbed 'covenant lite loans'. These were a clear reflection of relaxed lending standards prevailing at that time, unfortunately adding to losses when the financial crisis broke, since many banks were left holding loans they originally intended to distribute to other investors. Qualitative risk limits detail financing principles, including a minimum borrower PD requirement for uncollateralized transactions, eligible collateral, transaction tenors, and other financing terms, such as currency or margin grids, use of proceeds from borrowing, ranking of the claim (i.e. no subordination), covenants, eligible borrowers under a transaction (e.g. holding company versus subsidiaries), and constraints concerning credit products (i.e. term loans, revolving credit facilities, guarantees, etc.). While the financing principles are very detailed and act more as a business restriction than a limit, they

[32] See also CEBS (2009). The guidelines provide further information and clarity as regards the definition of connected groups.

complement the quantitative limits to fine-tune daily operations with the objective of shaping the credit portfolio to a predefined target by actively selecting new business that meets the characteristics set out by the target portfolio.

2.4.3.2.3 Consistency check. Once the limits have determined the bank's capital position, conformance to the business and risk strategy must be proved. As a general rule, limits must allow business model operations to execute the business plan to which the risk appetite and credit risk strategy correspond while observing the respective limits. Since in some cases volatile moves of FX (foreign exchange) rates or seasonal patterns of the drawing of credit lines can have a measurable impact on the limit usage, the setting of limits must take into account expected or simulated trends to avoid 'passive' limit breaches. In general, the limit headroom reflects the relative attractiveness and strategic relevance of the subsegment. In particular in areas where the bank feels less comfortable with the exposure or the future prospects, a stricter limit may be set, accelerating the reduction of that segment and triggering counterbalancing measures earlier.

2.4.3.3 Limit monitoring

Regular and frequent limit reporting is a prerequisite for a portfolio development that complies with the approved credit risk strategy. In order to perform limit analyses, capable data systems must be in place. Weaknesses in the IT infrastructure result in unsustainable manual efforts to improve data quality, to the detriment of the timeliness and content focus of those limit reports. Highly automated report generation incorporates several layers of quality checks to reduce manual corrections to a minimum. High-quality limit reports, analysed and commented on by skilled experts, raise loan origination units' awareness of the relevant limits and support management in steering the organization on the path laid out by the credit risk strategy.

2.4.3.4 Management of limit breaches

The full circle of concentration-risk limits consists of four parts: limit setting, recognition of the limits within the credit approval process, regular limit monitoring and, finally, management of bulk risk-limit breaches.

Concentration-risk-limit breaches occur for different reasons:

- New business
- Drawing under existing credit commitments
- Deterioration of credit quality

- Automatic rating downgrade when the regular credit review timeline has been missed
- Stuck syndications
- Merger or takeover to form a larger entity

Countermeasures can be categorized into two groups: organic and active mitigations. Organic solutions include a credit review with the potential for a better credit quality assessment and assigning of a higher limit that would cover the actual risk. Requesting collateral mitigates the net EAD and EL and is usually the first attempt to solve bulk risk limit breaches for clients for which no capital market hedges are available. Optimizing the credit product mix so that corresponding risk measures, such as gross EAD and net EAD improve, are other solutions which can be considered for larger firms that use a broad spectrum of credit products. Depending on the procedure used to derive the relevant PD for a borrower group, an internal reallocation of credit lines to obligors having a better credit quality may also help to eliminate concentration-risk limit breaches. Active risk mitigations refer to credit risk transfer techniques which include outright sale or syndication, hedging via credit derivatives, subparticipations, and financial guarantees and securitization. Since the objective of all these measures is to reduce the EAD, the PD, or the LDG of a borrower, the same holds in principle for industry concentration-risk limit breaches as long as the limits are expressed in risk measures which are sensitive to the techniques listed.

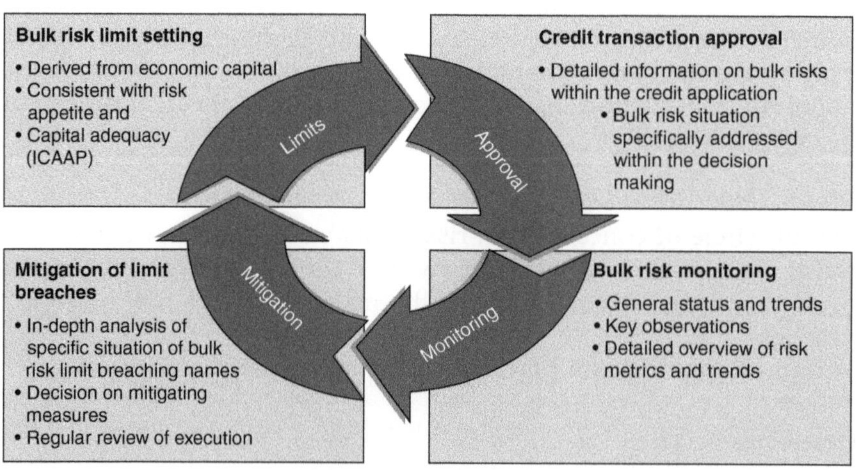

Figure 2.2 Concentration-risk limit circle

2.4.4 Syndication risk limits

Syndicated loans are defined as those loans which are provided by more than one lender, the so-called syndicate, to one borrower or a group of related borrowers under a common legal documentation framework. Unlike bilateral loans, which are characterized by highly individual loan agreements between a bank and a client, syndicated loans benefit from comparably higher standardization and tradability. They are most often larger transactions in which the client's core banks provide the borrower with the requested funds; that is, the banks keep a chunk of the loans financing M&A transactions on their books to retain the client relationship and orchestrate the further distribution of the rest of the loan to other lenders. An exception is the club deal, where a group of banks jointly originate a loan with the intention of holding the asset to maturity. The terms and legal documentation of a syndicated loan are negotiated by the mandated lead arranger(s) while the bookrunners are in charge of managing the distribution, or syndication, of the loan. During the primary syndication phase, the lenders that are part of the syndicate either underwrite the loan or commit to sell the loan on a best efforts basis. After completion of the general syndication, when the participating lenders receive their allocations, a secondary market sell-down starts. Hence, the underwriter of a syndicated loan takes the risk that either the loan may be undersubscribed or that the subsequent selling of the loan in full or in parts may fail if no other investor emerges to buy the asset at the suggested price. In general, the syndication process takes place within three months. However, if the loan is severely mispriced or the demand for syndicated loans drops due to a significant adverse change in market conditions, the bank may be left with a commitment to the client. Although at that stage the loan itself is not signed, the bank would run a substantial legal and reputational risk by walking away from the deal. Moreover, when a transaction has been fully underwritten, in some cases the loan was signed even before the syndication phase, which exposes the underwriter to the risk of having to fund the drawdowns under the terms of the loan.

Even though the market for syndicated loans is only loosely connected to and correlated with other debt markets, a general risk-off attitude will negatively affect the trading liquidity of those loans, too. When this happened during the financial crisis, banks had to digest stuck loans which sometimes greatly exceeded their risk appetite and limits. Nevertheless, syndicated loan limits serve to restrict business operations to avoid the piling up of new underwriting risks before the pipeline of deals has been cleared. They do not per se prevent larger transactions from being kept on the bank's books for a considerable length of time when they become unmarketable once the internal credit approval has been granted and the loan underwritten. It should be noted that the phrase limit does not imply any capital consumption. In contrast to concentration-risk limits, for which capital to cover the risk has to be set aside, syndicated loan limits aim at prudent and precautionary restrictions to avoid ongoing loan origination when the market is effectively shut, preventing successful syndication. Since syndicated loans refer to different asset classes, such as asset-backed financing – that is, leveraged loans or project and commodity finance – and large corporate debt, limits may be applied on a transactional and asset class level. An aggregated limit further complements the limit system. Additionally, a bridge to bond limit for loans which will be replaced by bonds issued at a later stage provides protection against market conditions that do not allow for bond issuance, thus hindering a refinancing of the loan.

3
What If: Credit Risk Stress Testing

In many credit risk managing organizations there is a rift between fundamental and quantitatively oriented portfolio managers. This partly reflects a belief in real facts versus questionable data manipulating, or empirical versus statistical analysis. The mathy quants rely more on the view from the top when constructing portfolios; in part to avoid getting carried away with micro level convictions and losing sight of the balancing and construction of portfolios. So it's never been easy to find the right mixture or interface of top-down to bottom-up, quantitative to fundamental portfolio management. It is in fact a challenge to make the best use of the expert know-how of credit analysts, who specialize in single name and transaction analysis from not only a credit risk perspective but also a market risk perspective. In the current environment, where major economic and financial trends are met with unpredictable political actions, making the right call is a much tougher proposition than ever before. As a direct result, it is essential to correctly assess the consequences of positioning the portfolio. This has led to a building-in of quant analysis as a core part of the portfolio managing process. Quant tools have been developed to provide an additional lens for the portfolio manager, to slice and dice through the different dimensions of a portfolio, adding new perspectives or raising awareness of hidden or underestimated risks. The more high-quality and timely the available data, the better a sound quantitative portfolio model can help to reveal built-in biases, confirming or opposing the manager's intention. However, modelling and data are identified as recurrent pain points by a study by Moody's[1] on best practices of banks regarding stress tests, hence they deserve both close attention and improvements to make the exercise viable. Better insights into sources of risk and return help the fundamentalists to better align themselves with their strategic convictions by providing obvious reality checks of their performance. However,

[1] See Moody's (2011).

incorporating risk models into the investment process to improve risk analysis and management is a key ingredient of sound portfolio management, but it does not stop there. Portfolio models can also help to answer the what-if-I-am-wrong question, a base requirement for portfolio managers and one that is especially valuable at times of heightened volatility and market disruption. Here, model-based stress tests can provide a picture of possible outcomes for any given scenario. This gives managers a better feel for unwanted consequences, which can be mitigated by trimming positions down to the level of acceptable risk in line with a clearly defined risk tolerance. Stress tests also encourage a higher degree of discipline in formulating potential scenarios and in thinking through the chain of events, cascading down from high-level macroeconomic moves into effects on the micro level, therefore ultimately on the credit quality of borrowers and the value of their debt. When the unexpected defaults of Enron and WorldCom rattled financial markets, investors were faced with unprecedented losses from their holdings in these firms, but worse, spillover effects throughout the debt capital markets were felt for a long period of time. The shock waves from the downfall of these large corporations contributed to a substantial rise in credit spreads around the globe. Portfolio managers who correctly anticipated the credit events but did not consider second-round effects trumped the performance of their competitors only for a short period of time. A similar fate was suffered by Morgan Stanley, when, at the height of the financial crises, a combination of a hedge position in ABS equity and an investment in an ABS super senior position first showed tremendous gains; but when credit losses began to eat through the capital structure of those ABSs, the losses on the long position far exceeded the gains from the short position, resulting in substantial net losses.[2] In this chapter, approaches to stress tests and the specific stress scenarios which form the basis for purposeful stress tests are explained. It describes the types of stress tests and explains their managerial applications.

3.1 Definition and objective of stress tests

Stress tests are an essential managerial tool to define and confirm a sustainable strategy, and thus they receive close attention from

[2] In 2007, Morgan Stanley CEO John J. Mack wrote in his annual letter to shareholders, '*The writedown that Morgan Stanley announced at year end in our mortgage-related business was the result of an error in judgment made by a small team in one area of fixed income and a failure to manage that risk appropriately. It was deeply disappointing to me – as I know it was to all of our shareholders.*' (See www.morganstanley.com.) On November 8, 2007, Morgan Stanley had to announce a $3.7 bn loss related to its U.S. subprime mortgage exposure, which was the largest write-down in the history of the firm. See www.reuters.com, 'Morgan Stanley sees $3.7 billion subprime hit'.

supervisors. They are ultimately located within the area of responsibility of the management body[3] and serve the purpose of revealing the connectivity of macroeconomic changes to key credit portfolio risk measures and of assessing the implications of unfavourable developments for the resilience of a financial institution. A precise qualitatively and quantitatively defined scenario, whether hypothetical, historical, or worst case, helps to quantify potential losses and to define trigger levels which, when reached, should activate countermeasures to limit further losses – as required by the bank's regulators. Specifically, the capital requirements directive (CRD) and supervisory review process, the second pillar of the Basel II capital adequacy framework, requires banks to conduct rigorous stress testing to introduce a forward-looking view in risk management and strategic and capital planning, thereby identifying possible events or changes in market conditions related to all the relevant risks (credit, market, operational, liquidity, financial investments, real estate, business) that could adversely impact the bank. Under Pillar 1, banks qualifying for the internal ratings-based (IRB) approach perform stress tests to assess the robustness of their supervisor-approved internal models and the cushions above the regulatory minimum capital.[4] That capital level is set to ensure solvency by covering unexpected losses, defined as unexpected tail risks at a specified confidence level. It should not be confused with the stress testing of capital under Pillar 2, where stress tests reveal whether a bank is able to satisfy internal capital requirements when adverse conditions, as outlined in the stress scenario, materialize.

Stressing a portfolio or investment strategy and testing for sustainability have become very popular lately as a result of the financial crisis. Most market participants agree that, if the consequences had been known beforehand, Lehman probably would not have been allowed to go bankrupt. Consequently, banks as well as their supervisors have questioned whether the stress-testing practices prevailing at that time were sufficient to cope with the crisis. The introduction of the CEBS or EBA stress test gained widespread attention from market professionals. From the perspective of a bank's management, however, these official stress tests are often of little value in steering risk management. It should come as no surprise, given the intention of EBA to calm the fears of financial markets, that the vulnerability of various banks to certain adverse economic or

[3] See CEBS (2010b). 'Management body' is defined as top management level of an institution, whereas 'senior management' is the level of management below the management body.

[4] Banks applying an IRB approach are required to conduct stress tests as requested by CRD, Article 124.

financial developments might be unacceptably high and require a capital increase or other capital-strengthening measures to avoid a systemic collapse of the financial industry. Consequently, the focus has been more on comparing the results of the participating banks and providing decent transparency, especially because only shortly after passing the CEBS stress test, four Irish banks went bust in 2010. The stress scenario defined by EBA in 2011 did recognize the rising risk of sovereign defaults in Europe but was not able to keep pace with the deteriorating situation in Greece. Also, the specific portfolio characteristics of each bank, in particular the big differences between wholesale and retail banks, were not considered appropriately. For a risk manager, the attention is on what can hurt the most, which is different for every financial institution and does not comport with a one-size-fits-all approach.

Stress tests that are governed by top management as requested by CEBS and firmly embedded into the risk-management framework and senior management decision making improve the competitiveness of the organization. Banks that established stress tests as a standard procedure, with clearly defined roles and processes, and that secured management attention are perceived to have better withstood the crisis. Two major factors that contributed to the comparatively superior resilience of those institutions can be identified. First, regular and frequent stress tests allow risk and business managers to better anticipate the effects from downturns or shocks, regarding both the sequence and magnitude of events, and to not get paralysed when caught by surprise. This enables institutions to take informed and timely decisions, and to respond appropriately as circumstances develop. The other advantage stems from consciously incorporating stress test results into the risk appetite and limit framework, which, if appropriately tested and set, diminishes the need for costly corrective actions when adverse scenarios materialize. A bank might be comfortable with the risk/return profile of a proposed business plan given the historical and expected conditions, but hidden inherent tail risks might be intolerable for the bank. An example of such a case is the demise of leveraged structured credit products. Some banks which were active in this business because of the very attractive margins prevailing at that time later lost multiyear revenues when the market collapsed. With the benefit of hindsight, it seems clear that for some, the decision to enter that business segment would not have been taken if appropriate stress tests had been conducted and deemed plausible and the results taken seriously by the management.

Definition: a stress test assesses the financial health of a firm under a severe but plausible scenario. By quantifying the implications of those adverse conditions, in particular on key risk metrics such as loan losses and economic capital, stress tests help the organization better withstand the effects of a downturn or shock and contribute to better decision making.

Objective: the key objective is to alert a firm's management to adverse unexpected outcomes related to a range of risks and to indicate the amount of capital needed to absorb losses when large shocks occur.[5]

Supporting a bank's risk management, stress tests

- provide **forward-looking assessments of risk**, which are a key ingredient in meaningful risk management, in particular with respect to budgeting and strategy definition. To derive a robust risk strategy which flanks a proposed business plan, the sensitivity and viability of the budget to significantly worse-than-assumed operating conditions are tested to reveal hidden weaknesses in the business plan.
- contribute to **capital and liquidity planning** and to the **determination** of the risk appetite or tolerance and **capital adequacy**, as required by ICAAP. Determining of the necessary level of capital to hold against severe deterioration of the economic environment[6] can ensure the solvency of a bank even during times of crisis and stress.
- enhance external information by **increasing transparency** of the risk profile and capital position of the stress-testing institution under certain adverse circumstances.
- help to develop solution-oriented **risk mitigation** measures and **contingency plans** as part of an effective crisis management, either pre-emptive or as a coordinated process to regain stability based on in-depth information on risk sensitivities and interconnectedness.

Stress tests cover firm-wide risks, either as a whole or as separate component; that is, subportfolios by region or business line or by type of risk. 'Firm-wide' means all material risks to which an organization is exposed, but not as a simple aggregation of stress tests for parts. Although no specific frequency[7] has been outlined by regulators, CEBS asks firms to stress-test certain risk areas more often while firm-wide stress tests are performed less frequently. Besides that, ad hoc stress tests are part of the stress-testing program. The time horizon of stress tests is typically set in relation to the maturity profile and degree

---

[5] See BCBS (2009).

[6] In other words, stress tests identify the amount of capital needed to restore the capital ratios to the pre-crisis level.

[7] CEBS (2010b) states that '*stress tests should be undertaken with appropriate frequency*', which should be proportionate to risk areas and the need of an institution for firm-wide stress tests – i.e. higher for large, complex banks that have a number of risk areas requiring stress tests. It seems reasonable to assume that conducting an ICAAP stress test at least twice a year complies with this requirement.

of liquidity of the stressed portfolio but also recognizes an assumed duration until the economy returns to some kind of equilibrium after the applied shock.

In order to measure the erosion of regulatory or economic capital of a financial institution resulting from the stress scenario, the level of increase in RWA due to rising obligor PDs, loan loss provisions, valuation adjustments, and the shortfall are observed. Changes in credit quality metrics such as EAD, PDs[8] and LGDs[9] are determined either by the elements of the stress scenario that are factored into the rating of the obligors or through the parameterization of the credit portfolio model defining the dynamic interaction of macroeconomic variables and the risk profile of the portfolio, as well as by interdependencies in the form of correlation structures. Portfolio models also make it possible to assess changes in the value of collateral and credit quality migrations, including any deterioration within the non-performing part of the portfolio.[10] Alternatively, the transmission of moves of economic factors and corresponding losses or changes in related risk metrics could be derived from judgemental assessment and internal or external expertise. Effects on revenues or off–balance sheet positions are evaluated similarly. The decision to base the transformation of scenario into impact on a model very much hinges on the availability of a sophisticated portfolio model and sufficient data of decent quality. However, a credit portfolio model might be better suited to deal with non-linear changes in macroeconomic factors and the corresponding stress on parameters, meaning that an acceleration of effects might result in an overproportionate impact, often observable as a domino effect. Credit portfolio correlations are defined as asset or default correlations, ensuring a consistent approach throughout the credit portfolio; this is necessary to correctly estimate the stress impact on default rates, which in turn contributes to deriving the corresponding impairments. On a portfolio level, the impact of stress is determined by the delta in conditional expected loss and other portfolio statistics. Stress tests are regularly performed at the single-risk level as well as on an integrated level and subsequently disclosed to the senior management. Stress tests come in a variety of approaches, with equally diverse goals based on specific stressed scenarios.

[8] For those institutions permitted to take the IRB approach.

[9] Provided that the bank uses its own LGD estimates for capital requirements calculation.

[10] These effects may be material and deserve attention.

3.2 Stressed scenarios

Stressed macroeconomic scenarios are designed to reveal the vulnerability of a bank's portfolio to *extreme* or *exceptional* but *plausible* events – although this description, originally introduced by the IMF, is not clear-cut as to how *exceptional* and *plausible* are defined. Scenarios are developed to address specific questions or concerns. In that sense, they can relate to a wider macroeconomic crisis or downturn or to specific events or shocks which will directly affect certain portfolio segments or risk types, and others indirectly through second- and third-round or spillover effects. Scenarios chosen for stress tests are discussed among research analysts, economists, portfolio managers, senior risk officers, and industry and business specialists to assure economic relevance and to foster general acceptance. In particular, industry specialists can provide valuable insights as to whether a scenario and the chain of events are plausible. In general, stress test scenarios can be grouped into[11]

a) **hypothetical** or macroeconomic scenarios
b) **historical** or shock scenarios
c) **worst-case** scenarios

3.2.1 Hypothetical or macroeconomic scenarios

For a broader assessment of the resilience of banks or the financial system as a whole to economic downturns, a corresponding scenario has to be developed and translated consistently by a macroeconomic model into changes in various economic variables, such as GDP growth, inflation, interest rates, oil prices, and unemployment. Thus, in a hypothetical scenario, banks and corporates are affected by simultaneous large moves of those factors. This kind of scenario is used most often because it has the flexibility to test a broad range of combinations of changes in macroeconomic factors, of unlimited severity, as long as the scenario remains plausible. A baseline scenario with only moderate changes can serve as a benchmark putting the results of severe stress into perspective. Alternative scenarios with different directions – for instance, a spike in oil prices that results either in a significant rise in output and inflation as rising costs are passed through, or in a major decline in economic growth due to a price-driven collapse in consumer demand – provide additional information about the consequences if certain assumptions on the build-up of the scenario do not hold. A probability weighting of the alternative scenarios according to the expectation that the defined

[11] See also Bonti et al. (2006).

scenarios materialize enables portfolio management to position the credit portfolio accordingly. A complete scenario definition entails a 'story', with trigger events that are politically or financially motivated, such as an introduction of a capital control by a government or a ban on certain hedging instruments, or natural catastrophes, or isolated events – such as a terrorist attack. Related movements of macroeconomic and other factors are then examined to provide a consistent and full picture of an unfolding adverse development, whose impact is felt across a broad range of factors, and corresponding market reactions. The knock-on effects that ripple through following the initial events – such as increased margin and collateral requirements; prudent valuation haircuts because a market segment is drying up, thus accounting for illiquidity; or built-in convexity of credit default swap (CDS) hedges – are further considerations in an exhaustive scenario. Alternatively, a hypothetical scenario might use historical risk drivers and risk relationships and then be modified to account for actual developments and connections, mitigating the pure backward-looking nature of historical scenarios.

3.2.2 Historical or shock scenarios

While history does not tend to repeat itself, some historical events provide a detailed picture of the transmission mechanisms of a singular trigger event onto a whole economy, creating a complete and, by definition, a plausible and realistic scenario. However, the way macroeconomic variables were affected when the initial shock filtered through the economy at the time might be very different from today's world. A practical example is the oil crisis of the 1970s, which had significant credit-related effects because of its unexpectedness, whereas today a substantial rise in oil prices would trigger immediate concern because of the globalization of trade. The Lehman default and, more recently, the sovereign debt crisis became popular shock scenarios for both credit and market risk. At the same time, the aftermath of the Lehman event demonstrated the shortcoming of historical scenarios: the unprecedented aggregated losses in the financial industry and the resulting economic downturn exceeded those of all other historical events by far, meaning that applying pre-Lehman shocks would have substantially underestimated those risks.

3.2.3 Worst-case scenarios

The goal of worst-case scenarios is to provide information on effects in a highly adverse situation, based on expert judgement or quantitative techniques, thereby creating awareness of the magnitude of potential problems. For example, a bank might be interested in how its liquidity would be affected if certain clients – say, large corporates or customers in certain sectors or regions, like those on the European periphery – fully drew on their committed credit lines because of concerns of a looming credit crunch. While this assumption may be exaggerated, it nevertheless enables the bank's management to identify the impact of maximized stress and to set corresponding trigger levels which, once reached, activate counterbalancing measures.

3.2.4 Stress scenario requirements

Stress scenarios, in order to be meaningful and relevant in a strategic context, have to be[12]

- **extreme:** the level of stress should create a meaningful impact which does not underestimate real threats. For example, the economic downturn in 2009 was so severe that economic forecasts few captured its full magnitude, thus leaving banks wondering how to plug the holes in their capital resulting from both losses and the rapidly rising risk weights of their assets.
- **plausible:** although extreme, the stress scenario still must be realistic to be accepted by a bank's management as a basis for risk-mitigating measures. Ultimately, there is a fine balance between pre-emptive measures to protect the bank from an unlikely but possible event and the costs attached to those measures, which could put a bank into a competitive disadvantage.
- **consistent:** the consideration of the interconnectedness of stressed variables should be consistent with the model framework but also reflect economic reality. This allows the interpretation of scenario results with intuition gained from experience.
- **specific:** in order to reveal both material and hidden weaknesses in a credit portfolio, the individual portfolio characteristics should be sufficiently recognized. For example, a credit portfolio consisting of loans to private individuals of below-average credit quality might be more severely affected by a significant rise in unemployment, than that of a financial institution that is primarily engaged in wholesale banking. Thus, a stress scenario needs to adequately incorporate the observed sensitivities of the portfolio and stress those variables which determine the quality of the portfolio.

[12] See also Bonti et al. (2006).

3.3 Types of stress tests

Stress test approaches differ in terms of their objectives and frequency. To address the complex nature of interconnected risks,[13] their drivers, and relevance for the portfolio of a bank, multiple layers and combinations of stress tests are performed. An overview of (complementary) stress tests is provided by Table 3.1.

All approaches should entail qualitative and quantitative elements, where larger and more complex organizations focus on the latter as per the principle of proportionality. Common to both larger and smaller institutions is a narrative running through the stress-testing programme that links the risk appetite, business strategy, and impact of the stressed events (internal and external) on the business model, as highlighted by the test results.[14]

3.3.1 Sensitivity analysis

A sensitivity analysis is a simplified stress test approach where one factor, identified as a key risk driver, is used to assess the sensitivity of portfolio

Table 3.1 Types of stress tests

Type of Stress	Short Description
Sensitivity analysis	Analysis of the impact of a *single stressed factor* on the risk profile of a portfolio
Scenario analysis	Analysis of the impact of a *stressed scenario*, historical or hypothetical, on the risk profile of a portfolio. The scenario addresses all risk drivers relevant to the individual portfolio, as well as interconnectedness and spillover effects (second- and third-round effects)
What-if analysis	Analysis of the impact of a specific *hypothesis* relative to risk metrics, parameters, or developments of the portfolio or parts of the portfolio
Concentration-risk analysis	Analysis of the effects of *portfolio concentrations*, by region, industry, single name or asset type, on the portfolio's key risk metrics
Reverse stress testing	Simulation of *trigger event* and transmission mechanism causing a predefined significantly adverse outcome

[13] Potential interactions between risks, such as intra- or inter-risk concentrations, have to be explicitly recognized rather than isolating single-risk factors.
[14] See CEBS (2010b).

risk metrics to that factor. It generally starts with the definition of relevant key risk drivers, such as macroeconomic, credit risk, and financial risk drivers, as well as external effects[15] and their changes under stress. Typically, individual risk types, business lines, or subportfolios are subjected to a sensitivity analysis to address questions specifically related to those portfolio segments. If stress tests are performed using a credit portfolio model, a sensitivity analysis considers the macroeconomic variables input to the portfolio model. A comparison of credit risk metrics – that is, PD, EL, EC and RWA – before and after a shock reveals how sensitive they are in relation to the stressed variables. Several rounds of tests with varying degrees of severity provide a comprehensive picture of how the stressed factor affects the outcome on a portfolio. An extension of the sensitivity analysis is the multifactor approach, which assumes a combination of events. However, unlike a scenario analysis, this type of stress test intentionally ignores the interconnectedness of macroeconomic variables and second- or third-round effects to determine the relevance of a single factor to the risk profile of a portfolio.

3.3.2 Scenario analysis

A scenario analysis is the most complex type of stress test and should cover all material risks throughout the organization. It is based on forward-looking hypothetical or historical scenarios, although using only historical scenarios has proved to be insufficient.[16] Typically, a set of scenarios is defined, incorporating various events with increasing levels of severity. Factors not directly addressed under the stress scenarios – which usually encompass only a small number of systematic factors – respond to the stress through correlations to the stressed factors. This generates a consistent set of stressed PDs for the total portfolio, since the change in PDs depends on the correlation of the individual credit exposure to the stressed factors. A scenario analysis has to consider the *risk types* that are most relevant for the institution, the institution's predominant

---

[15] CEBS (2010b) lists interest rates as an example for macroeconomic risk drivers, change in bankruptcy law or shift in PDs for credit risk drivers, increased volatility in financial instrument markets for financial risk drivers and operational risk events, market events, events affecting regional areas or industry sectors for external events.

[16] Shortcomings of historical scenarios relate to the observed magnitude of the shock impact that may be well below effects triggered by an identical event that happens today. Also, transmission chains and spillover effects may differ substantially due to the globalized nature of the modern world economy.

risk factors, and the individual, institution-specific vulnerabilities, in particular intra- and inter-risk concentrations.[17]

3.3.3 What-if analysis

In some cases a stress scenario is defined by events channelling through special macroeconomic factors which are not encompassed by the credit portfolio model, the specification of which usually recognizes only broader systemic factors. Stress assumptions are then applied directly to certain parameters, such as PDs, LGDs, and EAD, on the whole portfolio or portfolio segments to isolate effects at the subportfolio level, which are then focused on as part of the scenario. For example, a multifactor credit portfolio model may take into account major macroeconomic variables which describe the general state of the economy, but only a few risk drivers that are relevant for the performance of specific sectors. For instance, the credit portfolio of a typical German bank may be representative of the dominant automotive industry in Germany. As was seen in 2009, the decline in global economic growth severely affected the demand for both new and used cars, leading to significant stress in that particular sector, stress mitigated only by a political initiative, in the form of a scrappage bonus, which provided consumers with the incentive to buy new cars. However, in order to isolate the effect of a collapse in the automotive output from that of a global recession, that is, to model the hypothesis of saturated markets or shifts in consumer preferences, risk measures of that portfolio subset are directly adjusted. This can be done by significantly increasing obligor PDs and EAD, reflecting both the deteriorated operating profit as well as the additional refinancing needs of the borrowers concerned. A decrease of the LGD corresponds to lower valuations of assets of automotive producers and their suppliers. A what-if analysis also complements a scenario analysis–based stress test when certain portfolio or asset characteristics or discretionary actions are not fully addressed by the portfolio model specification. Examples include the agreement of investors to accept haircuts on their Greek government bond holdings[18] and the losses related to mortgages denominated in Swiss francs imposed on banks by the Hungarian government.[19] In those cases, losses can be directly simulated by adjusting the credit risk measures concerned.

---

[17] See CEBS (2010b). Institution-specific vulnerabilities include regional and sectoral portfolio characteristics, as well as specific product or business line exposures or funding policies.

[18] As a result of the private sector initiative (PSI), holders of Greek government bonds issued under Greek domestic law agreed in 2012 to a cut of the bond principal.

[19] In 2011, Hungary allowed its citizens to repay Swiss franc–denominated mortgages in a lump sum and at an exchange rate substantially below the actual rate, with the resulting loss to be taken by the lending banks.

3.3.4 Concentration-risk analysis

Risk concentrations in a bank's credit portfolio are a key source of concern and determine the level of credit risk capital. A credit portfolio may exhibit concentrations in countries or regions, industries, single names, or credit products or may be due to high correlation among those factors. Since the Basel II approach does not cover risk concentration in its assessment of regulatory capital based on the risk weighting of assets, regulators strongly emphasize the importance of internal or economic capital to determine a bank's risk appetite. Stress tests on portfolio concentrations are designed to reveal whether the portfolio concentration characteristics under stress is consistent with stated risk tolerance and also to identify hidden sources of portfolio weaknesses due to material risk concentrations. In a complete setting and because of the interconnectedness of risks, concentration-risk stress tests should cover risks across the different booking locations and risk types. However, since credit risks are typically the predominant source of risks for most banks, a stress test on credit risk may already provide valuable insights on inherent vulnerabilities and reveal undesired sensitivities of the credit portfolio to a macroeconomic downturn or other sources of stress.

Concentration risks are stressed either by measuring the impact of a stress scenario on key portfolio metrics or by imposing worst-case assumptions directly on selected risk measures, with the stressed outcome then observed on a portfolio level. The aggregation of risks and corresponding losses serves as a basis for evaluating specific corrective managerial actions.

3.3.4.1 Single name concentration-risk stress test

Single name concentrations arising from the deteriorating risk profile of a portfolio are usually stressed within the scenario analysis. However, the prevailing obligor concentration can become significantly more severe when those clients decide to raise the amount drawn under the committed lines to counter a looming credit crunch or as a general pre-emptive measure. This assumption can be applied to borrowers domiciled in regions affected the most – namely, the European periphery at the time of the sovereign debt crisis – or to corporates operating in industries that exhibit structural weaknesses or downturns. A worst-case scenario would entail all large and bulk risk relevant obligors drawing up to the granted amounts. While this might serve as a benchmark measure to put other stress test assumptions and results into perspective, it fails to meet the condition that stress tests be plausible and realistic. The effect on capital in this particular test is more pronounced for economic capital, as a consequence of the rising level of portfolio concentration, as opposed to regulatory capital, which is impacted by the increase of RWA only. A rise in amounts drawn under commitments is consistent with deteriorating PDs from a scenario analysis–based stress test and reveals a hidden portfolio vulnerability from concentration. To move the stress a little further, the scenario may incorporate the default of one or more of the largest customer groups. In this case, the bank's capital position is not only affected by the additional loan losses, thereby reducing the total capital and capital ratios; it also suffers a meaningful loss of current and future client revenues, which will no longer materialize as assumed.

3.3.4.2 Sector concentration-risk stress test

Although the sensitivity of obligors to systemic risks varies, in general the majority of them are exposed to the economic conditions prevailing in their respective industries or regions. When a stress test on sector concentration is being conducted by applying economic stress on a credit portfolio, stressed economic variables should be representative of or have a direct link to those areas which should be tested, such as countries or industries. A scenario to stress regional or industry concentration-risk assumes a severe increase of risk in that particular area. Other factors that are not directly stressed respond via the specified dependence structure of the model. The advantage of this approach, compared to a simple aggregation of exposures by sector, is that risk concentrations also become visible through the correlation structure.[20]

3.3.5 Reverse stress testing

Reverse stress tests aim at identifying causes and scenarios which ultimately result in a predefined outcome, typically the failure of the firm or, less extreme, a breach of specific triggers, such as maximum loan losses or minimum capital ratios. Trigger levels are set to reflect the case where the thresholds are breached and a bank may no longer be in a position to perform its regular operations, which may be well in advance of undercutting the regulatory capital minimum requirement. At this point, a combination of risks, such as credit, market, and liquidity risk, may respond simultaneously to the situation, eventually preventing the bank from tapping the capital markets for funds or capital. In general, a range of simulations is performed, since various reasons or constellations can ultimately result in the insolvency of a bank or the breach of a predefined trigger level, significantly restricting on the manoeuvrability of the institution. Events sufficiently adverse to the capital of a bank are assessed according to their likelihood of materializing. Risks or flaws

[20] See Bonti et al. (2006).

within business lines or concentrated subportfolios resulting in losses inconsistent with the bank's risk tolerance are analysed in order to identify plausible and *economically relevant* scenarios or shocks that are able to generate those impacts. Reverse stress tests can be either qualitative or quantitative, depending on the aspirations and complexity of the financial institution. However, while regulators point out the importance of reverse stress tests to identify weaknesses in business operations, they may be used for monitoring and contingency planning purposes but are not expected to be considered in the context of capital planning or for capital buffers.[21]

3.4 Stress test information and subsequent mitigation

Stress test results provide managerial value when presented in an understandable format, with a clear description of the scenario – including rationale for the formulation of the scenario, the impact on the portfolio, and its key metrics – and finally with recommendations for the conclusion-based actions to be taken. The responsibility of the management for stress test program of a bank includes the ability to understand

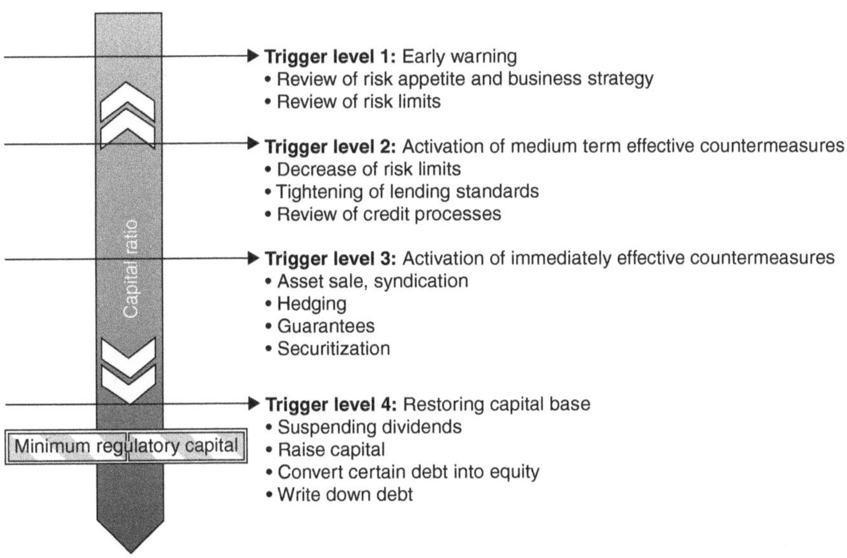

Figure 3.1 Stylized cascading approach of predefined trigger levels and corresponding risk-mitigating measures to counter a decline of the capital ratio

[21] See CEBS (2010b).

the impact of stress events on the bank's firm-wide risk profile and, based on that, to take appropriate actions to assure ongoing solvency.[22] As required by their supervisors, banks have to demonstrate their ability to maintain sound capital ratios even under adverse circumstances and thus to develop contingency plans in case regular actions prove to be insufficient and to take mitigating actions to ensure the survival of the organization for an extreme but plausible scenario. Contingency plans entail a set of counterbalancing measures, incorporating a description of the type and timing of the actions as well as an assessment of the feasibility of those measures under stress. A waterfall approach cascades considerable mitigations, as follows:

- revision of risk appetite, strategy, and business plan, closing business lines or regions where necessary;
- de-risking actions which take effect medium term; that is, a review of the credit process, a tightening of lending criteria, and adjustments to risk limits;
- de-risking actions taking effect immediately, such as hedging, selling, and securitizing assets;
- capital-restoring actions, such as capital increase or halt in capital outflow; that is, eliminating dividends.

The stress test framework includes the management's responsibility to agree on intervention and mitigation and to question whether the assumptions underlying the mitigations are realistic.

3.5 Conclusion

Stress tests are a useful and necessary tool in risk and business management. As such, they are embedded in capital adequacy assessment and business and capital planning, as well as in the determination of the risk appetite of the institution. Governed by top management and with its active involvement, stress tests emerged from a regulatory box-ticking exercise to a business and risk-management connecting instrument where views and thoughts on economic outlooks and scenarios are actively shared and controversially discussed. Although details such as modelling assumptions, incorporated correlations and model and infrastructure limitations play a major role in the stress test's outcome, the awareness of the management body and senior management is often too focused on by the scenario selection and the outcome itself. Stress test committees

[22] See CEBS (2010b).

are the right place to address both those limitations and the design and implications of the stress-testing program in general. This is of particular importance because when business and strategic decisions take into consideration stress test results, the shortcomings of stress tests must likewise be factored into the decision.

Part II

Credit Portfolio Management in Practice

The evolution of credit portfolio management largely reflects the change in traditional banking to a more active, value-oriented approach, driven by a combination of economic and regulatory forces. Since for most banks credit risk consumes a dominant part of economic and regulatory capital, it comes as no surprise that efforts of both financial institutions and regulators focus on the management of credit-risky assets. Regulators expect financial institutions to provide evidence of adequate steering and management of their portfolios of credit risks, including a regular and frequently updated overview of portfolio characteristics and dynamics. Emphasis must be placed on the analysis of consistency of portfolio developments with the approved strategy and relevant credit risk parameters. Furthermore, banks are requested to perform an analysis, taking into account stress test results and to define trigger levels which initiate actions and contingency plans that detail possible active and organic measures that can be employed to change the portfolio characteristics and trends and regain a sound, sustainable credit portfolio. The focus of regulators is on risk containment; that is, controlling risk and avoiding tenuous losses. Stakeholder interests, in particular those of bondholders, are geared to preserving the value of investments, while shareholders additionally expect optimal return on equity. Both require an active approach to portfolio management in order to create value. The board of a financial institution and the senior management have a common interest in effectively managing and communicating the level of credit portfolio risk because of its direct implications for funding costs and equity valuation. Perceived weaknesses in a bank's credit portfolio may ultimately result in higher funding costs, which in turn can make it difficult to do business with better-rated clients, forcing the bank into investments at the lower end of the rating scale to maintain its market position. Because of the costs of this vicious circle, a business model may become unsustainable.

The objective of active credit portfolio management is therefore to optimize the risk/return balance and economic capital of the bank's credit portfolio and to support a business model that complies with the firm's risk appetite. In this part, we discuss the evolution of active credit portfolio management business models and outline the objectives decisive for its set-up, as well as a full credit cycle value proposition. Since portfolio managers effectively connect different segments of debt capital markets, a description of convergence of bank debt with other debt securities follows. Loan transfer prices, which serve as market price–based loan valuations and profitability measures of a lending relationship, are explained. Organizational aspects more often than not contribute to the success of a portfolio management unit. Key considerations are highlighted, with emphasis being put on defining the mandate. Valuing loans in line with CDS and bond spreads is also at the core of solutions to the problem of accounting asymmetry arising from credit derivatives measured at fair value and from loans carried at costs. An in-depth discussion of the alternatives to mitigate the CDS hedging–induced volatility in financial results covers hedge accounting for credit risk, fair value option and financial guarantees. Part II concludes with an overview of regulatory capital relief achieved through credit risk transfer, which is a primary motivation for financial institutions to engage in hedging.

4
Evolution of Portfolio Management Business Models

Credit portfolio management consists of a variety of activities, many of which, like portfolio risk modelling, measuring, reporting, and monitoring, are rather passive. The business models of credit portfolio management can be described according to the activities performed and the level of sophistication and autonomy. The role of a '**risk controller**' is to provide intelligence on key risk measures and developments as well as on the usage of limits. Setting portfolio risk limits and developing risk strategies for performing loans are the responsibilities of the '**risk protector**'. The focus here is on risk reduction or risk containment rather than risk/return optimization. The '**risk optimizer**' defines a target portfolio and optimizes growth based on risk-adjusted returns. Stress tests are performed to confirm the feasibility of various strategies and to discover any hidden vulnerabilities in the portfolio and the strategy. Until this point, all portfolio management measures target the new flow of business, which includes asset origination as well as refinancing of existing stock due to repayments, amortizations and prepayments. In contrast, the '**value creator**', or **Active Credit Portfolio Management** (**ACPM**), can be defined as actively reshaping and changing the risk/return profile of a given portfolio of credit risk to improve key portfolio measures, such as value at risk (VaR) and conditional value at risk (CVaR), to a level consistent with the loss tolerance of the respective financial institution.

The evolution of the active approach to credit portfolio management mirrors the impressive growth of credit markets since the 1980s. It received another boost when tradable debt products, sophisticated debt packaging, and risk transfer techniques emerged. New quantitative models, combined with – until recently – hugely increased liquidity in credit markets, enabled loan portfolio managers to reshape almost any portfolio to a target risk profile at minimal transaction costs, like an asset manager. For many financial institutions, especially those with investment banking aspirations, the shift from a 'buy-and-hold' model to an

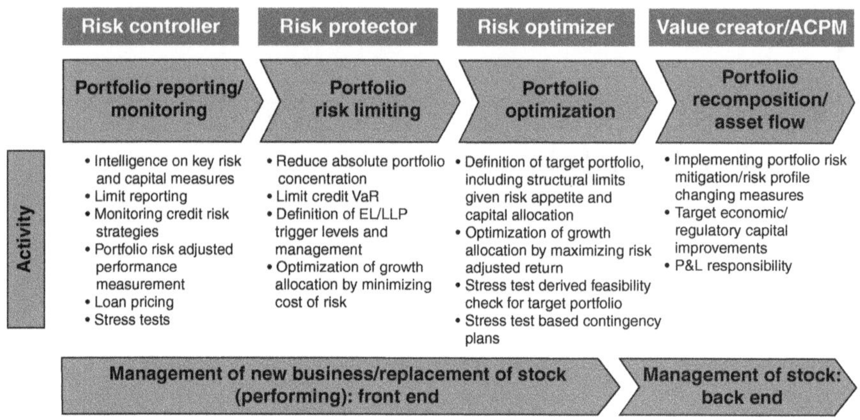

Figure 4.1 Business models of credit portfolio management

'originate-to-distribute' one, where assets do not remain on balance sheet or at least the credit risks attached to them get neutralized, is synonymous with the creation of active credit portfolio management. However, since the spectrum of credit assets encompasses a diverse range of loan products, with different risk and cash flow profiles as well as specific funding requirements and the presence of secondary markets, there are numerous approaches and models for managing credit assets, sometimes even within one organization. With secondary-market liquidity for loans, bonds, CLOs, and credit derivatives as the criteria for segmenting assets into liquid, less liquid, and illiquid categories, the dividing line is often blurred. Liquidity of debt capital markets tends to suddenly disappear in times of market volatility, which can unexpectedly limit the flexibility of portfolio managers and thus hamper the portfolio management model of choice. Consequently, a clearly formulated mandate, shared targets, and senior management governance proved to be the elements of a successful and stable credit portfolio management operation, especially during the financial crisis. Furthermore, a consistent loan pricing concept prevents internal arbitrage, where assets are directed to the books with the most beneficial pricing scheme from the point of view of the client-relationship manager, who is charged the transfer price.

Besides selection of the best-fitting portfolio management model, the real challenge lies in implementing the corresponding organizational structures, policies, and processes and then maintaining the approach through the different phases of the credit cycle. Thus, this chapter is structured in five parts. First, it describes the factors to be considered when designing the ACPM model. The model of choice (section 2) is determined to a certain extent by the type of assets under management, which is described in the third section, covering the connectivity of loans, bonds and CDSs. An in-depth analysis of the important role of the transfer price for an enhancement of origination discipline and transparency in profitability follows. The chapter closes with a review of organizational and infrastructure aspects, implementation issues, and a case study for an implementation of ACPM at a fictive wholesale bank.

4.1 From credit advisory to active credit portfolio management

It's fair to say that no major financial institution can claim to be adequately equipped to weather financial storms without having some kind of credit portfolio management in place. At the same time, the overwhelming emphasis observed at the time of the advent of ACPM, both at banks and consultant firms, may to some look exaggerated these days. One could argue that did ACPM not fully protect banks from the impact of the downturn, and neither do today's market conditions for risk distribution allow ACPM to exploit its full value. However, a closer look at the performance of banks reveals that those that managed their assets in a more sophisticated way were hit less hard by the crisis. Also, in many cases portfolio management focused largely on corporate loans, for which a meaningful secondary-market activity existed. Losses, however, stemmed predominantly from credit assets that were traditionally outside the scope of ACPM. The conclusion is twofold. First, the concept of ACPM has been proved to work under extreme conditions. Second, an extension of ACPM to other, less liquid assets can improve the resilience of financial institutions in times of market stress. Given the series of once-in-a-lifetime events which have plagued financial markets since the start of the century, the importance of taking an active approach to credit risk management – rather than performing a credit advisory function only – may have never been higher.

Nevertheless, the challenging environment in which banks operate calls for fundamental adjustments to the role of ACPM. The scarcity of capital and liquidity and the repricing of credit risk in general, as well as the languishing market for asset securitization, necessitate a new way of thinking. The subprime crisis also uncovered the inherent moral hazard aspect of the originate-to-distribute model. Essentially, if originators do not have to be afraid of any repercussions from insufficient credit standards and low-quality loan origination, there is no shared goal with the ultimate investor of these assets. To find a balanced approach that serves best the individual needs of the institution and its stakeholders, a number of strategic issues have to be fixed. The appropriate level of risk that a bank should target and respect – the risk appetite, aligned with business objectives and incentive schemes for managers[1] – provides a framework in which portfolio managers can act. The bank's mission and strategy, its risk culture as well as the market environment, are key determinants of success for the credit portfolio management unit, which in turn must be visible and authorized to perform its defined role within the organization. Generally, two categories of credit portfolio management models can be observed: those that aim to be highly effective and those designed to cover the portfolio to the largest extent possible. Effectiveness comes with a higher degree of specialization, with a focus on fewer assets that are more liquid and marketable, such as multinational and large corporate loans or certain leveraged buyout (LBO) transactions. Here, pricing, market timing, and time to market matter most. In contrast, a holistic approach covering the full range of diverse credit assets on a bank's balance sheets calls for a longer-term solution and is driven less by secondary market conditions than appropriate lending standards. The two approaches' models usually find their expression in the location of the portfolio management unit within the organization. For about half of 49 international banks, the CPM (credit portfolio management) unit resides within a business line, whereas for the others CPM is part of a finance or risk function.[2] Being part of a business line naturally limits the scope of portfolio management to assets owned by the respective line. On the other hand, asset ownership and profit and loss responsibility typically make for stronger and more active CPMs, whereas the focus of risk or finance CPMs is more on risk reduction and capital management than risk/return optimization. As a result, there is no one-size-fits-all model which is appropriate to each and every bank, given the individual balance sheet composition and ambitions of financial institutions. What is common to all these concepts, however, is the need for intensified and target-oriented, sometimes less technical, communication between senior management and portfolio and risk managers. But also within the credit chain, which involves loan origination, credit analysts, loan officers, portfolio managers, quants, traders, and syndication, a common language and understanding of the mission is the key to letting portfolio management become a strategic advantage.

Consequently, the starting point in designing the ideal ACPM is to identify the key objectives, which can be grouped into six areas of value creation levers. Enhancement of portfolio transparency on aggregated

---

[1] By incentive schemes, we mean not just monetary compensation and awards but more generally the key performance indicators and motivation of managers, which are determined by high-level goals and serve as key drivers for consistent execution and success.

[2] See Stegemann and Jamin (2008).

Areas of Responsibilities	***Value Creation***
(1) Portfolio transparency	• Enhance **portfolio transparency** with integrated risk/return view • Identify and monitor portfolio **key risk drivers** • Evaluate impact of **origination trends** and targets • **Stress** analysis and **early warning** systems
(2) Asset selection	• First level of asset **selection**/investment **rationalization** • Loan/transfer pricing to create **pricing transparency** and to enhance **origination discipline** • **Steering** of origination activity to achieve target portfolio
(3) Portfolio balancing	• Identify **target portfolio** and manage portfolio accordingly, set structural portfolio limits • Develop **proactive risk mitigation** measures for portfolio vulnerabilities • **Reduce** portfolio **concentration** by hedges and investments • Integrate and manage connected risks (liquidity, market, volatility, accounting asymmetry)
(4) Risk/return	• **Improve risk/return** profile of credit portfolio • **Increase risk-adjusted returns** • Increase absolute amount of revenues (through **balance sheet velocity** or pricing discipline) • Generate revenues
(5) Capital	• Economic/regulatory capital **management and allocation** • Economic/regulatory capital **optimization** • Economic/regulatory capital **preservation (downturn protection)**
(6) Asset distribution	• Develop **new distribution channels** • **Tailorize portfolio transactions** to the specific needs of both bank and investor • Reduce transaction costs by introducing best practice and regular **presence in capital markets** • Increase level of **standardization** of loans to improve transferability/tradability

Figure 4.2 Portfolio management value creation levers

and granular level for a 'deep dive', close monitoring of origination and portfolio trends, as well as stress analysis and early warning systems, are base objectives. The need for improvement in those areas has often been cited as a lesson learnt from the financial crisis.[3] Asset selection based on proper risk assessment and pricing and profitability considerations, as well as portfolio aspects, is another value creation lever, one often subject to dedicated investment committees. Improving origination discipline to achieve satisfactory loan margins and to identify the gap to internal hurdle rates or risk transfer costs, which must be filled by revenues from ancillary business, requires a methodologically sound and accepted loan pricing scheme. (Re)balancing the credit portfolio by setting structural limits (see also 'Risk limits: Framing the credit risk strategy' in Chapter 2), which aims at reduction of economic capital and portfolio vulnerability, is a standard task for most portfolio managers on the risk-management side. Hedging operations or other risk-mitigating measures to mitigate concentration and counterparty or issuer risks require more advanced portfolio management operations and usually reside with the business

[3] For example, see Schuh (2009).

units. Corresponding to regular and frequent risk transfer, loans must be priced in line with market conditions. Value-adding credit portfolio management targets an improvement in the risk/return characteristics of the credit portfolio via specific front-end and back-end measures. 'Front end' describes the asset selection process, which begins with client-relationship management and ends with the credit approval decision. Client managers and loan officers who apply credit standards to route through or sort out new business are the first line of defence against risks that do not comply with the financing principles or lending standards. 'Back-end' management, however, denotes measures that change the composition of an existing portfolio by way of risk transfer. These activities have a significant influence on the competitiveness and success of financial institutions. An empirical analysis confirmed that financial institutions that follow a specialized lending strategy, combined with back-end portfolio diversification activities, can enhance shareholder value or maximize risk-adjusted return on (economic) capital.[4] Disadvantages resulting from a higher level of specialization – that is, a portfolio exhibiting concentration risks in the form of regional, industry, client, or credit products exposure – can be offset while preserving the competitive advantages of a price setter or a know-how leader, provided sufficient risk distribution capabilities exist. These efforts also help to protect or optimize the capital position, which was the primary objective when banks suffered serious losses during the financial crisis. The shortage of capital in the financial industry has been singled out and addressed by the recommendation on the bank recapitalization plan published by the European Banking Authority (EBA)[5], adding to the prevalent pressure on banks. Capital optimization is seen as one of the most important value propositions of credit portfolio management units, as they are in a unique position to offer an integrated view on risk-weighted assets and their drivers. Regular and frequent distribution of risks requires access to relevant capital markets, processes, and regulations for products concerned, as well as the expertise to cope with tailorized and complex risk transfer transactions. Developing these distribution channels, thereby building on best practices and a regular presence in debt capital markets, is another value creation lever for credit portfolio management. These back-end portfolio reshaping and capital-releasing activities often make the difference between active and passive management of a credit portfolio in the relevant literature, which

[4] Gann and Hofmann (2005).

[5] See www.eba.europe.eu. The 2011 EU Capital Exercise performed by EBA recommended requiring banks to build up an exceptional and temporary capital buffer to reach a core Tier 1 capital ratio of 9%. Banks were asked to respond to the recommendation by submitting plans for achieving the target capital ratios by January 2012 and to meet the requirement by June 2012.

promotes consistent and regular risk transfer. However, in this book, the term 'active' is descriptive of any activities which intentionally optimize the risk/return characteristics of a credit portfolio. By definition, this includes front-end measures for asset origination, which are complemented by capital market–driven risk mitigation.

The main credit portfolio management objectives naturally differ in relation to the business model of the respective financial institution. Investment banks are usually more sensitive to capital consumption from corporate loans and consequently more active in distributing credit assets into the market. The capital, once freed up, is again available for new business. The repeated usage of capital allows for increasing non-loan revenues and achieving a comparably higher return on equity. The ability to turn over the balance sheet or the velocity of capital is a major determinant of the future profitability of investment banks and wholesale banks alike. Wholesale banks generally use their large balance sheets to achieve a dominant position with the client, thereby gaining fee income and improving the loan to non-loan revenues ratio. Since risk reduction or distribution is mostly seen as unfavourable or even harmful to the client-relationship (if client becomes aware of it), active credit portfolio management has to develop risk mitigation concepts which have no detrimental effect on the clients' perception of the bank. Unfortunately, the credit product of choice to manage credit risks, the credit default swap (CDS), introduces market risks because CDSs have to be measured at fair value, according to IAS 39. Many financial institutions are less comfortable with taking market risks as opposed to credit risks, which are seen generally as the bread and butter business for commercial banks. Finding appropriate solutions to balance hedging-induced market risks can be a key decision factor for the implementation of an active credit portfolio management unit. Banks that actively hedge their credit portfolios use CDS spreads as a measure for opportunity costs to enhance loan origination pricing transparency, or even as a pricing source for fair-valuing loans. The focus on origination discipline is just a natural consequence of hedging, as loan margins are often below CDS spreads and other market-based risk prices. Client profitability assessment is generally one of the main activities for the CPMs of wholesale banks. For regionally active or specialized lenders, ACPM can help to reduce the portfolio bias to certain regions or industries. Since bilateral credit is characterized by a low level of standardization, ACPM improves the process efficiency for traditional credit risk mitigations, such as sub-participations, guarantees, or collateral, by standardizing and bundling the loan structuring and documentation. This is particularly relevant for client-focused banks, which have a reasonable comparative advantage in mitigating information asymmetries between lender and borrower, given the close relationship to their clients. Specialization benefits, resulting from better client information to overcome the problem of adverse selection, as well as qualified assessment of collateral value, advanced workout processes, and timely anticipation of negative credit trends due to superior market insights, are counterbalanced by concentration effects.[6] Thus, preserving the advantages of specialization while mitigating the increase in risks from regional, industry, or collateral concentration ultimately enhances the risk-adjusted return of financial institutions.

4.2 A full-cycle approach to credit portfolio management

In economic theory, business cycles are defined by the degree of utilization of the production potential of an economy, mostly represented by changes in GDP as the most aggregated output measure. Cycles are characterized by a similar and recurring wave-like pattern, although these vary substantially by length and depth. Financial markets, both stock and debt, respond to the economic cycles and are generally perceived as anticipating rather than following trends.

Figure 4.3 Dax index and IFO pan-Germany business climate
Data source: Bloomberg.

[6] See Böve, Düllmann and Pfingsten (2010).

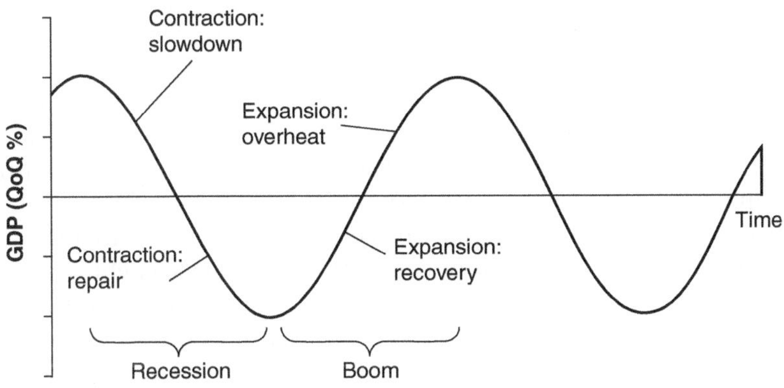

Figure 4.4 The four phases of the business cycle

Consequently, a well-positioned portfolio management needs to be prepared to adjust its activities to the specific credit environment and requirements of these different phases. A stylized graphical representation charts the boom phase as positive GDP growth, while a recession indicates negative GDP growth. Two consecutive quarters of real GDP decline is often referred to as the beginning of a recession. Other variables used for assessing economic cycles include gross domestic income, employment, various output measures and consumer spending.

The National Bureau of Economic Research (NBER), which officially reports U.S. business cycles,[7] defines recessions or contractions as starting at the peak of the cycle and ending at the trough. Out of 11 cycles since 1945, NBER identified three business cycles (contraction, peak to trough) for the more recent history: from July 1990 to March 1991, from March 2001 to November 2001, and from December 2007 to June 2009.

Various four-quadrant schemes monitor the developments of economic activity in relation to business and consumer survey–based assessments of current economic climate and outlook, among which are the European business cycle clock of Eurostat,[8] the OECD business cycle clock[9] and the German Federal Statistical Office.[10] Because business cycle clocks not only provide an intuitive visualization of recent and historical economic trends but also give some hints about potential future developments, they receive a fair deal of attention from the financial industry. For Germany, a significant correlation between business expectations and climate,

[7] For reference, see www.nber.org/cycles.html.

[8] See http://epp.eurostat.ec.europa.eu/cache/BCC2/group1/xdis_en.html.

[9] See http://stats.oecd.org/mei/bcc/default.html.

[10] See www.destatis.de.

displayed by the *IFO business cycle clock*, and economic activity, described by the *Monitor for Real GDP* by the German Federal Statistical Office, has been proved.[11]

The recurring pattern of economic cycles has led to the invention of simple but useful methodologies for cycle-sensitive asset allocation. Research analysts from Morgan Stanley, Merrill Lynch, and Citigroup, among others, are using investment clocks which suggest portfolio positioning relative to the phases of an economic cycle. Coordinates are either leverage versus GDP growth or corporate profits versus debt.

However, credit markets do not tend to correspond in similar ways to recessions or slowdowns in economic activity. Despite eight months of contraction in 2001, caused by the burst of the dot-com bubble, credit spreads were largely stable, with the exception of a major widening for a shorter period of time that can be attributed to the 9/11 terrorist attacks. A substantial widening occurred only in 2002, when stocks retreated, reflecting concerns about the brewing Iraq conflict, which also depressed economic growth later. In both cases, markets anticipated the economic slowdown–induced deterioration of average borrower credit quality, with an increase in credit risk premium well before the economic downturn, while during the slowdown itself spreads were stable or even tightened. Prior to the most recent 18-month economic slump, which, according to

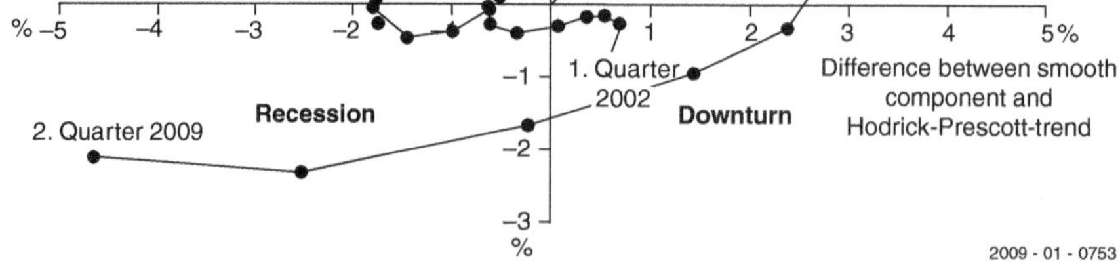

Figure 4.5 Monitor for real gross domestic product, Germany
Source: Oltmanns (2009).[12]

[11] See Abberger and Nierhaus (2010).

[12] Statistisches Bundesamt, Wiesbaden. Dr. Erich Oltmanns: 'Das Bruttoinlandsprodukt im Konjunkturzyklus', in Wirtschaft und Statistik, 61. Jahrgang, Heft 10/2009, pp. 963ff.; here, p. 968.

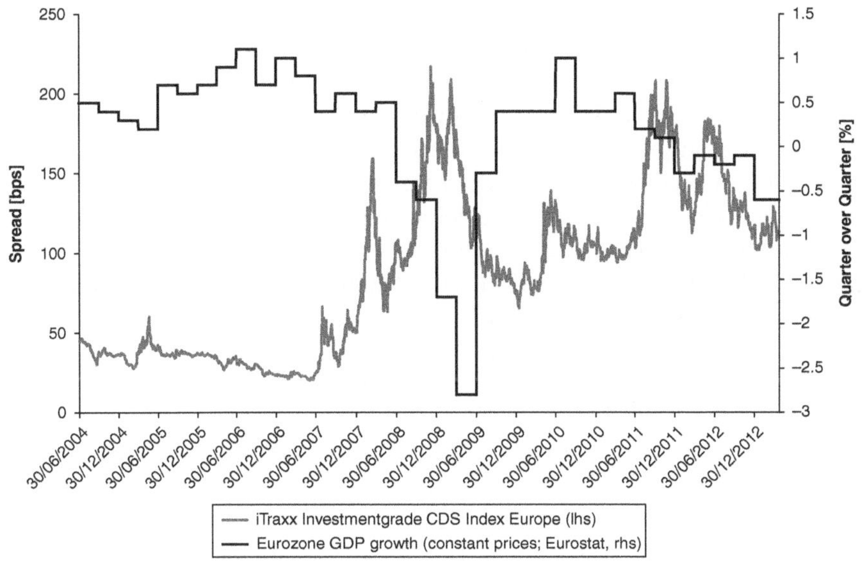

Figure 4.6 Credit spreads versus Eurozone GDP growth
Data source: Bloomberg.

NBER, started in December 2007, spreads widened again from a record high of around 20 bps for iTraxx to 65 bps, which was massive at that time. Spreads reversed the widening in late 2007, but then corporate and bank bonds plunged, together with stocks, when the housing and subprime bubble collapsed, further accelerated by the default of Lehman and the bailout of Bear Stearns, Merrill Lynch, and Bank of America. Both in 2001 and 2008 the accumulation of stress, either because of the impact propensity of global interconnectedness or due to idiosyncratic events, underscored the value of tail-risk protection.

Certainly, the phases of the cycle cannot be easily forecast, nor can the implications for corporate credit quality and credit spreads. Nevertheless, supported by cycle monitoring, proactive credit portfolio management should be able to chart the corresponding activities to the phases of a cycle and determine trigger points for timely portfolio positioning and pre-emptive measures.

Countercyclical credit portfolio management builds up downside and tail-risk protection that is already in the **overheat phase**, when fostering origination discipline is also necessary to offset a weakening in lending standards. Rigorous asset pricing, based on risk transfer costs, increases transparency in the risk-adjusted profitability of lending. During the slowdown phase, portfolio de-risking can be supported by an improved asset standardization to broaden the channel for risk transfer. Consequent capital market information enhances transparency to build a stable investor base. The repair phase often corresponds to a decline in capital ratios, which results in capital relief and optimization initiatives. ACPM contributes here through balance-sheet management and capital optimization efforts. In the recovery phase, with an improvement in risk and return, the focus shifts to increasing the velocity of the balance sheet in order to further boost profits to cost of equity.

Full-cycle active credit portfolio management highlights the advantage of continuous focus adjustment for ACPM activities and, equally important, of consistency within the intention of measures. This is notable, as different objectives exhibit time effects, with some measures lagging behind others. For example, since credit spreads already regularly anticipate economic downturns and rises during the expansion phase, hedges may become too expensive in relation to expected losses when borrower credit quality deteriorates in the downturn phase. On the other hand, when business cycle enters the downturn and repair phase, related de-leveraging and de-risking initiatives often prevent closing hedges because of their contribution to capital release and loss protection. This may mean giving up earlier mark-to-market gains from hedges when spreads tighten again. CDS hedges are quite often hugely mark-to-market

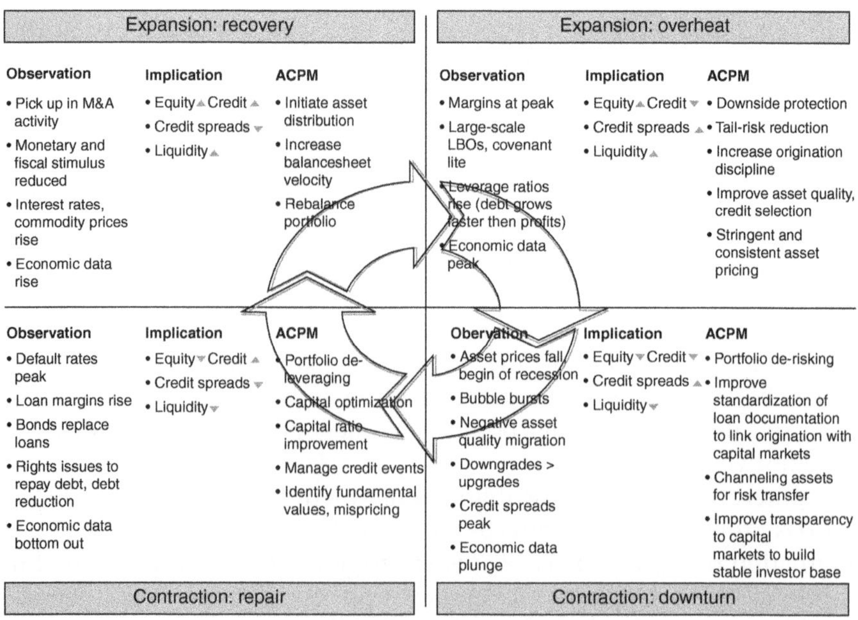

Figure 4.7 Full-cycle approach to credit portfolio management

positive before internal and external ratings start to deteriorate, with subsequent loan-loss provisioning. The diverging timing of loss compensation due to rising spreads from hedges booked in the trading profit and loss account, and potential loan losses from a credit event at the hedged borrower at a later point in time, requires continuous review of the hedge strategy. The review needs to be clear about the prime objective of the hedge, which could be profit and loss maximization, net credit loss minimization, avoidance of loan loss provisions or capital conservation, among others. Profit and loss maximization is different from net credit loss minimization. At the time of a credit event, buying the cheapest CDS deliverable, delivering it into the CDS, and receiving par from the hedge often overcompensate losses on a loan to the same borrower but leave the bank with the unprotected loan on the balance sheet. From a purely economic point of view this procedure is optimal, but it could foil the strategy of the workout department, which might make CDS hedges part of their negotiations with other banks or with the borrower in a restructuring. Clear guidance on priorities is a prerequisite to achieving the best results – and not only from CDS hedges. Since there are alternatives to transfer risk and optimizing capital, and since timing matters for most of them, ACPM should offer advice on potential risk-mitigating measures and their corresponding strategy throughout both the different phases of the business cycle and the lifetime of the underlying transactions. This includes articulating the purpose and goals of the risk-management measures, developing exit strategies, and defining decision making and procedural roles; for example the right to call in new risk mitigants, like hedges, and veto rights when it comes to unwinding them.

4.3 Bridging distinct worlds: Loans, bonds and credit derivatives

The changing environment in which financial institutions operate has deep implications for traditional client relationship–driven banking. The availability of cheap central bank funding, which has become a common worldwide response to economic and financial stress, has tremendously increased competition among banks, on the one hand, and between banks and markets, on the other. Financial disintermediation is gathering momentum and will further accelerate the integration of banks and financial markets. In the hunt for yield, third-party investors – pension and mutual funds, hedge funds, insurance companies, and private investors, to name but a few – turn to markets to source assets. These investors depend on loans originated and distributed by banks and debt securities directly issued by individual borrowers to achieve their target asset allocation. The rapid growth of corporate bond issuance and the emergence of electronic trading platforms where those debt securities are frequently quoted and traded, as well as derivatives used to insure and distribute credit risk, have transformed once-separated markets, with observable spillover effects on pricing. For banks, synergies exist because of the complementary nature of lending and capital market underwriting. When bank loans compete with corporate bond or equity issuance, a bank specializing in investment banking ultimately benefits from additional revenues sourced from client advisory on capital structure, rating, and debt issuance. The scarcity of bank capital may actually result in banks *guiding* rather than *losing* borrowers to the market. Active credit portfolio management contributes to the trend of converging loan and bond markets, since it amends the lending function, which consists of originating, servicing, and managing credit assets, by distributing risk, thereby connecting otherwise distinct markets. Credit risk processing to capital markets increases interdisciplinary price transparency, which allows direct comparison of the costs to borrowers of different funding alternatives.

4.3.1 Asymmetric information in bank loans

Banks are better suited for lending, as they can minimize the problem of asymmetric information and moral hazard between borrower and lender. According to the theory of financial intermediation, two mistakes arise from lending based on imperfect information: declining good borrowers or approving bad borrowers. Because of their closeness to customers, in particular relationship-driven lending, banks are expected to have better information about their clients. Thus, the problem of information asymmetry can be reduced if banks gain access to higher-quality and more timely financial data, as well as to soft (i.e. non-quantitative) information. Lower loan losses compensate for the costs of sourcing and screening additional information and subsequent monitoring – so-called agency costs. Furthermore, higher returns can be generated when banks have superior information, as financiers gain a better understanding of the client's needs and thus are able to deliver tailored funding solutions which further tie the client to the bank. Relationship banking contrasts with pure transaction banking, where no such close relationship exists because of intense client or price competition or because of the transactional focus of the customer's business, to the exclusion of other business areas. At the other extreme, a bank securing an information monopoly may improve loan portfolio performance and generate higher returns, but that comes at the expense of the borrower. Long-lasting bank-borrower relationships might allow lenders to extract monopoly rents by charging higher loan margins due to their exclusive position with the client. Consequently, it is common for larger firms to have multiple lending relationships or core banks to reduce the costs of borrowing. This, however, may also motivate lenders to demonstrate their financing expertise, becoming more client-focused to preserve their customer proximity and to counterbalance the effects of price competition. Banks with close customer relationships may retain a competitive advantage because they are able to take more timely decisions and to intervene when the borrower's strategy changes or when its credit quality deteriorates. To the contrary, the ongoing internationalization of banking may have a detrimental effect on the quality of originated loans, since it increases the distance to the customer.[13] From an economic point of view, the concept of a single core bank creates information-cost efficiency; otherwise, each of the multiple lenders incurs monitoring costs, which can add up. For debt securities with a broad investor base such as corporate bonds, the monitoring of issuers by many lenders could lead to unnecessary costs and free-riding problems.[14] Rating agencies basically coordinate the fragmented investor base by providing a kind of information certificate – a role banks otherwise implicitly perform by providing loans. Based on a theory initially developed by Boot and colleagues (2006), Bannier and Hirsch (2009) find evidence that rating agencies effectively perform a monitoring function via the credit watch procedure. Ratings for issuers and securities are supplemented by outlooks and reviews, or watch lists, which express the agency's opinion on short- to medium-term credit rating developments. Market reactions to rating changes increase after the introduction of watch lists, suggesting that market participants accept the role of the agencies as a central information source.[15] A review for downgrade by a rating agency may be seen as a warning shot; thus it increases the issuer's motivation to take active measures to defend the rating. Boot and colleagues (2006) introduced the concept of an *implicit contract* between

[13] DeYoung, Glennon and Nigro (2006) show that for small business financing with opaque information, loan performance suffers from extended borrower-lending distance.

[14] See Altunbas et al. (2009).

[15] Although there is no common sense both in literature and among financial market participants that rating agencies are economically relevant and that ratings contain any valuable information, the recent efforts to strictly regulate the agencies strongly suggest that ratings do matter for financial markets' stability in the view of regulators and authorities. For more information, see European Commission, Proposal for a Regulation of the European Parliament and of the Council, amending Regulation (EC) No. 1060/2009 on credit rating agencies; Regulation No. 1060/2009 and Regulation No. 513/2011, www.ec.europa.eu; Center for European Policy (CEP), *Credit Rating Agencies*, cep policy Brief No. 2012–2007, www.cep.eu; European Banking Federation (EBF), Comments on the European Commission's proposal regarding the regulation of Credit Rating Agencies (CRAs), www.ebf-fbe.eu; European Securities and Markets Authority (ESMA), Annual report on the application of the regulation on credit rating agencies as provided by Article 21(5) and Article 39a of the regulation (EU) No. 1060/2009b as amended by Regulation No. 1095/2010, www.esma.europa.eu. Securities and Exchange Commission (SEC), *Report on Review of Reliance on Credit Ratings*, www.sec.gov.

the issuer and the rating agency, where the borrower commits to making 'recovery efforts' to counteract possible deteriorations of credit quality. If the attempt fails, the rating review ends in a downgrade. This is similar to the threat by banks to terminate or to not refinance loans if an obligor does not comply with the previously agreed credit development path thereby creating an incentive for the borrower to maintain the credit grade.

4.3.2 Convergence of bank loans and debt capital market instruments

The certification role of both bank loans and credit ratings is credible and also facilitates the access of borrowers to public debt markets by building up the reputation and by 'establishing' the borrower.[16] Hale and Santos (2008) show that costs of external funding decrease because of the extended reputation, visibility, and transparency that come with the listing of bonds. Put another way, the delegated agency costs and reduced information asymmetry, as well as debt issuer coverage initiated by research analysts after a bond IPO, lower the loan margins requested by banks. Borrowers that tap the bond markets may also consider syndicated loans the closest substitute to corporate bonds. In particular, larger and more profitable firms that are highly leveraged prefer syndicated loans, which have emerged as an asset class of their own, over corporate bonds for medium- and long-term funding.[17] Smaller borrowers, however, may find it easier to negotiate with a single bank and are less likely to tap the public debt markets; this is also because of the significant costs and disclosure requirements attached to the listing of debt securities.[18] Bonds from non-frequent issuers typically are more illiquid and trade at comparably higher credit spread levels, reflecting both the limited investor base and the greater investment uncertainty arising from the information asymmetry, which is sometimes mitigated by restrictive covenants. The life-cycle theory describes a firm that switches from borrowing in the form of a bilateral loan from a single bank to a syndicated loans provided by multiple lender, and, as often observed for publicly listed companies,

---

[16] For many mutual and pension funds, the requirement of a rating is often regulated by investment guidelines.

[17] See Altunbas et al. (2009).

[18] Although the requirements are less onerous for Eurobonds, which are offered exclusively to institutional rather than retail investors, listing of securities at an exchange like the London Stock Exchange requires the provision of comprehensive information about the financial conditions of the issuer, such as independently audited annual accounts for past years, as well as on an ongoing basis for the duration of the listing. Private information, which may affect the pricing of the listed security or the ability of the issuer to fulfil its obligations, has to be provided.

finally issuing bonds. There is extensive literature available on the competitive, complementary, or coexisting nature of bank loans and private and public debt capital markets.[19] While debt markets and bank loans appear to have become increasingly integrated and codependent,[20] a firm's financing choice is only one determinant of the convergence process. Another driving factor is the emergence of active credit portfolio management, which accelerates the process by structuring, standardizing, bundling, transforming, and dispersing risks. Since credit portfolio managers engage in

- selling or syndicating loans,
- buying derivative protection for loans,
- investing in CDSs and corporate bonds, and
- securitizing credit risk, as well as
- receiving (sub)participations and guarantees,

valuations of different credit risk products become directly comparable because of market observable prices and credit spreads.

CDSs are a bridging element, smoothing price discrepancies of loans and bonds, and have been publicly acknowledged by some multinational corporates as the benchmark for their loan and bond pricing. Linking loan margins to CDS spreads is more widespread among companies in the United States, but it has also been considered by European corporates to overcome difficult funding market conditions.[21] Norden and Wagner (2008) find that CDS spreads are a dominant factor in determining prices of syndicated loans to U.S. corporates. They conclude that CDS spreads in turn incorporate loan-specific information; this should not come as a surprise given that the CDS was invented as an instrument to transfer credit risks from loans. Rather than just absorb risks, banks' credit risk distribution activities allow external investors to diversify their portfolios by investing in assets which would otherwise not be available for them, and, at the same time, to delegate to a certain extent the monitoring function to the asset-originating bank. A

[19] Song and Thakor (2010) present a thesis of complement and co-evolving banks and capital markets that contrasts with other views of competition between the two, where the growth of one comes at the expense of the other. Due to their specialization, banks and markets each have their merits and comparative advantages, which play out when interacting with each other.

[20] See Boot and Thakor (2009).

[21] For example, in 2008 both Nokia and Nestlé expressed an interest in linking the margin of their commercial paper backstop facilities to the respective CDSs spread while a French state-owned utility company switched the loan base rate from LIBOR to a reference bank rate setting. See www.uk/reuters.com.

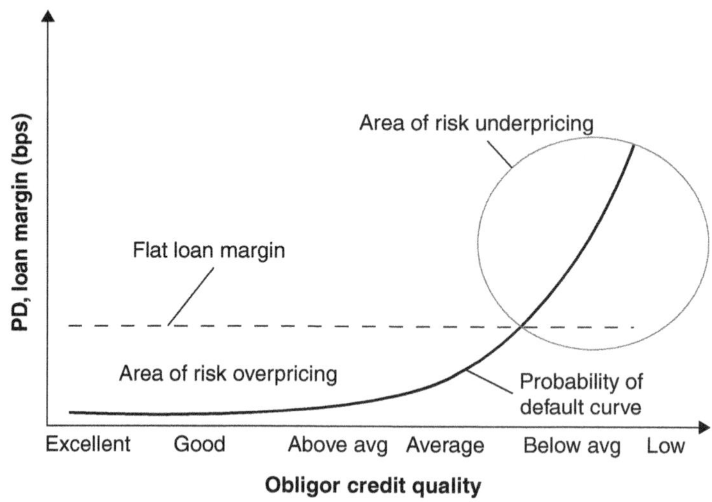

Figure 4.8 Flat loan margin versus increasing probability of default

higher degree of standardization improves the transferability of assets, thereby increasing pricing transparency. From a socio-economic perspective, the European economy benefits from an accelerated integration of the still-fragmented European bank loan market, as well as from converging loan and bond interest rates in the non-financial corporate sector, due to enhanced competition and innovation.[22] The next chapter explains how loan transfer pricing contributes to a consistent and harmonized approach to credit asset pricing. We will show that using market spreads to price loans is a linchpin of regular risk processing. It improves loan origination discipline and is a prerequisite in the context of mitigating the accounting mismatch created by hedging loans with CDSs.

4.4 The role of loan transfer pricing

Loan pricing is a key determinant of success of a financial institution. If margins are consistently set too low, thus underpricing the risk of assets, the result over a longer period of time will be net losses from credit operations, as lending income fails to cover losses from materialized risks. If risks are overpriced, an institution will be forced out of the market,[23] since eventually a borrower will opt for lenders that

[22] Wagenvoort et al. (2009) found that while there is a complete integration of the primary euro-denominated bond market, the market for bank loans remains segmented, albeit to various degrees depending on type and size of the loan. In particular, retail lending appears to be a national affair.

offer cheaper conditions. For instance, a combination of over- and underpricing, which can be caused by flat loan margins – that is, a constant margin regardless of borrower risks or non-risk-adjusted pricing – will have the effect of adverse selection. Pricing will be too high for better-rated customers and will keep these clients from borrowing at the bank, while the same loan margins will attract debtors with lower credit quality, as spreads are cheap compared to risk-adjusted pricing prevalent at other banks.

Very often, in implementating credit portfolio management, an internal market–based credit risk pricing is established at which an asset is transferred from loan origination to portfolio management – effectively replacing the bank's internal risk–adjusted pricing by making reference to market spreads. The transfer price makes it possible to isolate of the economic benefit from portfolio management and also allows better measurement of the profitability of loan origination. But even if the portfolio management is not run as a profit center,[24] usually banks for measurement purposes typically apply a rule-based transfer pricing which aims at risk-adjusting the price in line with observable market prices for tradable debt securities. Assets which are priced too generously relative to these market prices and do not compensate for the risk taken, have to be either subsidized by other incremental income or otherwise strategically justified to avoid being dismissed. On the other hand, if assets are priced so that losses are more than covered, the responsible client-relationship manager will be rewarded accordingly. Consequently, transfer pricing of loans helps to create transparency regarding the profitability of a credit asset relative to prevailing debt capital market prices. If consistently applied, transfer pricing highlights the cost of relationship-driven lending, including the profitability driver and total customer profitability over time. A financial institution is free to choose the benchmark for risk adjustments, which can be anything from observable market spreads to generic pricing, which is defined by net profitability hurdle rates or capital efficiency or just reflects incentives based on strategic decisions for higher- and lower-growth areas. However, it is critical that the pricing scheme be compatible with the business model in order to create incentives which best support the established goals.

[23] Assuming the institution is a price taker, not a price setter.

[24] See §4.5, 'Practical implementation: Organizational and infrastructure challenges'.

4.4.1 Risk-adjusted loan pricing

Non-market-based risk-adjusted loan pricing includes elements determined by the credit quality of the loan debtor; that is, the expected loss[25] and the additional capital to be held against the risk of the loan, as well as costs which are specific to the bank, such as the internally assessed cost of equity,[26] funding costs, and operating costs. Commercial adjustments are used for strategic purposes – for instance, for setting a negative value to subsidize a business that is entering a new market where established competitors defend their market share. In a market where the bank is already heavily exposed and unwilling to extend its market share, or where concerns exist about the market's future prospects, which are likely precipitated by rising PDs, the financial institution may decide to raise the bar and add to the commercial adjustment as a precautionary measure.

The basic idea of risk-adjusted prices is to enhance the motivation of client-relationship managers to negotiate loan margins which are profitable net of costs. If the client manager cannot meet the hurdle rate, the gap between the internal price and the loan margin needs to be filled by revenues from an ancillary business. In a more sophisticated portfolio management, a sponsor – that is, the business unit which benefits from cross-selling, for example the debt capital markets area benefiting from a bond issue of the borrower – has to advance the shortfall from its own profit and loss. This is clearly superior to a promises register of future revenues. A sponsor will emerge only if the prospects of that future business are convincing; if not, the deal has little chance of going through. Besides the absolute level of net revenues, banks also often set rules on the quality of income. The lower the share of lending-based revenues, the higher the return of equity, because non-lending revenues such as advisory fees do not consume capital. Defining a maximum ratio of interest to non-interest income creates a certain sensitivity to deploying the bank's capital, which is naturally a scarce resource. By definition, any kind of benchmarking will face scepticism from client managers who can claim to

[25] Since expected loss is composed of probability of default and loss given default (and in some cases the loss confirmation period), it is of great importance for the financial institution that these parameters are correctly derived to remain competitive with respect to pricing and ultimately remunerate the shareholder's investments.

[26] Cost of equity usually relates to regulatory capital. It should be noted that the capital weights of assets under Basel II, although these rules represent a significant improvement over Basel I, are still somewhat simplistic and insufficient for assessing capital adequacy or for pricing purposes. By contrast, under Basel I the risk weight for assets has been categorized only into five weights: 0, 10, 20, 50 and 100%. At that time the BCBS already pointed out that '*... the weightings should not be regarded as a substitute for commercial judgement for purposes of market pricing of the different instruments.*' See BCBS (1988), II, 29.

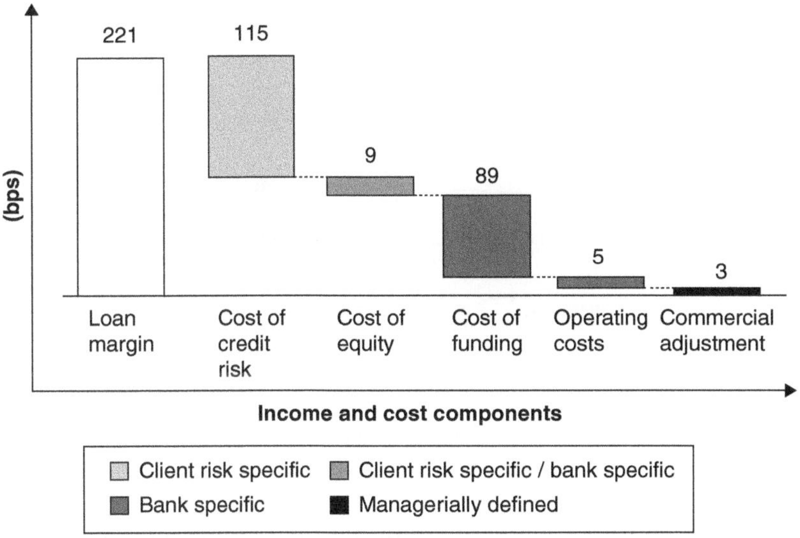

Figure 4.9 Risk-adjusted internal pricing

be autonomous with respect to pricing. On the other hand, risk-adjusted pricing also removes subjectivity and creates reliability when it comes to defending the loan to investment councils or credit approval committees. For loans which surpass the hurdle rate, provided all other loan features comply with internal rules and requirements, as well as the client strategy, credit approval will most likely be easily and consistently obtained.

4.4.2 Loan transfer pricing

The term *transfer pricing* emerged in the context of active credit portfolio management being set up as an independent internal asset manager. The transfer of a loan from origination to credit portfolio management takes place at the clearing price, which is the price at which the asset-taking unit is willing to receive the loan because it can distribute the asset into the market by selling or hedging at zero net profit and loss. A cascading approach illustrates the steps for pricing loans, using market prices and spreads.

In the first step, a loan is priced at the prevailing secondary-market price, provided that such a price exists. Furthermore, applying secondary-market prices is conditional on receiving permission from the client manager to sell down the asset and on loan documentation that does not prevent such a sale. If these conditions are not fulfilled, a transfer price will be derived from the costs of hedging, which can be CDS spreads or the costs at which an investor would take the risk by way of a financial guarantee, a subparticipation, or the costs of securitization. Since the universe of liquid CDSs

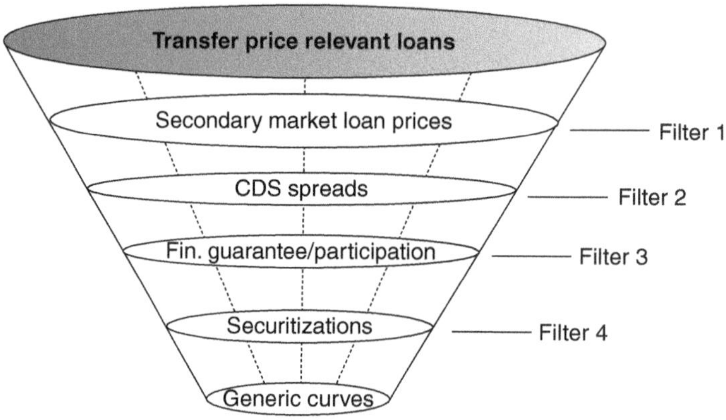

Figure 4.10 Cascading approach for transfer prices

and bonds is concentrated on large, multinational companies, a generic curve pricing based on market quotes ensures consistency in pricing the loan of smaller corporates. In any case, the introduction of a new concept of loan pricing needs to be transparent, well communicated, and supported by top management to secure the buy-in of involved units. This is even more important when the concept encompasses corporate loans only partially; that is, when the bank's internal risk-adjusted pricing is chosen for small and medium enterprises, whereas loans for larger corporates are priced using market quotes. Internal arbitrage of pricing approaches by allocating customers among the different categories depending on the better outcome for the client-relationship manager, may be the result of lack of acceptance of transfer pricing. For most banks, the cost of funding is another significant contributor to the transfer price. The funding spread is often provided by an internal funding desk in charge of calculating the funding cost for a specific transaction, given its characteristics. Banks fund themselves from different sources – deposits, bank bonds, collateralized or covered bonds, and central bank funding. The blended funding costs can vary significantly over time, and given their share of the total transaction costs, the effect on the profitability of a transaction can be substantial. An alternative is to use the bank's own CDS spread as an indicator for cost of funding. Although this is transparent and consistent, the real funding costs usually differ from the CDS spread. Thus, loan profitability calculated using the bank's CDS spreads can be materially different from the real economic value of a transaction, affecting the ability to take informed decisions when approving a credit request. Because of those implications, the sensitivity of transfer prices and loan approvals to funding costs has to be taken into account.

Transfer pricing plays an important role in the context of fair-valuing financial assets to overcome the accounting asymmetry arising from measuring loans at amortized costs while CDSs used for hedging are valued to market for financial reporting. Since changes in values of credit derivatives affect the profit and loss statement, adopting fair value for loans can substantially reduce the mismatch, which otherwise leads to unintended volatility from hedging activities. While measuring changes in hedged loans under hedge accounting for credit risk (HACR) reflects corresponding spread changes from the hedged CDSs, loans valued in line with the requirements of the fair value option (FVO) could be measured using market prices for loans, CDSs or other debt instruments, or be derived from models. If a bank chooses to apply either HACR or FVO, it needs to ensure that the approach is as consistent as possible to the transfer price. Even though the objectives of accounting might differ from the those of internal market–based loan pricing, they have the common goal of creating transparency as to the actual economic substance of the loans that are valued.

4.4.3 Loan transfer pricing based on observable loan market prices

Even though the last few years witnessed a pickup in secondary loan trading for large corporates, the depth of this market is still seen as an insufficient pricing source for valuing loans other than the ones trading. However, if a loan price can be observed in the market, and the contractual terms of the loan permit syndication or loan sale, this price is understood to be a fair price at which an asset can be cleared. Prices are quoted by brokers and dealers and provided through financial information servicers such as Bloomberg and Reuters. Quotes indicate bid and offer and are mostly indicative rather than firm prices which will be updated upon request. Rule-based pricing requires a minimum amount of regular quotes and a minimum frequency to eliminate distorting outliers. Loans trading in the market are typically leveraged buyout (LBO) loans, syndicated loans, credit lines, and distressed debt.

In some cases a loan cannot be sold at par into the market. This means that the cash price–implied secondary-market spread is different from the loan margin, with the difference between the two being the residual spread or settlement margin. The net present value of the residual spread equates to the discount to par at which the loan trades. If a loan can be sold only at a loss, the client manager has to reimburse the portfolio management unit accordingly, and vice versa. A loss can be interpreted as the cost of the client-relationship, which must be compensated by other

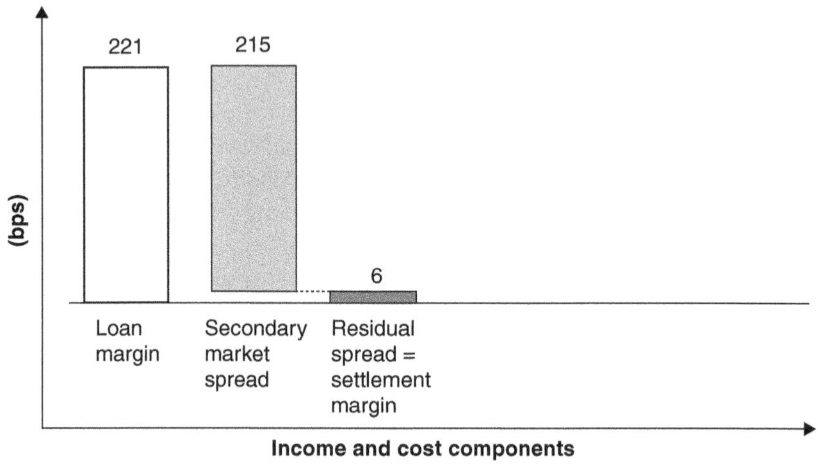

Figure 4.11 Transfer price for loan which can be sold into secondary market

client income.[27] If a transaction is prevented form being sold because legally binding contract terms, then a credit portfolio manager's discretion is restricted. This is often the case when a client wants the bank's full commitment to the financing or is concerned about a change of the final creditor without explicit prior consent. Because syndicated loans often trade at par at the time of origination, an asset sale does not have immediate profit and loss implications. In contrast, when there are restrictions on selling the loan, a different transfer pricing scheme has to be applied, one which could result in a significantly more negative transfer price. An alternative to selling a loan is to keep the asset on the books but transfer the credit risk to an investor. This typically takes place in the form of CDS hedge, a financial guarantee, or an open or silent subparticipation, all of which are in most cases more costly. An origination unit measured by the transfer price is thus incentivized to negotiate with the client the terms permitting a sale of such loan, which is also a prerequisite for an originate-to-distribute model. However, the outright selling of loans is not always a suitable alternative. A client manager is often wary of potentially negative implications for the customer relationship if the client becomes aware of the sale. Also, most loans do not trade frequently enough or the tradeable

[27] This holds true for the pricing gap at the time of loan underwriting and subsequent syndication. If the loan gets sold at a later point in time, the price can deviate substantially from par because of market conditions or because of changes in the credit quality of the borrower. A transfer price, however, is calculated solely at the time of underwriting. If the portfolio management unit is authorized to take the decisions to sell down assets at its own discretion, it is also accountable for the resulting profit and loss resulting from the trades.

sizes are insufficient, sometimes due to market conditions, to make these quotes useful as a reference for transfer price purposes.

4.4.4 Loan transfer pricing based on observable credit spreads

If loan prices cannot be applied, a hedge cost–based transfer price is the next step in the pricing cascade. In general, using CDS spreads for loan pricing is widely accepted by portfolio managers. Thus, via this transmission mechanism, CDS spreads may influence the cost of refinancing and, eventually, also the access to funding of loan borrowers as well. Credit agencies benchmark their fundamental credit assessment with market-implied ratings derived from spreads of trading credit assets, namely CDSs. But CDS spreads and stock prices also become interlinked because of trading strategies which aim to generate low risk but steady returns by arbitraging deviating developments between credit and equity risk – that is, by selling CDS protection on a listed company and simultaneously hedging the credit exposure by selling the stock, or vice versa. As a consequence, the liquidity of the CDS market and its interconnectedness to other capital market instruments qualify CDS as an objective source for pricing information. When portfolio managers rebalance a credit portfolio by hedging and reinvesting, the hedge spread also corresponds to the price at which portfolio managers can invest in equivalent assets of the same borrower, ensuring consistency of the approach.[28] A market spread–based transfer price is comparable to an insurance premium and should therefore cover both expected loss (EL) and unexpected loss (UL).[29] Market spreads reflect a fair price at which market participants agree to trade based on their asset valuations given publicly available information[30] and, by definition, do not take into account the contribution of said asset to the risk profile of an individual portfolio.

Spreads of CDSs refer to deliverable assets, bonds, or loans of a specified borrower. In many cases, a loan product encompasses a variety of features which have to be considered for pricing. Unlike bonds, which have a predefined and mostly non-changeable maturity[31] and exposure,

[28] For comparison, the investment has to be treated the same way from an accounting perspective.

[29] Goebel (2007). This is a fundamental difference from the internal risk assessment, limiting the direct comparability of market spreads to internal PDs.

[30] Assuming efficient markets. That assumption may not always hold true, in particular for less-regulated over-the-counter (OTC) markets, which is the case in particular for corporate debt and CDS.

[31] It should be noted, though, that high yield bonds can be redeemed at a predefined price before maturity.

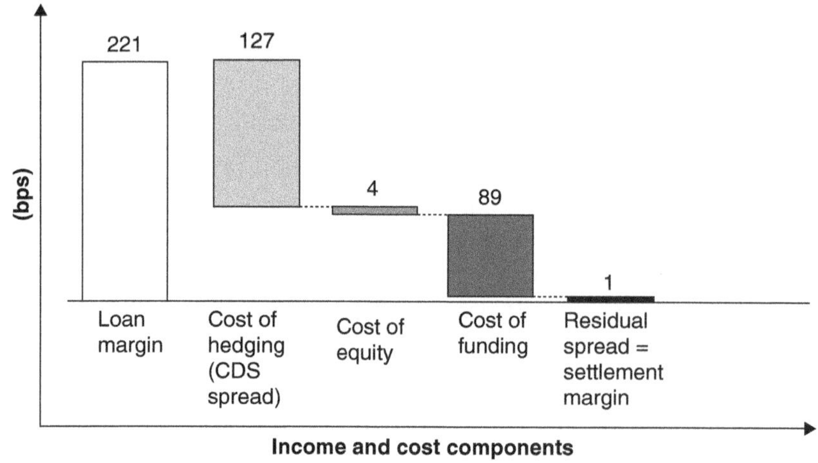

Figure 4.12 Components of hedge spread–based transfer price

for many loans, assumptions on both have to be taken, since, for instance, prepayment and extension options alter the maturity and some contract terms give the borrower the right to flexibly draw money under the loan. For non-plain-vanilla loans, a credit conversion factor helps to recognize the loan specifics, usually with respect to expected cash flow profile and maturity features. Exposure of undrawn credit lines, backup facilities, revolvers, or guarantees, for example, are typically estimated in relation to the borrower credit quality and maturity, determining both the amount of risk to be funded and hedged as well as the potential income from the loan, as interest is usually paid only on the drawn part. The likelihood of committed lines being drawn ranges from 25 per cent for a BBB-rated customer to 80 per cent for a B-rated one. Sensitivity of drawing to maturity increases with decreasing credit quality. If the transfer pricing approach is a net present value of revenues and costs, the default probability has to be considered, since it is less likely that future revenues will be realized for lower-rated customers. Put another way, the timing of default matters. Financial covenants have a risk-mitigating effect and are taken into account in calculating the usage of lines at default and the loss given default. A negative pledge clause, for example, prevents a borrower from providing collateral to another lender, which would put existing creditors into a subordinated position in the event of the liquidation of the borrower. Collateral provided by the client has to be subtracted to calculate the net exposure that needs to be hedged. Optionalities of loans include grid pricing, term out and prepayment options, as well as an extension clause.

Prepayments of loans are a particular concern, since for risk, accounting, and regulatory reasons the maturity of the loan must be matched by the maturity of a hedge.[32] If a loan is prepaid, the hedge and the funding continue minus the other leg of the pair, the hedged item. Even without considering the market value effects from the hedge and funding, which are no longer offset by the corresponding value changes of the loan, the costs of both are also no longer compensated by the loan income. It seems natural that borrowers often make use of a better credit environment to lower the average costs of borrowing. But prepayment risks do not exist only at times of declining market spreads. Very similarly, debtors tend to refinance their debt on time and before maturity, when they expect that refinancing could become difficult. In that case, loans are prepaid or terminated early to secure new funding even if interest costs for the new loan are substantially higher. However, once the transfer price has been calculated and agreed to, the risk of deviations from actual to estimated cash flows remains with the portfolio manager. Therefore, the transfer price must take into consideration breakage costs so that, at least on the portfolio level, the portfolio manager is compensated for those costs that are

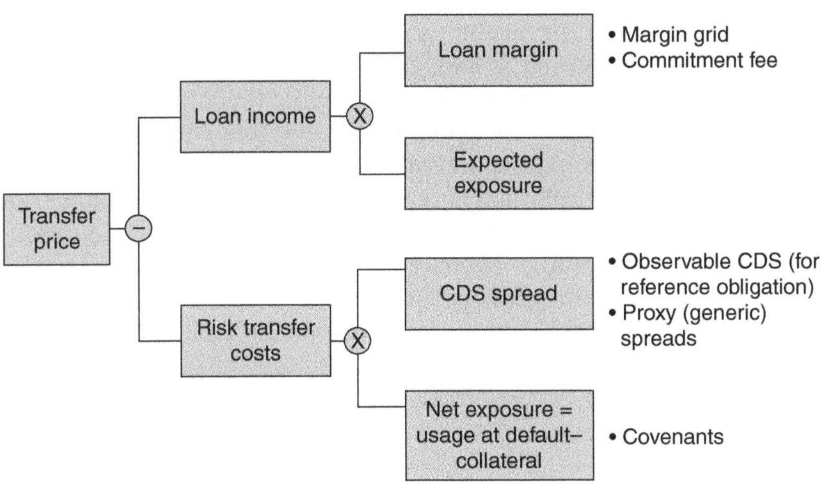

Figure 4.13 Determinants of loan income and risk transfer costs
Source: McKinsey.

[32] For example, to qualify for HACR, the CDS maturity must not exceed the maturity of the loan. The opposite holds for regulatory requirements regarding capital release via CDS hedges.

the result of options which have been granted to the borrower by the responsible client-relationship manager.

4.4.5 Transfer pricing based on generic curves

If no risk transfer takes place, either by intention or because of a lack of investor interest in a particular asset, the loan gets priced against a benchmark to derive the transfer price. Applying market spreads to loans for pricing purposes highlights the sometimes differing views of the bank's internal credit analysis and the capital markets. Even for borrowers whose credit quality assessment does not differ between a bank and the rating agencies or the markets, as measured by spread implied default probability, loans are often priced below the corresponding credit spreads for tradable debt securities. In particular, the pricing for loans of larger companies and multinationals is mostly relationship driven, and only to a lesser extent reflective of the cost of risk corresponding to the external and internal ratings. In the absence of cross-selling revenues, a bank would earn a higher income when investing in the client's bonds while taking identical credit risks and capital charges.[33] Consequently, loan transfer pricing based on market spreads is often used by financial institutions as a shadow pricing to quantify the pricing gap between the loan margin and the risk compensation demanded by other investors to foster origination discipline, thus keeping the gap as narrow as possible. However, market prices can be directly observed for larger, listed corporates and frequent borrowers, while for the others, a generic pricing scheme has to be developed. Usually, benchmarks for rating classes and industries can be established and used for generic pricing. Input into these benchmarks are typically CDS spreads, corporate bond spreads, and spreads of securitizations. Even though the introduction of TRACE®[34] has substantially improved the trading and pricing transparency in corporate bond markets, CDSs are still referred to as the most liquid element for generic pricing. Since securitizations became quite rare, and the pricing of structured credit products depends on not only the type and quality of collateral but also other important features, such as the risk of the originator and servicer, using structured credit

---

[33] Assuming all else is equal (i.e. exposure, maturity, debt ranking, accounting treatment, etc.).

[34] TRACE®: Trade Reporting and Compliance Engine®. The Trade Reporting and Compliance Engine is the FINRA-developed vehicle that facilitates the mandatory reporting of over-the-counter secondary-market transactions in eligible fixed income securities. Since 2002, all broker/dealers who are FINRA member firms have an obligation to report transactions in corporate bonds to TRACE under an SEC-approved set of rules. Current TRACE reporting time is 15 minutes. See www.finra.org.

transactions as a benchmark for pricing loans is less common today. Furthermore, extracting the risk component of the individual asset out of the securitized pool is challenging. Nonetheless, CDS spreads have some pitfalls, too. The universe of actively traded CDSs is comparatively small. Within the CDS universe, index constituents are the most liquid. Because indices are by definition a small sample[35], the number of spreads for some industries or rating classes may not be sufficient to generate a full rating/maturity curve for each rating class and data points for at least 1, 2, 3, 5 and 7 years.

Generic pricing for loans using market spreads can be performed as follows. To obtain a large enough number of issuers for which prices can be observed on a daily basis, CDS spreads as well as corporate bond quotes are used. Although basis risk exists for bonds and CDS and can be substantial, as during times of financial stress, the basis risk is not considered here. U.S.-domiciled companies represent the biggest share of corporate bond issuers, with some 5,000 to 6,000 bonds frequently quoted. By comparison, around 1,000 quotes can be retrieved for euro-denominated bonds. When comparing bonds to CDS spreads, the equivalent par spread of bonds is taken into account.[36] Bonds from financial institutions are removed. Corporate bonds denominated in different currencies are adjusted by adding the basis swap quote for the respective maturity and currency. Short-dated bonds with a maturity of less than one year are excluded from the sample, as they tend to be more illiquid, and their prices are sometimes not updated frequently. Maturities in excess of 10 years are also discarded, as there will be only few bonds outstanding. Callable bonds, which are often issued by non-investment-grade corporates, should be included in order to enrich the sample if the embedded call is significantly out of money. Since CDS spreads are considered to be more liquid than to corporate bonds, bond spreads are replaced by CDSs if CDS spreads are available. Mapping of bond issuers to CDSs can be done using the Bloomberg corporate ticker for each issuer. Removing outliers further cleans up the sample. Bonds with negative spreads are excluded, as we assume that borrowers cannot fund themselves below LIBOR, indicating that the spread is distorted by an embedded option

[35] The iTraxx Europe index, for example, consists of 100 industrial and 25 financial names, while the high-yield index crossover is composed of 40 constituents.

[36] Bloomberg, a financial information servicer, provides various bond spreads, among others the par asset swap spreads and z-spreads, to compare bonds to credit default swaps. However, these spreads are prone to a certain bias as they do not incorporate recovery rates or probabilities of default, which prevents a like-for-like comparison of bond and CDS spreads. A methodology developed by JPMorgan, called equivalent par CDS spreads, offers a more accurate and robust comparison between bonds and CDSs. See JPMorgan (2003).

or the bond has been simply mispriced. To compute a generic curve, the remaining spreads are clustered by rating and maturity. A composite rating scale analogous to the ones used by the rating agencies is taken to construct rating buckets. An example for a bucket would be all spreads for issuers with a rating of AA[37] and maturity of a CDS or bond between 4 and 5 years. For each bucket down to BBB, all spreads lower than the 5 per cent quantile and higher than the 90 per cent quantile are excluded. Below BBB, all spreads lower than the 5 per cent quantile and higher than the 80 per cent quantile are discarded. The spreads of some names may not be representative for their rating classes because of pending downgrades or upgrades, or simply because of a significantly diverging view of the riskiness of the CDS reference entity by market participants versus rating agencies. To arrive at generic rating/spread curves, a Nelson-Siegel curve is fitted, using the Levenberg-Marquardt algorithm. The Nelson-Siegel parametric approach is widely used and is a standard to perform generic curves. For comparison, a more in-depth analysis of pricing using Nelson-Siegel is provided by Oricchio (2011). All curves that are not strictly monotonic increasing with respect to maturity are excluded. Overlapping curves have to be avoided. For example, the generic curve for AA-rated industrials over the 1- to 10-year time horizon should never cross the curve of AAA- or A-rated industrials. Missing curves are interpolated using the geometric mean of the two neighbour rating curves. An illiquidity premium, which reflects the illiquid nature of loans, could be added to spreads across the rating spectrum but should be more pronounced for investment grade. Empirical data suggest that illiquid high-grade bonds offer 20 to 40 per cent higher spreads to compensate for illiquidity. High-yield bonds are usually smaller by issue size and trade with a larger bid-offer spread, which makes them more comparable to loans; thus there is less need to add a premium for illiquidity. Borrowers not externally rated have to be mapped to the corresponding rating category by comparing the internal default probabilities attached to internal ratings to those of the external ratings. Ratings are allocated to default probability ranges rather than to a single PD value. Overlapping default probability ranges between internal and external ratings have to be harmonized. It should be noted, though, that on a single obligor level, the pricing will most likely not be exactly representative but rather indicative of a theoretical average risk compensation that an investor would demand for those assets. In other words, if an obligor-specific market spread existed, it would very likely be different from the generic

[37] In case more than one rating exists and they do not correspond, the lower rating will be used.

spread, although the deviation should be insignificant. On a portfolio level, those differences may cancel each other out, meaning the prices on average are fair.

While a generic pricing scheme for loans within different categories (e.g. industry, country, currency) can be established, its application may be limited, since the generic curve is highly representative of the composition of the CDS and bond markets. Thus, the pricing might be suitable for some industrial countries (e.g. the U.S., UK, Germany, France) with a high share of listed corporates[38] but less so for those, like Italy and Spain, dominated by smaller-sized corporates. Given the significant country risk premium incorporated in CDS and bond spreads, as well as the loan margin for corporates domiciled on the European periphery, their low share in the generic pricing may lead to a systematic underpricing of the corporates of those countries. Interestingly, for pricing credit risks in non-liquid markets, Oricchio (2011) suggests incorporating a market view into the fundamental risk assessment. Additional sources of information are macroeconomic indicators, research from established investment banks, default rate forecasts of rating agencies, and credit indices. The main advantage over an internal rating model–based (IRB) pricing is its currentness with respect to the business cycle, since the majority of rating systems are point-in-time (PIT) and calibrated using a backward-looking anchor point, which by design tags behind actual economic developments. In contrast, rating agencies take a forward-looking through-the-cycle (TTC) approach. Blending the two approaches preserves the memory of rating sensitivity to previous credit cycles while anticipating future developments. Although the rationale has its merits, the concept is a compromise between pure, market-driven pricing and rating model–based credit pricing and is therefore well suited to a portfolio management which is front-end oriented but to a less well suited to an originate-to-distribute model, which is by definition ultimately determined by prevailing market prices. Because of the subjective nature of forward-looking assumptions, the approach does not have the objectivity of market spreads as a measure for origination success, and leaves transfer prices open to discussion about whether the price is fair. However, since the assumption of efficient capital markets with indefinite liquidity – allowing distribution of assets to investors at the discretion of the portfolio manager at all times – does not hold, the forward-looking nature of Oricchio's approach provides a clear advantage.

---

[38] Very often, CDS reference entities and bond issuers are publicly listed companies, because issuing securities involves a significant burden and costs of public disclosure which may not be suitable for smaller corporates.

4.4.6 Risk-adjusted versus transfer pricing

Unlike transfer pricing, buy-and-hold strategies and internal risk cost–based loan pricing have to explicitly incorporate the loan portfolio structure. Assets which remain on the bank's balance sheet should be priced so that the loan origination unit benefits from improvement in the portfolio's value-at-risk due to the asset added to the portfolio, whereas a penalty should be imposed on prices for assets which deteriorate the portfolio risk metrics because they contribute to an increase of the portfolio's concentration or correlation risks. It then follows that market-based transfer pricing, if it is not used solely for benchmarking or shadow pricing but for profit and loss measurement, is only applicable for assets which are ultimately hedged or sold at these prices. Pricing for all other assets has to be determined by their contribution to the portfolio risk.[39] A market-based credit pricing for a buy-and-hold strategy without any back-end portfolio management – that is, risk distribution into the market – will not meet a shareholder value orientation. Even if the loan margin is in line with the hedge spread, it may not compensate for a potential disproportionate rise in the cost of equity driven by the increase in the portfolio's economic risk and capital given the increase of the portfolio concentration risks from the single asset.[40] It becomes clear that for loan origination units, an originate-to-distribute approach and subsequent market-based loan pricing allows them to originate loans to one customer or to correlated customers at constant prices[41] regardless of the amounts already originated, while the asset may become prohibitively expensive under a buy-and-hold regime once the asset has added too much concentration risk to the portfolio. In practice, this creates problems, as a pure originate-to-distribute model, in which all originated assets are distributed into the markets by portfolio managers, rarely exists. Also, in many cases assets remain on the balance sheet for some time, until they are sold or hedged because the size of loans exceeds the liquidity of hedge instruments or because of time-consuming negotiation phases for asset sale or participations. In particular, securitizations raise some uncertainty about the saleability and conditions of portfolio transactions and require an asset warehousing before a transaction can be executed. During that time, the eligibility of loans for an intended securitization is subject to negotiations with potential investors, especially with lower-quality assets, so that applying illiquid prices calculated from expected or observed

[39] See Steinmüller (2007).

[40] See Gann (2008). While the risk weights of Basel II are insensitive to any correlation effects, regulators expect banks to consider correlation risks when assessing the capital adequacy and therefore to hold additional capital to cover those risks.

[41] Assuming all other pricing determinants – i.e. funding and market spreads – remain unchanged.

securitization costs carries some uncertainty. To solve the conflict between bank internal risk–adjusted versus market-based transfer pricing, which has the potential to generate intense discussions between the loan origination unit and portfolio management because of the possible distortion of the profit and loss measures of both, portfolio managers must issue an opinion about the intentions to distribute the asset during the origination phase and also lay out the proposed transaction's impact on the portfolio. This way, client managers are incentivized to originate loans that remain on the bank's balance sheet and add economic value to the portfolio, even though market spreads might be higher than the loan margin. Therefore, if the asset has a negative impact on the portfolio loss distribution, the internal price correctly reflects the increase of economic risk which the client manager must pass on to the client. For loans which will be distributed to investors, a market-based transfer price and subsequent hedging or selling allows the client manager to proceed with the transaction, even though its unfavourable portfolio implications or violation of concentration risk limits would otherwise lead to a refusal of the deal. The latter is in particular relevant for client relationships where a financial institution wants to position itself as a core or house bank to a client because of its strategic relevance or because the bank wants to protect its home market but cannot afford to keep all assets of said client on its books. A pure market-based pricing, outside the scope of portfolio considerations, will become more relevant again with accelerating financial disintermediation or the development of shadow banking, where the bank's credit value chain ultimately consists of asset origination and brokerage – for example, for project finance where banks have the expertise to originate assets but might not want to hold them because of an asset/liability term mismatch, while other investors have the funds but not the access to this asset class. Selling assets into the market immediately after origination implies that credit risk effectively becomes underwriting risk.

The relevance of market prices often challenged by client-relationship managers to traditional banking is, especially if market spread–implied default probabilities exceed the ones derived from the internal rating model, which are also not updated as frequently as credit markets reprice. Loan markets typically follow credit markets with some time delay, so rising credit spreads indicating the impending deterioration of credit quality are transformed into higher loan margins only with some delay. That leaves the loan originator with an increasing gap between loan interest income and hedging costs, to be filled with revenues from cross-selling. On the other hand, in times of tightening credit spreads, loan margins may not be renegotiated as quickly as spreads come in. This creates an opportunity to hedge out loans and preserve the residual income after hedging, which is then almost risk free and therefore significantly profitable from the perspective of return on equity. Market prices are used for the shadow-pricing of loans and, in some cases, to enhance origination discipline. Calculating transfer prices, which are based on market prices, makes the shortfall of loan income transparent and allows origination to assess the amount of additional income from a client-relationship needed to cover the shortfall. Clearly, transfer pricing is almost always viewed with some suspicion by client-relationship managers and loan origination units. Especially when ACPM is organized as a profit centre, the concerns are that portfolio managers will attempt to make profits to the detriment of loan origination. The conflict of interest when it comes to loan pricing – that is, pricing transactions away from current markets to create profits at portfolio management, while loan origination has to take an equivalent amount of losses – has to be considered appropriately when setting up an active credit portfolio management unit which is responsible for loan pricing. Ensuring full integrity and interest alignment of origination and portfolio management is difficult but a prerequisite to the introduction of any kind of transfer price.

4.5 Practical implementation: Organizational and infrastructure challenges

Unlike other areas in banking, there is no ideal ACPM model or best-practice design which serves all financial institutions alike. This should come as no surprise, given the widely differing strategic objectives and individual strengths and limitations of the financial institutions. The International Association of Credit Portfolio Managers (IACPM) developed a framework of principles and practices[42] against which an organization can benchmark its own activities and measure its portfolio management efforts. Their paper provides an excellent overview of the various aspects to be considered when designing portfolio management operations. Very often, active credit portfolio managers rely on the existence of liquid debt capital markets for risk transfer and risk-pricing purposes. However, in today's financial market environment, the credit portfolio must also be managed rigorously at the front end. That means setting incentives and restrictions sufficient to originate only assets which contribute to an improvement of the risk/return profile of the credit portfolio. Increasing the risk-adjusted performance of a credit portfolio through the credit cycle requires a long-term view complemented by short-term measures such as asset distribution and back-end portfolio rebalancing. In the transition towards active credit portfolio management, creating the correspondent organizational structures and portfolio management processes represents the

[42] See IACPM (2005).

most significant challenge.[43] Specifically, the key determinants for successful active credit portfolio management are

governance and mandate: precisely and fully defined objectives and competences, based on senior management understanding and sponsorship; full transparency on governance and principles and buy-in of concerned stakeholders;

organizational design: the design for ACPM must be chosen carefully based on the specific characteristics, strategic targets, risk culture and limitations of the institution, as well as the market-imposed constraints;

performance measurement and communication: performance measurement must be long-term oriented, based on a full credit cycle approach with regular and frequent review and focus adjustment;

portfolio analytics and IT infrastructure: guidance on portfolio developments which are of interest to the different stakeholders; timely, accurate, and complete data must be provided, using a sound IT structure, to allow combining of different data sources (i.e. external and internal data; markets and credit data).

4.5.1 Governance and mandate

By far the most decisive factor for the successful implementation of any credit portfolio management is top management governance and sponsorship. Where in the hierarchy the ACPM is located clearly reflects its strategic importance, whereas the reporting line is determined more by organizational aspects. A clearly formulated mandate and scope, which must be communicated to all relevant stakeholders and along the lines of cooperation, is another prerequisite for success. This may seem obvious, but the financial crisis laid bare that there is a striking gap here for many credit portfolio management activities and that it has potentially severe implications that can prevent the CPM function from exploiting its full potential. The latest example of a confusion mandate was the admission of JPMorgan Chase that it lost more than $2 bn due to 'errors, sloppiness and bad judgement'. The bank said in a statement on May 11, 2012, that its chief investment office had the mandate to generate profits, backed by CEO Jamie Dimon, although the primary role of the unit was to protect the credit portfolio. Unclear responsibilities generally result in internal competition, a fight over mandates and a lack of conviction in their execution. As there are various ways to define, implement, and run credit portfolio management, no one is organized like another, and all are largely dependent on and must be responsive to the individual goals and characteristics of the

43 See PricewaterhouseCoopers (1999).

Objectives	Improve origination discipline and loan pricing	Enhance portfolio transparency	Optimize portfolio risk/return and capital consumption	
Portfolio under management	Asset based lending (leveraged, project and commodity finance), commercial real estate, shipping, leasing, factoring	Multinational corporates/ large caps	SME	Private individuals
Involvement in credit approval process	Advisor	Voting right from portfolio perspective	Voting right from portfolio and credit risk perspective	Veto right
Risk sources	Borrower and issuer default risk, migration risk	Counterparty risk	Market risk (price risk)	Liquidity risk
Risk mitigation	CDS, LCDS, CDS based credit indices (linear and tranched), options	Syndication	Guarantees, participations	Securitization, portfolio transactions
Investments	Derivatives (CDS, LCDS, CDS based credit indices incl. tranches, options)	Bonds (corporates, high yield), promissory notes	Loans	Convertibles
Booking and risk limits	Trading books Trading (VaR) limits	Banking books Credit lines, plafonds, RWA	Combination	
Transfer price and asset transfer	Risk insurance: internally derived insurance premium covering expected loss and cost of capital or CDS quote. no asset transfer, only risk transfer	Pro rata credit risk asset transfer: transfer price based on net pro rata (i.e. yearly) value of cash flows, expected loss and capital costs, administrative costs; excluded are funding costs and funding risks (i.e. prepayments)	PV credit risk asset transfer: transfer price based on present value of cash flows, expected loss and capital costs, administrative costs; excluded are funding costs and risks (i.e. prepayment)	Full asset transfer: transfer price calculated as net present value of all cash flows and costs, with full transfer of asset to ACPM P&L

Figure 4.14 Key ACPM mandate definition criteria

Objective	Focus on risk mitigation with cost limits. Little connectivity to capital markets and no market timing.	Focus on risk mitigation and diversification while keeping costs low. Some activity in capital markets. Market trends and timing partially considered.	Focus on risk transformation, reshaping portfolio composition with complete allocation of all related P&L effects. Frequent access to capital markets with market timing aspirations and best practice for execution.	Focus on risk transformation and revenue generation combining imperfect credit markets with expert knowledge on debt origination and debt capital markets and products. Trading like approach to arbitraging price inefficiencies of derivatives and bonds, market timing. Discretionary trading VaR and P&L limits.
Profit and loss	Cost center:	Part profit center with zero P&L:	Full profit center:	Full profit center with budget:
	Costs of risk mitigation (spread costs and valuation changes) and P&L from asset transfer (transfer prices) booked at an segregated account.	Costs of risk mitigation should not exceed transfer prices and income from investments. Mark-to-Market from hedging and investments booked at an segregated account. Potentially DV01 neutral strategy for combination of hedges and investments.	Costs of risk mitigation, transfer prices, P&L from hedging and investments (carry and mark-to-market).	Costs of risk mitigation, P&L from hedging and transfer prices booked at an segregated account.
Market risk from CDS hedging	No mitigation	Offsetting with DV01 neutral investments	Hedge accounting for credit risk	Offsetting by Mark-to-Market valuation for loans

Figure 4.15 Combinations of portfolio management objectives with profit and loss implications and risk mitigants

respective financial institution. Specifying the mandate includes defining the scope of portfolio management, which could comprise loans (i.e. to multinational corporates, financial institutions, small and medium enterprises [SMEs] or private individuals), asset-based lending (such as acquisition and leveraged finance), project and commodity finance, commercial real estate and shipping, as well as investments (corporate bonds, promissory notes, CDSs). Different approaches to managing credit subportfolios can be taken, which clearly underscores the need to identify the relevant portfolios and the corresponding portfolio management style. Besides the asset under management, the risks that the portfolio manager is supposed to manage also have to be defined. Risks to be managed could include credit risk, migration risk, counterparty risk, market risk, and liquidity risk.

The objectives should be reflected in the competences granted; that is, authorizing portfolio manager to sell or buy assets in the secondary market or to execute hedges to rebalance the portfolio, provided the necessary credit lines and limits are available and the loan documentation does not prevent selling the asset. In some cases, the mandate includes investments to recover costs from risk transfer or for portfolio diversification purposes. Here, it is important to define investment guidelines, which detail instruments, strategies, and books to be used, as well as restrictions.

4.5.2 Organizational design

The contribution of CPM to the credit value chain is a key determinant of its organizational allocation. A portfolio management largely focused on hedging and enhancing origination discipline by applying transfer prices on loans is better located on the business side. On the other hand, if the focus is mostly on regulatory capital optimization, CPM is probably be better suited to the CFO area, but transactions are then executed by business specialists. In many cases, in particular for larger financial institutions, the balance sheet consists of a variety of loan products and clients. Portfolio management as a risk function offers the advantage of broader and consistent coverage of credit assets across the board.[44] Organizational allocation in turn determines whether the portfolio management unit is a cost or profit centre. The most powerful ACPM units are run as profit centres. This is so because profit and loss responsibility is ultimately the most direct measure and constraint to operate with and, at the same time, it reduces process-related inefficiencies. However, the design of the credit portfolio management unit must explicitly acknowledge the moral hazard when client management becomes completely detached from

[44] Stegemann and Jamin (2008) conclude that stronger CPMs are typically located in the business line, whereas weaker mandates can be found in the risk or finance function. They observed that *'the effectiveness of CPM grows with the assigned power....The optimal model depends on the strategic objective a firm wishes to pursue with CPM'*.

the profit and loss implications of its origination activity. It is of utmost importance to retain common responsibility and partnership.

Specific policies detail the role of portfolio management and its connectivity to other units which are part of the credit value chain (e.g. ALM, capital management, loan origination, trading, syndication). Cross-divisional and/or shared responsibilities must be underpinned by an agreement on the senior management level and, in cases where required by legal or formal aspects, also by service-level agreements (SLAs). Strict compliance rules must be respected. Since borrower credit analysis often contains non-public information, Chinese walls between the private and public sides of ACPM must be implemented, accompanied by clear rules and codes of conduct. Penalties for misconduct can be severe, and it is often difficult to prove that private information made available has not been incorporated into the decision and/or timing of risk mitigation when using capital market products. To avoid restrictions on the interaction between ACPM and capital markets, any execution or trading desk must be located on the public side. Tax, legal, and regulatory aspects play a significant role in the organizational set-up of ACPM. Cross-country internal risk transfer between subsidiaries or branches of a bank must follow tax laws; in many instances it takes place at fair value rather than book value. The qualifications of ACPM personnel must meet the specific requirements of the portfolio management process. Because active credit portfolio management combines elements of traditional banking and debt trading, banks often source expertise from units specializing in those areas – traders for execution, quantitative risk managers for portfolio analysis, and credit analysts for transfer pricing and single name management. However, the flood of new regulations with respect to risk management, capital adequacy, and accounting requires expertise in different disciplines.

Case Study 3. ACPM at a large, cross-border, universal bank with investment banking operations

Let us consider a large, cross-border financial institution with significant corporate and investment banking activities. Typically, the bank's portfolio displays a certain degree of borrower concentration risks due to its strong relationships with multinational corporates, but exposure to some regions is also substantial, as the bank aims at defending a reasonable market share in its home country. Portfolio diversification benefits from loans to private individuals with low cost of risk. Small and medium enterprises are underrepresented. The board decided to implement an ACPM function to

1. release regulatory capital (which could be reinvested),
2. achieve a reduction in economic capital to a predefined target level,
3. reduce potential loan loss provisions from large corporates,

4. mitigate portfolio sensitivity to certain geographical areas and industries,
5. reduce vulnerability to market downturn–related stress, and
6. improve origination discipline and loan pricing and increase non-loan revenues,

under the condition that risk transfer must be effective, profit and loss volatility induced from hedges must be contained, and the portfolio management must be self-financing, with limited revenues from investments. ACPM has been given full responsibility for profit and loss. The portfolio management mandate includes all corporate loans.

Due to the importance of ACPM to the strategic mission of the bank, ACPM has a direct reporting line to senior management. The decision to provide ACPM with a profit and loss responsibility, in combination with the desired improvement in origination discipline, suggests that it should reside with the business line. To reduce regulatory capital, diverse risk transfer products are used – for example, securitization, participations, syndications, and CDSs. Single name concentration risks are mitigated by CDSs, with the respective loan as deliverable obligation. Since the derivatives should not introduce profit and loss volatility, either hedge accounting for credit risk (HACR) or fair value (FVO) for loans have to be implemented to offset value changes. Both approaches are closely connected to a loan transfer pricing methodology, which enhances the origination discipline. An investment committee has been set up, where underpriced loans are discussed. The revenue shortfall due to underpricing is expressed by the difference of fair value to book value at the time of origination and must be covered by additional income from cross-selling. Business units benefitting from potential ancillary business have to sponsor the transaction; otherwise the loan will be rejected. Loan loss provisions are diminished via HACR and FVO, where the increase in hedge CDS value due to rising spreads compensates for decreasing loan fair values. Industry concentration risks are hedged using a combination of linear and tranched CDSs. Options on CDSs are opportunistically used in the context of the credit risk strategy to reduce tail risks. Investments balance the market risk of options and indices, albeit on the condition that the net position must be at least DV01 neutral or negative.[45] A trade execution desk has been set up to maintain hedging on the public side. For calculations of the effects of risk mitigation to economic and regulatory capital, the unit runs a vendor portfolio model, which benchmarks the internal model. Regulatory capital optimization is performed in close cooperation with CFO functions. To ensure consistency with CFO and CRO reporting, close, regular portfolio analysis has been performed with comprehensive information provided to senior management to allow for timely guidance. Stress tests are conducted as a joint effort with risk functions.

A stylized organizational chart, which represents the layers of ACPM in this case study, looks like the following:

[45] Introducing a zero DV01 limit means that the net profit and loss from a spread increase of one basis point should be zero. That means the value changes of hedges

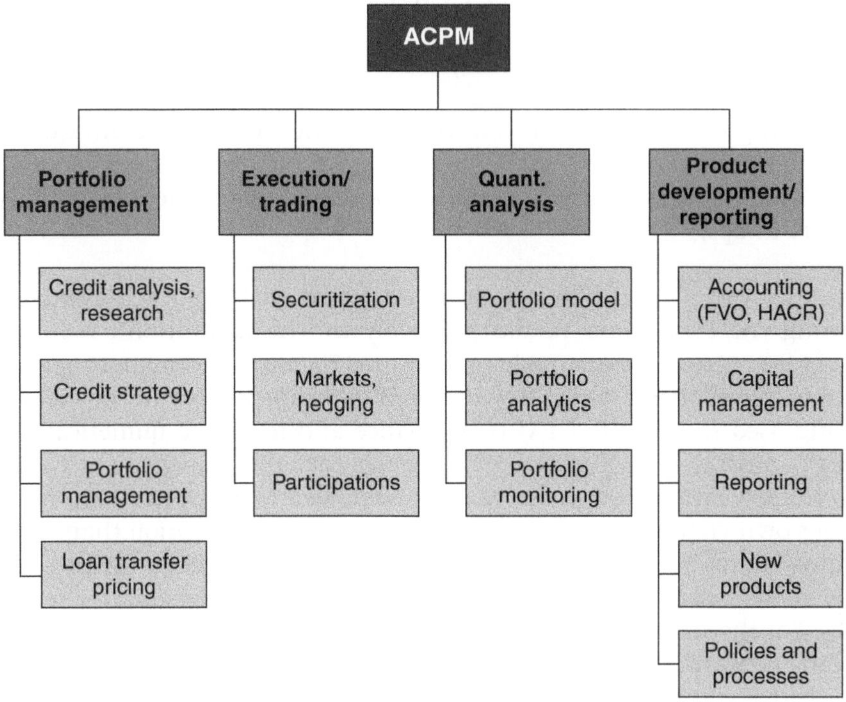

Figure 4.16 Stylized organizational ACPM chart

4.5.3 Performance measurement and communication

Portfolio managers need to report on their activities and communicate effectively. To a certain extent, portfolio reports also show the impact of portfolio management and support the measurement of the portfolio manager's performance, based on performance indicators that correspond to the mandate. It should be noted, though, that without a clear operating mandate no meaningful performance measurement can be set. In such cases it is sometimes delegated to the CPM units to propose and set targets and measurements used to ultimately determine the level of success. Based on interviews with dedicated bank CPMs, McKinsey[46] concluded that the definition of a clear and measurable vision for CPM hinges very much on its relevance for senior management. When asked

---

must at least amount to those of investments when credit spreads widen. A negative DV01 restriction requires that profit and loss effects from investments should not exceed those from hedges.

[46] See McKinsey and Company (2009).

- if the value contribution of CPM was questioned at the respective institution,
- if CPM was perceived as having a critical positive contribution during the crisis,
- if it is possible to measure a large part of the CPM value contribution in bps form, and
- what the value contribution of the measurable part of the CPM activity was in bps,

the majority of portfolio managers answered that their achievements during the crisis were valued positively by the institution's management but were not measurable or measured by any performance metrics. Furthermore, there was little evidence of full transparency in the metrics being used to measure CPM performance and to define numerical targets. Consequently, it is questionable whether the management's view on the role and achievements of CPM coincided with the portfolio manager's own view or whether it was more a matter of perception than facts. However, not having appropriate performance measures run the risk that the value contribution of ACPM may not be fully understood or recognized at the senior management level and throughout the organization. Going forward, financial institutions committed to raising the potential of their credit portfolio management will have to set cycle-consistent, non-contradictory, and intuitive performance measures that fit the business model and consider the long-term time horizon of the effects.

4.5.4 Portfolio analytics and IT infrastructure

Organizational considerations include information and technology. The aim is to provide a timely, complete, comprehensive and correct picture of the portfolio risks to all stakeholders, considering their individual area of interest. Portfolio reporting and management need to take into account the focus point of the various stakeholders, which is likely to differ from one to another, with the business side more interested in shorter-term metrics, especially revenues and risk-adjusted profitability, including regulatory capital; whereas risk management concentrates on such key risk measures as expected loss and economic capital, which are longer term and cycle oriented. Concepts to describe exposure vary, with the CFO taking the accounting view for granted loans (on and off balance risks) and the business perspective is on the maximum risk at stake (i.e. plafonds and granted amounts), while exposure at default serves as the measure of choice at risk management. Time horizons can be different with peak, average, and point-in-time exposure, which could have greater effects for clients generally doing end-of-period window dressing deals, as is common for financial institutions. Revenues consist of interest income, fees, and income from ancillary business. Usually, a customer relationship is characterized by some parts of the client's business subsidizing others, which is typically accepted as long as the overall revenues from that client satisfy the minimum thresholds defined. However, since larger customers consist of a number of subsidiaries, themselves clients of other divisions and probably regions, a meaningful credit portfolio reporting and analysis always needs to start at the most aggregated level and then break down into a higher granularity. In any case, it should reflect the way client business is organized; that is, centralized versus decentralized. Using different, sometimes disconnected databases stresses the need for a clearly defined cooperation mode between the units involved, shared responsibility, and full transparency on contribution and final product. To make the exercise worthwhile and to meet the expectations of the CPM sponsors, the set of metrics and particular focus points need to be defined and agreed on with the stakeholders in advance. The ability to elaborate on portfolio risks depends on the availability of complete, accurate, and timely data, sound IT infrastructure, models, and modelling expertise. However, users of model-based portfolio analytics not only have to understand their tools; they also have to have appropriate incentives to use them in a way that is consistent with the strategic objectives of their bank. As Bohn and Stein[47] point out, this also depends on the organizational structure and culture in which models are implemented and used. If loans are fair-valued or if HACR is used to mitigate volatility in profit and loss arising from an accounting mismatch for hedges, databases and systems for loans must communicate with those for market products. This is in particular challenging, since loan products display a wide range of loan-specific features, which are usually not present in capital market products and therefore not recognized in IT systems for trading.

4.5.5 Implementation of an ACPM function

Implementing a portfolio management function requires a sound plan that considers a range of credit risk management issues. Since most banks are advanced in managing their credit portfolios, their focus is probably more on reviewing and optimizing the business model of their portfolio management operations in light of a dramatically changed operating environment and regulatory and accounting rules than on defining a new setup. To maintain the most suitable model given the bank's specific targets and the nature of their loan business, continual review and

[47] See Bohn and Stein (2011).

refinement of organizational structures and portfolio management tools is essential. The non-exhaustive list of criteria that support a clear definition of the scope and purpose of credit portfolio management includes an outline of the objectives; identification and agreement on the assets to be managed; risk mitigation instruments and practices; the type of investments, if any; the trading and banking books allocated to the credit portfolio management, including respective limits; and finally, the determination of the transfer price system to be applied. While these factors are considered relevant for the design of the portfolio management activities, involving the concerned business and risk-management units early by introducing a portfolio management unit is likely to reveal other important aspects to be taken into account.

5
Accounting Complexity and Implications

Accounting standards and in particular their contribution to the financial crisis have been intensely debated for quite some time. A central aspect of accounting relates to the valuation of financial instruments. International financial reporting standards (IFRS) dictate that financial instruments are either carried at amortized costs or have to be valued mark-to-market (fair value). Both approaches have their merits and their drawbacks. Fair value enhances transparency on the worthiness of assets but has also been blamed for having intensified the downward spiral when the crisis broke. Significantly depreciating the value of assets led to banks experiencing capital shortage. Banks then sold assets to ensure that their capital position met the minimum regulatory requirements. Forced selling put additional pressure on market prices. As a result, asset valuations had to be reduced again, with pronounced detrimental effects on capital. These events led in October 2009 to an amendment to IAS 39 and IFRS 7 which did permit the reclassification of some assets out of the fair value through the profit and loss category to new cost or amortized cost. The pro-cyclicality of fair value was a major concern of politicians, who requested changes to the accounting rules. Under IAS 39, which deals with the recognition and measurement of financial instruments, financial assets are classified into four categories:

- Held for Trading, measured at *fair value* through profit and loss;
- Loans and Receivables, measured at *amortized costs* through profit and loss;
- Held to Maturity, measured at *amortized costs* through profit and loss; and
- Available for Sale, measured at *fair value* through equity.

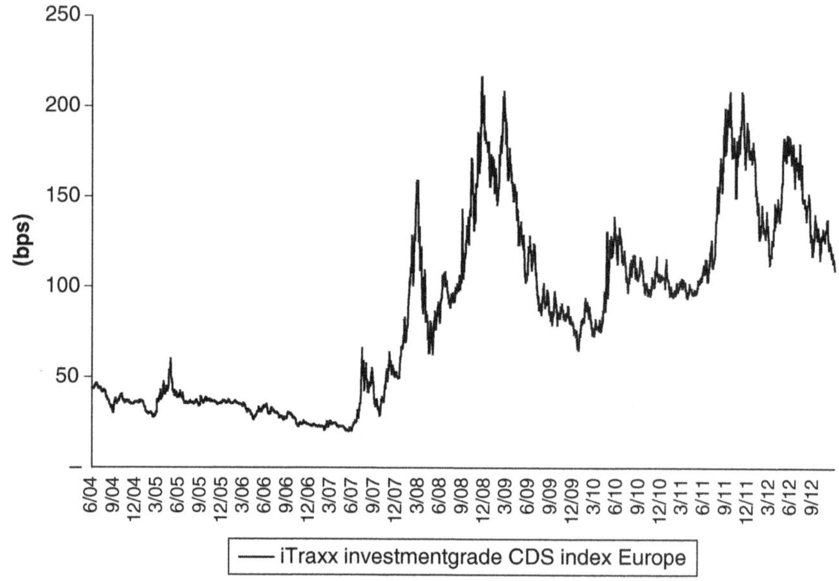

Figure 5.1 Markit iTraxx Europe spreads
Data source: Bloomberg.

IAS 39 will be replaced by IFRS 9, *Financial Instruments,* which covers classification and measurement of financial assets. The new accounting rule becomes effective on January 1, 2015; earlier adoption is permitted. Under IFRS 9, there will be only two measurement categories, *fair value* and *amortized costs*. Although IFRS 9 explicitly recognizes a bank's business model to determine the valuation approach for on-balance-sheet items, the mixed model problem of IAS 39 remains. Unlike traded securities, loans are usually booked into banking books and accounted for at *amortized costs* – so-called *accrual accounting*. On the other hand, credit default swaps, which are derivatives by design, have to be carried at *fair value*. The profit and loss from value changes of CDSs are recognized in the income statement. While economically, little risk[1] remains from a perfect name-specific credit risk hedge, the effects of an asymmetric accounting treatment of the value changes of the loan and the CDS pair creates headaches for risk managers. In a volatile capital market environment, those effects can be, and have been, very substantial.

[1] Residual risks arising from CDS hedging are explained in chapter 7.

Case Study 4. CDS Hedge–Induced Profit and Loss Volatility and Mitigation

The chart above shows the generic spread[2] for the Markit iTraxx Europe index, composed of 125 equally weighted credit default swaps on investment grade European corporate entities. (For details, refer to Chapter 7.) In the wake of the financial crisis, the index spread widened from a record low of 20 bps in 2007 to more than 200 bps at the end of 2008. It softened again in 2010 but did not reach levels as low as before the crisis. The sovereign debt crisis again contributed to rising corporate spreads in 2011. Financial institutions which run a meaningful CDS hedge portfolio to protect loans are exposed to substantial volatility from changes in CDS spreads. While some banks decided to take this risk unmitigated, others were more conservative and took appropriate measures.

Example 1. Société Générale

It appears that Société Générale's portfolio management opted to take the volatility from its CDS hedging activities unmitigated. The bank reported on February, 18th 2010 '... accounting effects related to the revaluation of debts linked specifically to the credit risk and credit derivative instruments used to hedge the loans and receivables portfolios.... These items, which reached an exceptional level on account of the crisis, made a contribution of EUR –2,324 million to gross operating income in 2009 (vs. EUR \+2,489 million in 2008).'[3]

Example 2. JPMorgan Chase & Co.

The bank's portfolio management unit, which was awarded the credit portfolio manager of the year 2012 by *Risk*,[4] takes an active stance towards managing wholesale credit risk, including hedging, but also to diversifying the portfolio by way of investments and portfolio transactions. In 2010, JPMorgan outlined the following in its annual report:[5]

Management of the Firm's wholesale exposure is accomplished through a number of means including loan syndication and participations, loan sales, securitizations, credit derivatives, use of master netting agreements, and collateral and other risk-reduction techniques. The Firm also manages its wholesale credit exposure by purchasing protection through single name and portfolio credit derivatives to manage the credit risk associated with loans, lending-related commitments and derivative receivables. Changes in credit risk on the credit derivatives are expected to offset changes in credit risk on the loans, lending-related commitments or derivative receivables. This activity does not reduce the reported level of assets on the balance sheet or the level of reported off-balance sheet commitments, although it

[2] The time series shows spreads of the then on-the-run iTraxx series; spread adjusted for the rollover.

[3] See www.societegenerale.com, Press release, 2009 Activities and Results.

[4] See www.risk.net.

[5] See www.jpmorgan.com, 2010 Annual Report.

does provide the Firm with credit risk protection. The Firm also diversifies its exposures by selling credit protection, which increases exposure to industries or clients where the Firm has little or no client-related exposure; however, this activity is not material to the Firm's overall credit exposure.

The credit derivatives used by JPMorgan Chase for credit portfolio management activities do not qualify for hedge accounting under U.S. GAAP; these derivatives are reported at fair value, with gains and losses recognized in principal transactions revenue. In contrast, the loans and lending-related commitments being risk-managed are accounted for on an accrual basis. This asymmetry in accounting treatment, between loans and lending-related commitments and the credit derivatives used in credit portfolio management activities, causes earnings volatility that is not representative, in the Firm's view, of the true changes in value of the Firm's overall credit exposure. The MtM value related to the Firm's credit derivatives used for managing credit exposure, as well as the MtM value related to the credit valuation adjustment (CVA) (which reflects the credit quality of derivatives counterparty exposure) are included in the gains and losses realized on credit derivatives disclosed in the table below. These results can vary from period to period due to market conditions that affect specific positions in the portfolio.

Example 3. Deutsche Bank

The German bank is well known for its proactive, disciplined, and comprehensive approach to managing credit risks from loans. Running a substantial hedge book, Deutsche Bank decided to make use of the fair value option for loans and commitments under IAS 39. In its annual review 2010, titled 'Delivering in the Face of Uncertainty', Deutsche Bank wrote[6]

Our Loan Exposure Management Group (LEMG) helps mitigate our corporate credit exposures.... As of year-end 2010, LEMG held credit derivatives with an underlying notional amount of €34.6 billion. The position totaled €32.7 billion as of December 31, 2009. The credit derivatives used for our portfolio management activities are accounted for at fair value.... LEMG has elected to use the fair value option under IAS 39 to report loans and commitments at fair value, provided the criteria for this option are met. The notional amount of LEMG loans and commitments reported at fair value increased during the year to €54.1 billion as of December 31, 2010, from €48.9 billion as of December 31, 2009. By reporting loans and commitments at fair value, LEMG has significantly reduced profit and loss volatility that resulted from the accounting mismatch that existed when all loans and commitments were reported at historical cost while derivative hedges were reported at fair value.

Example 4. Hypovereinsbank

Hypovereinsbank successfully developed and implemented a new concept, hedge accounting for credit risks, to mitigate the volatile effects from CDS

[6] See www.deutsche-bank.de. Annual Report 2010 (entire).

hedging onto the profit and loss. Since 2009, the bank applied a micro fair value hedge to reduce the volatility in its income statement, thus correcting existing inconsistencies of CDS and loan valuations. In its 2010 annual report, Hypovereinsbank describes the approach as follows:[7]

As part of hedge accounting for credit risks, in accordance with IAS 39.86 (a) the credit-induced changes in the fair value of selected hedged items such as loans and receivables with customers and irrevocable credit commitments (off-balance-sheet fixed commitments) and the full-induced changes in the fair value of the hedging instrument (credit default swap, CDS) are offset. Remaining-term effects need to be adjusted in this context.

These remaining-term effects lead to a change in the credit-induced fair value over time without the current market credit spread changing. Among other things, this includes a difference between the nominal amount and the credit-induced fair value at the inception of the hedge. Excluding the possibility of an impairment, the credit-induced fair value on the settlement date will correspond to the nominal amount of the hedged item. Any difference between the credit-risk-induced fair value and the nominal amount existing when the hedge is designated amortises over the remaining time (pull-to-par effect). Differences like this can arise when hedged items are designated at a later date rather than when originated, for instance, since the contractually agreed credit spread does not generally match the normal market credit spread at the inception of the hedge in such cases.

The change in the credit-induced fair value determined in this way (after adjustment for remaining-term effects) is taken to the income statement under effects arising from hedge accounting in net trading income. Where the hedged items are assets recognised in the balance sheet, the carrying amount is adjusted for the changes in the credit-induced fair value. Irrevocable credit commitments (fixed commitments not shown in the balance sheet), on the other hand, are not recognised in the balance sheet. The credit-related changes in the fair value relating to these are carried under other assets in the balance sheet.

We show the associated hedging instruments (CDSs) at their fair value as hedging derivatives; the changes in the fair value are similarly taken to the income statement as effects arising from hedge accounting in net trading income.

Concerning the approach towards managing credit risks from loans, Hypovereinsbank stated that

Default risk is managed on the basis of defined policies, approval authority structures and risk-assessment processes. The introduction of fair value hedge accounting for credit risk did not result in any changes in the management of default risk.

[7] See www.hypovereinsbank.de. HVB Group Annual Report 2010.

Unintended volatility in the income statement is not the only problem active portfolio managers face when hedging loans with CDSs. Another important aspect of the accounting asymmetry is that, because CDSs are generally classified as derivatives under IAS 39, they do not represent collateral in connection with the evaluation of loan loss provisions. Gains from hedges, which compensate economically for losses from the hedged item, are already reflected in the income statement and cannot be 'reserved' for loan losses. The absolute level of loan loss provisions is a key indicator for the success of risk management. CDS as a risk mitigation tool stands a much better chance of being taken seriously if these drawbacks are resolved. Accounting rules in their current form do not coincide with business practices and also decrease the transparency of financial reporting. The risk is that banks may decide not to engage in hedging, leaving risks unprotected.

As seen in the cases shown above, active credit portfolio managers make regular use of financial products to manage the risk profile of their credit portfolios, taking different approaches to mitigate the accounting effects. The rest of this chapter contemplates solutions which are tested in practice, closing with a discussion of the advantages and challenges associated with each approach.

5.1 Hedge accounting and other solutions for accounting asymmetry

Since accrual accounting for credit derivatives does not seem to be an option for the accounting standard setter, other alternatives to mitigate profit and loss volatility from CDS hedges have to be investigated. Potential solutions should encompass

- consistency with the business model and portfolio management approach;
- accounting intuition, meaning consistent results of financial accounting and economic performance; and
- technical simplicity.

First, business decisions should not be driven or restricted by the accounting regime. Ideally, accounting rules follow business practices. Accounting intuition suggests that there no need for excessive explanation in the financial statements to describe the economic situation behind the numbers. The purpose and effects of active portfolio management activities, using financial products to mitigate risks, should be clear from financial reporting. Appropriate solutions also imply that back office, monitoring and IT-related efforts are operationally feasible.

Currently, there are four options for addressing the diverging accounting value changes for loans and CDSs:

Financial guarantee: If a derivative contract can be restructured to meet the definition of a financial guarantee (FG) of IAS 39, then the contract is allowed to be carried at cost, with no volatility effects for the profit or loss statement. An FG is not a derivative; therefore it qualifies as collateral and protects against loan loss provisions. However, it should be noted that a borrower credit quality deterioration–driven impairment does not necessarily coincide, timing-wise, with a failure to pay, which is the only credit event that triggers a compensation payment under an FG. The accounting requirements for a financial guarantee are strict and difficult to meet, making an FG a fairly illiquid hedge transaction that is in general expected to be kept together with the hedged item until maturity.

Fair value option: Applying the fair value option allows measuring each instrument at fair value. The full fair value incorporates changes in credit spreads, interest rates, and/or liquidity, while the credit derivative only offsets the credit risk. Volatility in the profit or loss statement is reduced only to the extent of the offsetting effects from the CDS hedge, except for other risk sources being hedged in addition. Credit hedge–induced volatility in profit and loss is substantially decreased by the fair value option. However, the cash basis, where changes in the value of loans as funded assets deviates from value changes of unfunded derivatives, can become an issue. Effectively, impairments are implicitly determined by the fair value of the loan, thus replacing specific loan loss provisions. Accounting under the fair value option may significantly limit the flexibility of a portfolio manager.

Hedge accounting for credit risk: Under certain circumstances, the hedged loan valuation can be adjusted by the corresponding value changes in the hedge instrument. No other factors that determine the full fair value of a loan are considered; hence no cash basis risk arises, as under the FVO. If applicable, hedge accounting for credit risk serves the purpose of volatility reduction in the profit and loss statement very well. It also counters the problem that loan loss provisions have to be built for hedged loans when hedge gains are already being reported in the profit and loss. However, the approach is challenging to implement and critically assessed by the IASB; IFRS 9 promotes the application of a flexible FVO (phase 3).

No mitigation/combination of hedges and investments: Volatility in the profit or loss statement could be accepted. Offsetting investments, measured at fair value, can reduce the overall volatility induced by hedges, but such investments create new credit and market (basis) risk. These risks are introduced through cash investments versus derivative hedges or derivative investments with other reference entities than that of the hedge. Because of their favourable secondary market liquidity and low transaction costs, derivative indices, like the iTraxx index, are often used to counterbalance hedge profit and loss volatility which exposes the investor to the credit risks of the index constituents. Depending on the purpose of hedges – that is, for portfolio diversification versus outright risk reduction – this approach may be a suitable alternative, but it does not fit all portfolio management models. In contrast to the profit and loss volatility mitigating effect, the capital relief from hedges booked in the banking book, and derivative investments in trading book, is significantly reduced under the new Basel 2.5 rules.

In practice, all approaches are present, and are often used in combination by active credit portfolio managers. In the U.S. risk managers seem to prefer the fair value option, since U.S. GAAP does not consider hedge accounting for credit risk, which is not widespread yet. Practitioners such as the IACPM members debated the issue intensely. Some banks expressed interest and considered implementing hedge accounting. However, none of the listed solutions are without compromise or limitations. And even if CDS were to be measured at cost, which intuitively appears to be the best way, it would have some disadvantages. In many cases, portfolio managers do actively manage their hedge portfolio to adjust for fluctuations in exposure amounts – that is, due to drawing of revolving credit facilities or early prepayments or to changes in the maturity profile of the client exposure. Buying and selling CDS hedges take place at market spreads, regardless of whether that is consistent with internal valuation. If, for example, the spread tightens for a hedge position that is carried at cost, the resulting losses would not be visible in the profit and loss until the position is closed. However, when the portfolio manager unwinds the hedge and the losses materialize, they cannot be offset, because the other leg of the loan/hedge pair remains valued at cost (or in the case of a prepayment, disappears). Tightening CDS spreads are indicative of an increase in the credit quality of the reference borrower. Proactive risk managers may want to reduce the overall level of credit protection in times of improving credit conditions and to increase protection if things get worse. Unrealized losses from the spread tightening of hedges have the potential to severely hamper an active approach to risk management. Ideally, valuations of a hedge and hedged item change in full synchronicity to align economic performance with accounting treatment. If accounting becomes equivalent to the hedge strategy, then performance measurement and external reporting provides an adequate picture of the risk-management activity and success. Hedge accounting for credit risk and the fair value option for loans are closest to achieving this objective.

5.1.1 Hedge accounting for credit risk

Hedge accounting is well known to banks from its application to interest rates. Although hedge accounting for credit risk (HACR) is less widespread and more complex to implement, the two concepts have some commonalities. The advantage of hedge accounting is clearly that it aligns the strategic purpose and economic effects from hedging with its accounting representation. Hedge accounting offsets the effects on profit or loss due to changes in the value of the hedging instrument (derivative) by changes in the fair value of the hedged item (risk-bearing asset). The fair value change of the hedged item results from value changes of the hedged risk only; hence it is isolated from any other valuation-relevant parameters. The objective is to achieve a high level of negative correlation or offsetting effect.

5.1.1.1 Types of hedge accounting and requirements

The IFRS standard distinguishes three types of hedging relationships which may be applied to micro and portfolio hedges:

'Fair value hedge' denotes the hedge of changes in fair value of an asset or a portion of an asset. Fair value changes must result from a specific risk, termed *'hedged risk'* in IAS39; that is, credit risk, interest rate risk, or FX risk. Revaluation of the hedge remains recognized in profit and loss; the carrying amount of the hedged item is adjusted for the change in valuation due to hedged risk, and the value change is reported in profit and loss.

'Cash flow hedge' is a hedge of the exposure to protect from variability in cash flows resulting from a particular risk. The hedged item will be carried at cost while the hedge is split into an effective and ineffective portion of the gain or loss, recognized in other contingent income (OCI) respective profit and loss.

'Hedge of net investment in a foreign operation' describes a hedge of a portion of net investments of a foreign operation; that is, loans in foreign currency, currency options, or other derivatives. This is a special form of a cash flow hedge.

'Micro hedge' refers to hedged single financial assets. For credit risk, a micro hedge in the form of a fair value hedge comes into consideration. There are two important aspects to it. First, under a fair value hedge, the value change of both the hedge and hedged item are accounted for at the profit and loss statement. Thus, the netted amount is the residual gain or loss which ultimately determines the profit and loss volatility. Second, when the credit spread of a hedge rises, it results in gains. The loan amount is then reduced by an equivalent amount. Assuming efficient markets, any potential losses from a default of the reference borrower, together with its probability, will be reflected in the spread of a CDS. The carrying amount of the hedged loan will therefore be adjusted, very much like a write-down, which effectively replaces loan loss provisions unless the bank sees the need for additional reserves.[8] In this way, the economic objective of hedging – mitigating losses from credit risk – is mirrored in the accounting representation. However, some requirements have to be fulfilled in order to qualify for hedge accounting under IAS 39:

- *Formal designation of the hedge and hedged item at inception* (retrospective designation is not permitted). The hedging relationship has to be documented, including the hedge, the hedged item, and the hedged risk, as well as the hedge objective and strategy. Also, the method which will be used to assess the effectiveness of the hedge relationship has to be stated. Once the prospective and retrospective hedge effectiveness tests have been performed, the results have to be attached to the documentation.
- The hedged risk must be *separately identifiable* and *reliably measurable.* Since the hedged risk is credit risk, CDS spreads are an appropriate indicator to derive a discount curve (benchmark curve) in order to measure fair value changes of a loan by applying the discounted cash flow (DCF) model. However, only liquid CDSs,[9] referring to the loan borrower as the reference entity with a coincident level of seniority, ensure that credit risk of the hedged item can be reliably measured. Furthermore, to meet the requirement of 'separately identifiable and reliably measurable', the hedged item has to be a deliverable obligation into the CDS to ensure that the default of the borrower is a CDS trigger event. In this way, the loan can be physically delivered into the CDS, in line with corresponding Basel II rules. Designation of hedging relationship has to cover the lifetime of the hedging instrument. However, partial term hedging allows designation of a hedged item for only a portion of time. The hedge relationship must be highly effective throughout all financial reporting periods for which the hedge was designated. A hedge is highly effective if the changes in fair value (or cash flow) of the hedge compared to the change in value of the hedged item are within an 80–125 per cent range. Effectiveness has to be measured, both prospective and

[8] Specific loan loss provisions might occur as a result of timing differences between impairment and credit trigger event.

[9] A condition of a liquid CDS is that the CDS is a standardized contract under ISDA (International Swaps and Derivative Association) and regularly and frequently quoted in active markets.

retrospective. If the effectiveness criteria are not fulfilled, the hedge pair must be de-designated; that is, applying hedge accounting for credit risk cannot be continued.

5.1.1.2 *Assessing fair value changes and measuring hedge effectiveness*

Fair value changes of the hedged item (a loan or bond) are determined by the contractual cash flows (C_{ext}) which are discounted on an adjusted swap curve fixed at designation date ($Swap_{t_0}$) – adjusted for the actual credit spread (CS_t) and residual margin (Mar_{t_0}). Since both the swap curve and the loan margin remain constant over the lifetime of the hedge, only the hedged credit risk will induce changes in the fair value of the hedged item:[10]

$$\text{Hedged Fair Value} = \sum_t \frac{C_{ext}}{\left(1 + Swap_{t_0} + CS_t + Mar_{t_0}\right)^t}$$

The IFRS does not prescribe a single method for measuring hedge effectiveness, but the method used must be in accordance with the risk-management strategy of entity. Assessment of the effectiveness has to be performed on a monthly or quarterly basis. The following methods are applicable:

Dollar offset method – A hedge is highly effective if changes in fair value of a hedged item divided by changes in fair value of the hedge fall within the 80–125 per cent range. The dollar offset method consists of a period by period dollar offset and the cumulative dollar offset method. The advantage of this method is the comparably simpler application, but in the case of small changes in the fair values of hedge and hedged item, it may not be highly effective.

Regression analysis – A statistical method that measures the strength of the statistical relationship between the changes in hedge fair values of the hedged item and the changes in fair values of the hedging instrument, or vice versa. Effectiveness is measured by the slope of the regression line, which must be between –0.8 and –1.25. Furthermore, a t-Test should verify if the results for slope of the regression analysis are statistically significant, to prevent hedges being wrongly classified as effective.

Shift scenario (sensitivity analysis) – A quantitative method to analyse the effect of a shift in main risk factors onto the fair value of hedge and hedged item, which are then compared. For credit risk, the method should incorporate absolute shifts in a credit spread curve and changes in

[10] See Schubert (2009).

the structure of the credit spread curve, to take into account all relevant aspects of the risk factor. The shift scenario is applicable for the prospective test.

Historical simulation – An estimation of changes in fair values of hedge and hedged item based on historical changes of the risk factors, applicable for the prospective test.

Matching critical terms – A simple prospective test which compares principal terms; that is, borrower entity, notional amount, currency, maturity and the like.

The effectiveness tests have to be performed both prospectively and retrospectively. For the retrospective test, the dollar offset or regression analysis using historical data has to be applied. Going forward, the IFRS 9 will relax the requirements of the effectiveness test. In the current version, the retrospective test has to be performed solely for assessing the ineffectiveness of the hedge relationship for reporting purposes. To determine if a hedge pair qualifies for hedge accounting for credit risk, only the prospective test is of relevance. The fixed range of 80–125 per cent, which verifies the effectiveness of the hedge, has been dropped. The focus is now on the ratio of hedge to hedged instrument to minimize expected ineffectiveness. In the clear case of a 1:1 hedge ratio, the critical term match test, which is qualitative only, could be accepted. In case a hedge relationship proves to be ineffective prospectively, the hedge strategy could be rebalanced rather than de-designating the hedge, as under IAS 39. Instead, a de-designation could result from a change in the hedge objective or hedge strategy.

5.1.1.3 Hedge accounting–eligible assets and strategy

Assets which could be considered for hedge accounting for credit risk (HACR) must bear significant credit risk. Eligible assets for a fair value hedge are on-balance-sheet assets – that is, bonds, floating rate notes, term loans, or loan commitments – or off-balance-sheet items, such as (firm) loan commitments, in general, any financial instrument that is economically hedged with respect to credit risk if the requirements in connection with the economic risk transfer are met. Since a major prerequisite for applying HACR is that the CDS has to be liquid, the scope is effectively limited to the credit risks of large multinationals. Loans are often restricted by non-transferability clauses, which prevent a portfolio manager not only from selling the asset but also from physical delivery when it comes to the CDS trigger event restructuring. If no hedge accounting had been applied, the portfolio manager would buy the cheapest-to-deliver asset in the market, deliver it into the CDS, and receive par. The difference of the purchase price to par is thus the loss compensation for losses from the asset of the defaulted borrower that the portfolio manager owns. Since the value change under hedge accounting has been imposed directly onto the asset on the book, this approach is not feasible. Besides the transferability clause, loans usually exhibit features which could have a negative effect on effectiveness of hedge accounting:

- **Undrawn lines**: The right to draw a credit line by a borrower up to the granted amount at any time. *Problem*: Many portfolio managers take a notional-based approach when hedging credit risk. If the drawn amount of a credit line is significantly lower than the committed amount, the credit risk–induced value change of the loan may differ from the changes in value of the hedge. *Solution*: Statistics show that corporates usually almost fully draw the lines available before default to ensure a maximum of flexibility up to the last moment this company exists. Assuming that exposure at default is close to the granted amount, for lower-rated customers it is conservative and did hold in most of the corporate defaults of the current decade.
- **Term out option**: The right of the borrower to extend the maturity of the loan to a predefined date without the consent of the loan granting bank. *Problem*: A change in the final maturity may decrease the effectiveness of the hedge pair, as the maturity of the hedge does not match the maturity of the protected instrument. However, assumptions that companies in trouble would exercise this right to secure more time to breathe, in contrast to corporates with easy access to liquidity and improved refinancing rates, did not hold. To the contrary, some borrowers facing deterioration in their credit quality were keener to restructure their liabilities on time to avoid a liquidity crunch at (even extended) loan maturity. Nevertheless, as the extension does not need the bank's consent, the said financial institution is effectively short an option and has to be conservative in assuming the option will be exercised. *Solution*: Any term out has to be taken as the final maturity date of the loan.
- **Prepayment option**: The loan is repaid in part or in whole prior to maturity. *Problem*: This leads to either a reduction of the notional amount or the disappearance of the whole loan. *Solution*: Pricing the option or building a model reserve.
- **Multiple borrowers**: Under the terms of the loan contract, various borrowers are entitled to borrow from that loan. *Problem*: The most critical issue with respect to a hedged position is that the hedge will not hold. This would be the case if a credit event takes place at the borrower of a loan, an event that does not trigger the CDS because of a different

reference entity. The result would be losses from loans due to the credit event that are not offset by gains from the CDS. *Solution*: To avoid such problems, any of the multiple borrowers entitled to borrow under the scheme have to be linked to the reference entity of the CDS. In some cases, this creates problems even for larger, multinational corporates which tap the capital markets via a dedicated financing subsidiary that is not contractually bound to the holding company.

- **Multiple currency**: Under the terms of a loan, the borrower can tap the loan in various currencies. *Problem*: This could impose inconsistencies between hedged and borrowed amounts in the case of large-scale currency moves, since CDSs are usually denominated in USD or EUR. *Solution*: While these effects can be material, so far they have not been in themselves criteria for ruling out hedge accounting effectiveness. Nevertheless, in combination with other optionalities, they could become obstacles and should be handled with care.
- **Grid pricing**: Like a coupon step-up for corporate bonds, some loan contracts exhibit margin grids for a range of default probabilities or ratings where margins increase if certain thresholds of credit quality are not met. *Problem*: While the CDS spread is fixed at purchase of default protection, the loan margin can vary over the lifetime of a loan and thus create ineffectiveness. *Solution*: Pricing the option or building a model reserve.
- **Fixed rate coupons**: While the margins of most loans are floating, for example, a certain risk premium above LIBOR, some borrowers prefer fixed coupons, like those for corporate bonds.[11] *Problem*: Value changes for fixed coupon loans are determined by changes in credit and interest rate risk. *Solution*: Hedge accounting for credit risk generally targets exclusively the credit risk component of a loan. A combination of an interest rate swap and a CDS should be able to mirror the cash flows of a floating rate loan. Without the interest rate swap, valuing loans based on interest rate curves and CDSs will almost certainly create ineffectiveness at one point in time.

Even though loans are often very complex, individual products which contrast sharply with the standardized nature of CDSs, most active credit portfolio managers make regular use of the derivatives to manage credit portfolios, and single name credit risk in particular. If applied at inception, which means hedging a loan at the time the loan transaction is signed, hedge accounting for credit risk perfectly supports a static strategy

[11] Although many frequent issuers also have some floating rate notes (FRNs) outstanding, the vast majority of corporate bonds have been issued with a fixed coupon.

of risk protection. The profit and loss volatility induced by mark-to-market for CDS hedges has been substantially reduced. The residual profit and loss, the hedge ineffectiveness, arises from value changes of the CDS which are not completely offset by value changes in the hedged loan. Considering that loans for larger corporates, for which CDSs are available, are usually looked at as relationship-driven products, it is fair to assume that loans margins will almost never match CDS spreads. However, the difference may be small enough to ensure sufficient hedge effectiveness at origination even though some residual profit and loss effects will be still observable. Nevertheless, hedge accounting for credit risk also leaves room for portfolio management discretion regarding the timing of the hedging and subsequent application, provided the hedge relationship is effective. Here, timing is of the essence, since a major gap between the loan margin and CDS spread can restrict the application of hedge accounting because of ineffectiveness. This is typically the case when hedging takes place quite late, that is, when signs of credit problems can already be seen in elevated CDS spreads while the loan margin remains unchanged and low. A proportion hedge, where only parts of the loans are hedged and hedge accounting applied, is permitted. This is particularly useful, as management of concentration risk requires only the exposure amount that breaches the limits to be mitigated, not the borrower's full exposure amount. It was clearly stated by the IASB that the objective of IFRS 9 was to align hedge accounting more closely to risk-management activities so that they are properly reflected in financial statements. Unfortunately for HACR, a credit risk mitigation technique acknowledged by Basel II is not included under IFRS 9, which contradicts this 'mission statement' of the IASB. Hedge accounting for credit risk may not be suitable for very active strategies which involve frequent hedge adjustments and imperfect hedges, and curve and relative value positioning. These strategies aim at maximizing profit and loss from market dislocations in addition to managing underlying credit risk. Since the purpose of hedge accounting for credit risk is to reduce profit and loss volatility rather than maximize profit, those are conflicting objectives by design.

5.1.1.4 Conclusion

Hedge accounting for credit risk is a straightforward accounting concept and has successfully passed the practice test. However, HACR is complex and difficult to implement. Technical and methodological challenges – that is, new procedures to change loan values in the loan data system – are significant. Extensive monitoring, back office, and reporting processes have to be set up, and they come at a cost. The effectiveness tests have to be performed regularly; this presents an administrative burden.

Related effects on workout and impairment, although positive, have to be considered and discussed with the units involved. Also, hedge accounting has some limits and drawbacks, mostly imposed by various loan features. A major concern of the standard setter is that credit risk of a loan may not be separately identifiable and reliably measurable. Given sufficient liquidity in derivative markets, CDSs allow taking a position on a very credit specific, isolated view. Therefore, those concerns are not admissible. Hedge accounting for credit risk is a major step to value loans in line with market conditions, which creates transparency about the true economic substance of the credit portfolio and also increases managerial flexibility in managing credit risk.

Bottom line, HACR deserves a more open and positive reception from regulators and could prove to be a superior approach for tackling the issue of accounting asymmetry if some of the restrictions are relaxed, which is possible without compromising the economic rationale of those restrictions.

5.1.2 Fair-valuing loans

Under IAS 39, any financial asset[12] or financial liability may be designated at initial recognition as such and reported at fair value, and changes in fair value are included in the profit or loss statement. The option to fair-value financial assets or from liabilities is permitted only if (a) using it eliminates or significantly reduces an accounting mismatch arising from measuring assets or liabilities or recognizing the gains and losses on them on different bases; or (b) it is used for a group of assets or liabilities that is managed and whose performance is evaluated on a fair value basis, in accordance with a documented risk-management or investment strategy.[13] In principal, the Financial Accounting Standards Board (FASB) follows the IFRS standard, which makes the FVO the first choice of banks reporting under U.S. GAAP. The fair value option under IAS 39 or FAS 115 aims to alleviate the problem of accounting asymmetry for related financial instruments, that is, a loan or bond reported at amortized costs while a corresponding hedge is measured at market value. In this way, as with hedge accounting, the effectiveness of a hedge to mitigate interest rate or credit risk can be assessed. On that basis, hedging strategies can be revised at the full discretion of the portfolio manager if the economic objective

[12] IAS 39 does not permit election of the FVO for investments in equity instruments that do not have a quoted market price in an active market and whose fair value cannot be reliably measured.

[13] Tschirhart, O'Brian, Moise and Yang (2007). The paper provides a good high-level overview of the FVO and related issues at commercial banks.

has not been achieved. It also serves the purpose of reflecting the actual economic value of assets, which in turn creates transparency for loan pricing and origination discipline. However, the FVO implicitly assumes that markets for credit risks are infinitely liquid, which might not be true in all circumstances, thereby casting doubt on the accuracy of the derived fair value. In addition, if market prices for loans are observed, they have to be applied, giving rise to potentially significant basis risk resulting from differences between loan price and CDS-implied valuation. On the positive side, deteriorating loan values are recognized in a more timely way compared to the concept of provisioning; they can also send early warning signals to take proactive measures to mitigate the risk. If markets for those loans or related derivatives exist, measures to mitigate the risk on time can include forced selling or forced hedging once the value of the loan has fallen below a critical level. Often, market-based pricing anticipates burgeoning credit problems earlier than do internal credit analysts or external rating providers, but it also sends incorrect signals sometimes. Consistent pricing of credit risk across the books (i.e. trading and banking books) and instruments (i.e. loans, bonds, and derivatives) provides a comprehensive view of the overall risks taken and makes it possible to take educated decisions to actively manage those risks. Fair value of loans is deeply connected to loan transfer pricing. Effectively, fair-valuing loans replaces the bank's internal assessment of the loans' risk with those of the markets. However, based on the valuation, an immediate decision can be made as to the fairness of the loan price. To enhance origination discipline, a minimum fair value (as a per cent of notional) can be set as a threshold to be met. If it is not observed, the loan would face internal dismissal or approval conditional on selling the loan, or the client manager will have to cover the shortfall with other (non-lending) revenues from the customer.

5.1.2.1 FVO-eligible assets and pricing

Under the FVO, where a more flexible approach has been discussed by the IASB, it is possible to elect to measure almost all financial assets or liabilities, including loans and commitments, at fair value in the financial statement. Determining the fair value of a loan includes considering changes in credit risk but also interest rates and liquidity spreads. With respect to credit risk, a stepped approach, similar to the one outlined for transfer pricing, can be taken. Essentially, the approach follows the idea that credit assets are valued according to observable market prices for those or comparable assets. Hence, secondary market loan prices have to be directly applied in valuing a loan. If the loan does not trade, other sources of valuations, such as bond or CDS spreads, can be applied. In that case, the residual profit and loss volatility from changes in the credit risk of the borrower will be largely determined by the basis between the loan and bond or CDS, which is driven by

- *funding*: loans are funded, whereas CDSs are unfunded instruments. Therefore, a basis between loan prices and corresponding CDS spreads will arise since the basis reflects the different funding levels of market participants.
- *supply and demand*: while CDS and loan markets are loosely connected, they often exhibit varying supply and demand trends due to their specific market and product characteristics, which clearly impact their pricing relative to each other.
- *definition of default*: the definition of default for a loan and for CDS may differ since the loan often carries specific provisions, whereas the documentation for CDS is standardized and includes credit events definitions different from the concept of incurred losses.
- *CDS deliverable obligation*: a CDS contract defines the obligations which are deliverable into the auction after a credit event. The loan may or may not be eligible as a deliverable, which has a significant impact on the loan price. The liquidation proceeds, not the auction-determined recovery rate, determine the value of the loan if the loan cannot be physically delivered to the CDS protection seller.
- *loan optionalities*: unlike CDSs or bonds, loan documentations more often than not include various optionalities which are partly sensitive to interest rates. Embedded options have to be priced consistently, which may prove to be challenging and may result in meaningful differences to CDS and bond spreads.

Most loans do not trade regularly in the market. Instead, the valuing loans of a particular borrower can be derived from market prices for related tradable securities of the same reference entity, that is, a CDS or bonds. The basis risk described above gives rise to a potentially considerable profit and loss amplitude, especially when hedging larger loan amounts. This can be irritating at times, in particular when the credit risk of a loan is thought to be perfectly hedged. When no secondary market prices or spreads are available for a particular borrower, generic curves can be used for pricing illiquid loans. Banks can estimate the fair value of a loan using a discounted cash flow (DCF) model. In a very simplified way, the fair value of a fully drawn transaction – for example, a term loan or a bond – for a performing obligor can be computed as follows. Expected payments from the customer minus costs are multiplied by the survivorship probability (that is, 1 minus the probability of default) per each payment date t, resulting in the 'net risky payments'. Payments from the obligor include margin on the exposure outstanding, principal payment at maturity, and fees. Costs of the transaction are (among others) credit spread, funding costs, operating costs, and cost of equity. The probability of default rises over time so that the value of expected payments in the distant future is lower than the value of same amount expected payments near term. Net risky payments at each period *t* are then discounted according to the spot curve. The fair value of the financial transaction is then determined by the present value of the net future expected payments.

5.1.2.2 Regulatory requirements for application of FVO

It becomes clear that the FVO is very sensitive to price assumptions and pricing models. The BCBS expressed concerns about banks' ability to determine reliable fair values for instruments that do not have market prices which are observable from active markets. According to the BCBS, the lack of reliable fair measures may permit companies to manage earnings using self-service models in ways that are not easily detected by financial statement users.[14] In its guidelines released in June 2006,[15] BCBS laid out a number of supervisory expectations to users of the FVO. Specifically, banks may not apply the fair value option to instruments for which they are unable to reliably estimate fair values. In April 2009,[16] BCBS issued principles aimed at promoting a strong governance process around valuations, given the significance of fair value measurements for regulatory capital adequacy and internal bank risk management. Rigorous validation of models should be systematically applied, including evaluations of model soundness, appropriateness of model assumptions, and the benchmarking of model results with observed market prices.

5.1.2.3 Conclusion

Application of the FVO is an appropriate way to solve an accounting mismatch of hedged loans and CDS hedges. Compared to HACR, FVO is less complex but also effective, provided there are functioning and liquid credit markets, which is a condition for deriving reasonable fair values. Although profit and loss volatility is substantially reduced

---

[14] BCBS, Letter to Sir David Tweedie, Chairman of IASB, regarding comments on the IAS 30 fair value option proposal, July 30, 2004. See www.bis.org.

[15] BCBS, *Supervisory Guidance on the Use of the Fair Value Option for Financial Instruments by Banks*, June 2006. See www.bis.org. The guidance referred specifically to IAS 39 but assumed that the principles are generally applicable to similar fair value option regimes in other jurisdictions.

[16] BCBS, *Supervisory Guidance for Assessing Banks' Financial Instrument Fair Value Practices*, April 2009. See www.bis.org.

under the FVO, potentially significant residual effects arising from the cash basis may remain. In contrast to HACR, with an FVO imperfect, macro, or portfolio hedges can be employed to manage credit risk, as there is no requirement of a one-to-one hedge relationship or a specific hedge ratio between a particular loan and hedge. However, valuation models are under regulatory scrutiny, which may restrict the eligibility of illiquid assets. The FVO may be suitable for obligors where there is a sufficiently liquid CDS or, at least, a bond that trades publicly. Product-wise, the focus is on term loans, credit lines, and revolving credit facilities where there is little complexity from embedded options. Nonetheless, FVO constraints are so onerous that few banks have chosen to apply them. Three key limitations have prevented more widespread use of the FVO and have been addressed by the IASB to increase its flexibility:

- The ability to choose fair value only at inception
- The irreversibility of the decision to apply the FVO over the lifetime of a transaction
- The inability to fair-value only a portion of the hedged facility rather than the full amount

5.1.3 Financial guarantee

A common feature of most loans is illiquidity. Trading in bilateral loans almost never takes place, while larger syndicated loans trade mostly at the time of origination and rarely later on. Complex credit products are tailored to the specific needs of clients and are largely reflective of the banks' expertise to satisfy these needs. This comes with a lower level of standardization of the loan documentation, which on the other hand prevents the regular trading of those assets. In contrast, credit default swaps are the most liquid debt instrument precisely because of their high degree of standardization, regulated by the International Swaps and Derivatives Association (ISDA). Portfolio managers make active use of CDSs to protect the bank against credit-related losses. However, the accounting implications of CDS hedging is for many banks a constraint which prevents more active and rigorous risk management. To avoid the unintended volatility in profit and loss induced by CDS hedging, an alternative solution is a financial guarantee. The objective of this instrument is to protect against a loan loss due to obligor default, similar to CDS, while matching the accounting treatment of loans. For reasons of efficiency, CDS documentation is often used as a reference to design a financial guarantee. Nevertheless, a simple carbon copy of the CDS documentation will likely lead to a dismissal of the contract as a financial guarantee, as evidenced in the case of the Austrian bank Erste Group. In October 2011, the firm had to issue a profit warning, related to an abrupt change in the accounting treatment of their credit derivatives, which amounted to a €410 mn charge. It appears that Erste Group had to switch from accrual accounting to fair value accounting, claiming beforehand that the transactions were financial guarantees, although they had used standard CDS documentation.

5.1.3.1 Accounting rules for financial guarantees

Under IAS 39, a financial guarantee contract is defined as '*a contract that requires the issuer to make specified payments to reimburse the holder for a loss it incurs because a specified debtor fails to make payment when due in accordance with the original or modified terms of a debt instrument.*' The rules for designing financial guarantees according to IAS 39.9 are strict and focus principally potential losses from credit risk, while other risks such as market risk are excluded from the definition.[17] A financial guarantee requires a contractual agreement between a protection buyer and a protection seller. The contract must refer to defined payments of the debt instrument. The payments must be quantifiable, and the protection buyer must be exposed to the risk of non-payment Also, the debt instrument cannot be disposed of by a bank that wants to enter into a financial guarantee for hedging purposes. Schubert (2011a) rules out the notion that the debt instrument can be sold to a third party, with the holder of the financial guarantee claiming compensation from the guarantee provider for subsequent losses due to obligor default. As a precondition for a loss compensation payment, the contract holder must have incurred the loss because of the failure of a debtor to make payments when due. The important point here is that the definition is loss driven, not event driven. For example, a loss occurring from a decline in market value due to a deterioration of borrower credit quality is not covered by a financial guarantee under the IAS 39 definition. Furthermore, compensation payments under the financial guarantee must not exceed the loss incurred from the specified hedged instrument. Also for that reason, the standard CDS documentation cannot be applied. CDSs can be settled either by cash or by physical delivery of the defaulted asset. In a cash settlement, the CDS protection buyer receives the compensation payment once the recovery is determined. Then the CDS contract terminates. One reason protection buyers may prefer a cash settlement is when the loss compensation from the CDS is expected to exceed the loss incurred from the asset they own. The physical settlement option of the

[17] See Schubert (2011a).

CDS standard[18] permits the protection buyer to opportunistically purchase a deliverable defaulted asset (deliverable obligation of the reference entity) that is then settled into the CDS rather than the initially hedged asset. If the purchase cost for the deliverable asset is below the value of the hedged debt instrument, the protection holder is actually overcompensated for incurred losses. Like insurance, the financial guarantee, however, covers only losses associated with the insured item and insured event.[19] Any possibility of loss compensation which does not equal the loss incurred – which cannot be excluded if, in the case of cash settlement, the protection buyer retains the defaulted asset and the future cash flows associated with it – does not meet the definition of a financial guarantee. Thus, the restrictive accounting framework requires certain adjustments to the CDS documentation to qualify as a financial guarantee; that is, the exclusion of a cash settlement. Under physical delivery, the hedged debt instrument must be the reference obligation, which the protection holder is expected to keep on his books for the lifetime of the protection. A similar situation occurs with respect to the credit event definition of the financial guarantee. Common credit events according to market usance and ISDA credit derivative definitions include bankruptcy, failure to pay, and restructuring, of which only failure to pay meets the definition of a financial guarantee. This is so because ISDA provides event specifications that determine a credit event even though no loss to the holder of the reference obligation has actually occurred, thereby violating the insurance intention of a financial guarantee. With respect to credit events, the financial guarantee documentation has to ensure that the triggering event directly refers to the payments under the debt instrument and that no compensation in excess of the incurred losses is possible. As with hedge accounting for credit risk, the settlement date of the hedge contract must not be later than the maturity of the hedged item.

5.1.3.2 Conclusion

Financial guarantees are best suited for an insurance approach: the credit asset is insured against the exact amount of loss arising from a default. A financial guarantee qualifies as collateral under IAS39. The specific features of the loan asset can be recognized in the documentation, since financial guarantees are tailorized hedge products – a kind of 'restructured' CDS

[18] Assuming that the contract specifies 'borrowed money' rather than 'reference obligations only'. Under 'borrowed money' all outstanding obligations of the reference entity qualify for physical delivery.

[19] See Schubert (2010). The article provides a well-written and in-depth assessment of how to restructure a standard CDS into a financial guarantee.

designed to not conform with CDS standards, which otherwise would imply mark-to-market accounting recognition. This in turn results in the illiquidity of the hedge, which may not be appropriate for actively managed credit portfolios. Traders take a basis risk by hedging financial guarantees with standardized CDSs, which very few are willing to do and which comes at a significant premium. An early unwind of a financial guarantee when a loan is prepaid is fully dependent on the willingness of the counterpart, with no perfectly offsetting (netting) CDS investment possible due to the different transactional specifications. Hence, a contract design which fully complies with the accounting standards unduly restricts the flexibility of the portfolio manager. In addition, the protection buyer may still be exposed to risks that can result in loan loss provisioning, since the only credit event recognized by an FG is 'failure to pay'. Table 5.1 compares a CDS hedge booked into banking book with a CDS hedge where both HACR and a financial guarantee have been applied. Determining the most appropriate solution largely depends on the priorities and targets to be achieved. Some restrictions can lead to dismissal of the product for hedging purposes. For instance, since a financial guarantee encompasses only the credit event 'failure to pay', it is seen as incomplete by many risk managers and therefore ruled out, even though from an accounting perspective it might have been the optimal solution.

5.1.4 Combination of hedge and reinvestment portfolio

Some portfolio managers use a combination of hedges and investments to manage CDS-induced profit and loss volatility. That concept is mostly applied in diversification strategies. Value changes from hedges, which aim at compensating for loan losses, are balanced by those from investments. On a net basis, the overall risk in terms of exposure or expected portfolio loss does not decrease significantly under this approach; it may even increase. However, it is possible to reduce the economic capital consumption of a portfolio by hedging large bulk risks at comparably lower hedge costs.[20] Nevertheless, combining hedges with investments exposes the portfolio manager to substantial mark-to-market risks. The strategy works best for highly correlated hedges and investments, which is also the major drawback, since a diversification strategy aims at reducing the

[20] The reduction in economic capital consumption is driven by the improvement in the portfolio diversification. Since Basel II capital weights do not recognize correlation effects, there is no immediate equivalent reduction in regulatory capital from the strategies outlined here. However, since banks are required to hold additional capital against concentration risks, ultimately the hedge/investment combination has a positive effect on the capital adequacy of the firm. It should be noted, though, that Basel 2.5 penalizes investments booked into the trading book by charging higher risk weights.

Table 5.1 Schematic comparison of CDS hedge, CDS hedge with hedge accounting for credit risk applied and financial guarantee

	CDS	**CDS with HACR**	**Financial Guarantee**
Impact on RWA	Reduction of RWA can be achieved. The RWA reduction effect depends on the risk weight of the protection seller		Partial/no capital relief due to exclusion of restructuring and bankruptcy credit events
Impact on accounting treatment	Full mark-to-market (MtM)	MtM of the CDS significantly offset by fair value adjustment on the loan (hedge result). Reduction depends on effectiveness of hedge pair	At cost treatment (book value)
Mark-to-market risk	Full mark-to-market	Residual mark-to-market risk from hedge ineffectiveness	In case of early termination of the hedge instrument, mark-to-market compensation to the counterpart basis risk if a contact cannot be closed out and an offsetting transaction put in place
Impact on specific loan loss provisions (SLLP)	No effect	SLLP represented by fair value adjustments. Timing effects to be considered when impairment occurs before credit event, depending on the estimate of liquidation proceeds	In general on SLLP necessary but timing effects to be considered when impairment occurs before 'failure to pay' credit event
Impact on standard risk costs (SRC)	SRC only on counterpart risk (according to the regulatory view)		
Economic loss	Fully covered	Fully covered	Only losses from failure to pay credit event
Possible credit events	Failure to pay Bankruptcy Restructuring (not for the U.S.)	Failure to pay Bankruptcy Restructuring (not for the U.S.)	Failure to pay
Loss compensation in case of credit event	Full compensation of loss, determined by auction	Full compensation of loss, determined by auction	Full compensation of loss, as determined by internal workout

Failure to pay	Recovery for all deliverables determined by credit derivatives auction	Recovery for all deliverables determined by credit derivatives auction	Realized loss of the hedged underlying after workout
Bankruptcy	Recovery for all deliverables determined by credit derivatives auction; no differentiation for maturity buckets	Recovery for all deliverables determined by credit derivatives auction; no differentiation for maturity buckets	Not applicable
Restructuring	Separate auctions for different maturity buckets may result in different recoveries	Separate auctions for different maturity buckets may result in different recoveries	Not applicable
Profit and loss effects due to timing differences	P&L effects (SLLP, mark-market, recovery) will likely occur in different accounting periods	Efficient hedge relationships largely smooth the time effect	Timing effects may occur when impairment takes place before failure to pay credit event. The actual loss after workout is applied against the compensation payment of the hedge
Qualifying underlying for protection instrument	Reference obligation	Reference obligation	Reference obligation only specific debt instrument on the book of the protection buyer during the lifetime of the FG
Product liquidity	High for standard maturities	High for standard maturities	Illiquid

Continued

Table 5.1 Continued

	CDS	CDS with HACR	Financial Guarantee
Impact of early termination of the hedge instrument	Accounted for at market value, no impact	If loan still exists, FV adjustment is amortized over the remaining lifetime of the loan; If loan is repaid, FV adjustment is reversed immediately through P&L	In case of early termination of the hedge instrument MtM compensation to the counterpart. Protection buyer however is not allowed to receive any payments from protection seller in case of early termination
Consequence of prepayment of underlying	CDS can either be unwound, or reassigned to another asset (also in work-out situation)	CDS can either be unwound, or reassigned to another asset (also in work-out situation); however former hedge pair terminates and therefore goes out of HACR; FV adjustments are reversed immediately through P&L	If loan terminates early the FG has to be terminated as well. (No mark-to-market compensation payment will be triggered – either from protection seller or protection buyer side)
Costs	Carry costs. Mark-to-market value changes	Carry costs. Residual mark-to-market from hedge ineffectiveness. Pull to zero effect of FV adjustments. In case of de-designation: amortization or immediately reflected in P&L (as described above under 'early termination')	Carry costs. Mark-to-market compensation payment in case of early termination
Physical or cash settlement	Both, contractual agreement	Both, contractual agreement	Physical settlement only
Qualifying underlying for physical settlement	Any underlying which is determined as deliverable obligation by Credit Derivatives Determinations Committee (can be cheapest to deliver)	Any underlying which is determined as deliverable obligation by Credit Derivatives Determinations Committee (can be cheapest to deliver)	Reference obligation only. Specified debt instrument on the book of the protecting buyer during the lifetime of the FG

correlation between portfolio constituents. There are four main applications for a combination of hedges and investments:

1. DV01 neutral
2. Beta neutral
3. Notional neutral
4. Cost (cash flow) neutral

Let us assume that a portfolio manager wants to hedge €100 mn of a five-year senior unsecured, fully drawn loan of the Italian corporate ENEL, using a corresponding CDS of equal duration. To counterbalance the profit and loss volatility arising from spread changes in the CDS hedge, the portfolio manager considers a maturity matching investment in the similarly rated German utility company E.ON. In order to test the four approaches and to compare the results, we use the CDS spreads of five-year CDSs of ENEL and E.ON for a full year, from January 2 to December 31, 2011. A combination of hedge and investment for one year will be put in place on January 1, 2011. However, even though the two

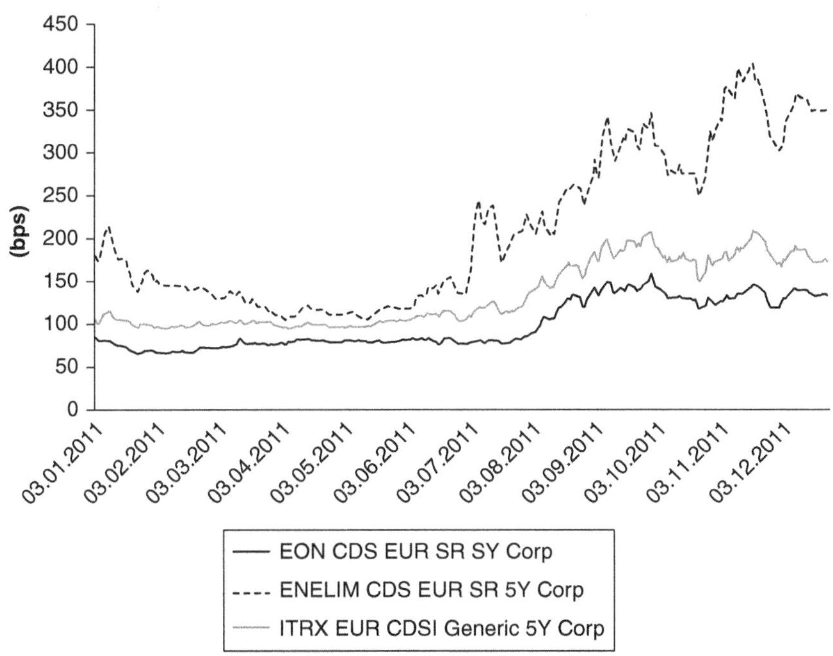

Figure 5.2 ENEL, E.ON and iTraxx five-year CDS spreads
Data source: Bloomberg.

Table 5.2 Profit and loss effects from combined hedge and reinvestment strategies

	Hedge	Investment	Combined
Company	ENEL	E.ON	
Rating	A3/A–	A3/A	
Ticker	CENEL1E5	CEON1E5	
Duration	5Y	5Y	
Seniority	Sen unsec	Sen unsec	
DV01 (€)*	42.453	47.918	
Coupon (bps)	100	100	
Spread at January 3, 2011 (bps)	179	83	
Spread at December 30, 2011 (bps)	350	134	
Δ spread (mn €)	172	50	
Beta		0.28	
Notional amount (mn €)			
DV01 neutral	100	–89	11.41
Beta neutral	100	–355	-255.17
Notional neutral	100	–100	0.00
Cost neutral	100	–214	-114.30
Carry amount (mn €)			
DV01 neutral	–1.79	0.74	–1.05
Beta neutral	–1.79	2.96	1.17
Notional neutral	–1.79	0.83	–0.95
Cost neutral	–1.79	1.79	0.00
P&L from Δ spread (mn €)			
DV01 neutral	7.29	–2.14	5.15
Beta neutral	7.29	–8.56	–1.28
Notional neutral	7.29	–2.41	4.87
Cost neutral	7.29	–5.17	2.12
Total P&L (mn €)			
DV01 neutral	5.50	–1.40	4.10
Beta neutral	5.50	–5.60	–0.10
Notional neutral	5.50	–1.58	3.92
Cost neutral	5.50	–3.38	2.12
P&L volatility (mn €)	Max	Min	
DV01 neutral	2.13	–1.17	
Beta neutral	2.13	–1.24	
Notional neutral	2.13	–1.17	
Cost neutral	2.13–1.20		
Cumulative P&L (mn €)	Max	Min	
DV01 neutral	6.19	–3.39	
Beta neutral	4.07	–4.78	
Notional neutral	4.04	–3.34	
Cost neutral	4.04	–2.83	

* DV01 per €100mn notional.

corporates belong to the same industry and have almost the same probability of default as assessed by external rating agencies, their spread moves differ significantly.

Table 5.2 illustrates the corresponding amounts to be invested in E.ON five-year senior unsecured CDSs. The DV01 denotes the change in value of each respective CDS for a 1 basis-point change in the CDS spread. Profit and loss effects arising under the different approaches are detailed by the contribution from cost of carry and value changes. Maximum and minimum values are shown for daily and cumulative profit and loss. The objective of any of hedge/investment strategy is to reduce both daily value changes and the cumulative profit and loss from the combined position as much as possible. The following examples illustrate the key concepts, but they may not be representative for other hedge and investment combinations.

5.1.4.1 DV01 neutral hedge and reinvestment strategy

The DV01 neutral strategy aims at achieving a balanced development of the hedge/investment pair based on their sensitivity to changes in spreads. The relevant DV01 measure for the CDS contract is the change in value of the CDS contract when the CDS quoted spread increases by 1 basis point. Since the DV01 for ENEL is lower than that of E.ON, an investment of €89 mn in E.ON CDSs would be DV01 neutral for a €100

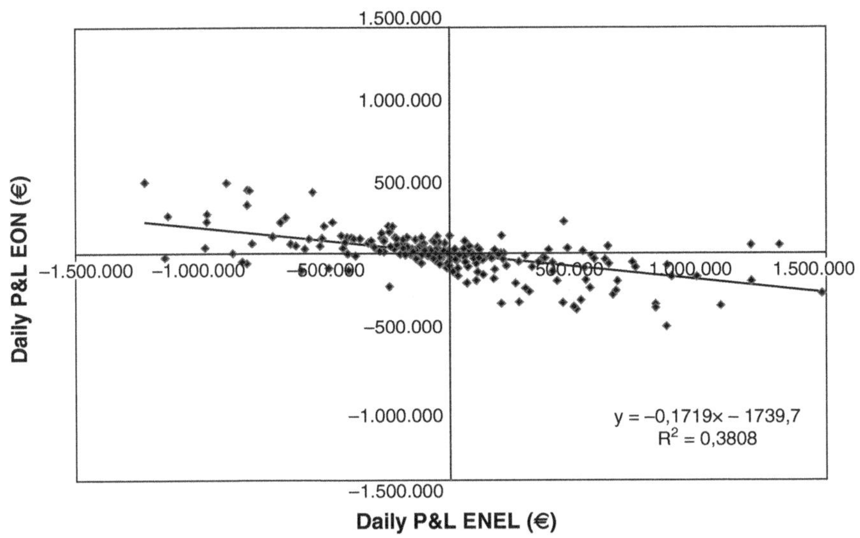

Figure 5.3 Correlation of daily P&L changes from hedge and investment under the DV01 neutral approach

Data source: Bloomberg.

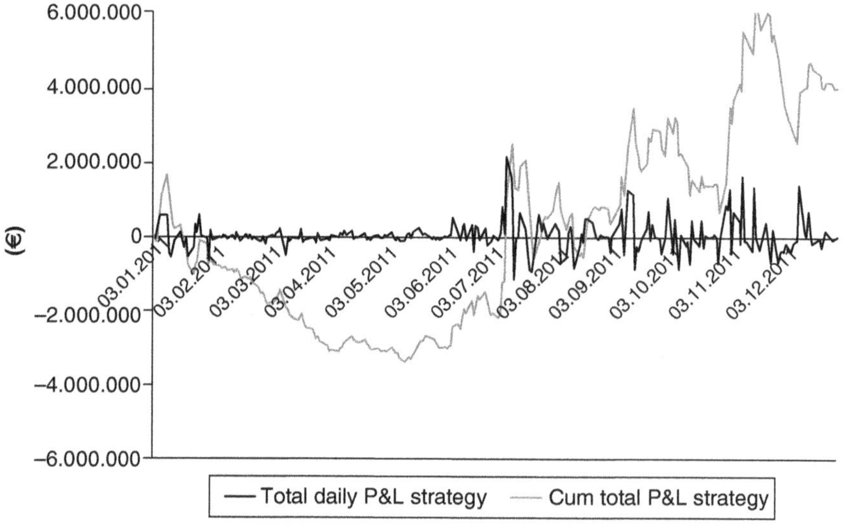

Figure 5.4 Daily and cumulative P&L of the DV01 neutral hedge and reinvestment strategy

Data source: Bloomberg.

mn ENEL hedge.[21] That means that if E.ON and ENEL spreads move in perfect synchronicity, the residual profit and loss (P&L) from spread changes would be zero.

However, during the tested period (2011), losses from spread widening for E.ON were more than compensated for by gains from the spread widening of the hedge. Figure 5.1 shows that daily profit and loss moves are dispersed to larger moves, positive and negative for the ENEL hedge, which are not counterbalanced by similar changes from the investment. Although the carry to protect for a default of ENEL largely exceeds the income from selling protection on E.ON, the total profit and loss for the combined position for the full year would have been a gain of €4.10 mn. Over the course of the year, the cumulative profit and loss from the pair ranges from €–3.39 mn to €6.19 mn. The chart shown in Figure 5.4 depicts the daily value changes from spread moves and carry costs for the hedge and the investment, as well as the cumulative profit and loss.

[21] This example assumes that the ratio remains static over the lifetime of the trade, i.e. no delta hedging or any dynamic or curve adjustment will be made. Although this restriction contrasts with the strategy employed by market makers or other traders, the intention here is to recognize the different objective of a portfolio manager, who aims at a longer-term stable hedge/investment relationship that does not inflict notable corrections of the positions which create transaction costs and consume resources.

A DV01 neutral strategy in theory has to be rebalanced frequently as DV01 sensitivities change, ideally on a daily basis. In our example, no such dynamic adjustment has been considered since (a) the purpose of the outline is to illustrate the basic concept and (b) the transaction costs and operating inefficiencies resulting from regular rebalancing have to be weighed against the incremental benefit from the permanently adjusted hedge ratio.

5.1.4.2 Beta-neutral hedge and reinvestment strategy

Higher-risk names typically exhibit greater volatility than do safer companies. A beta-neutral strategy explicitly takes the correlation of both names to an index or to each other into account in order to balance the profit and loss from market moves. The investment amount of €355 mn is equal to the hedge amount divided by the correlation weighting factor, which is 0.28[22] in this case. Unfortunately, the correlation is mostly unstable over time. So even in a beta-neutral strategy, the residual profit and loss from spread moves will be uncertain and will deviate from zero, which is a form of basis risk. For the chosen hedge and investment pair,

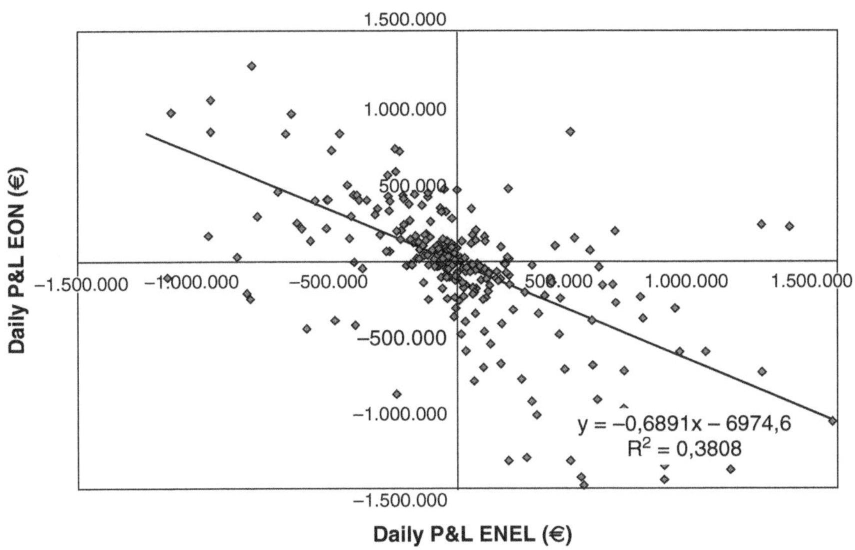

Figure 5.5 Correlation of daily P&L changes from hedge and investment under the beta-neutral approach
Data source: Bloomberg.

[22] For simplification, the regression has been performed on the time horizon of one year (2011 data).

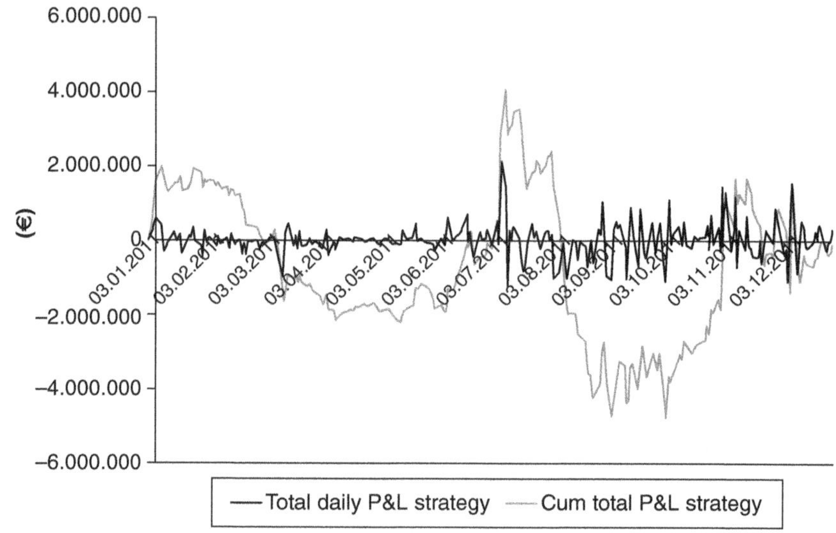

Figure 5.6 Daily and cumulative P&L of the beta-neutral hedge and reinvestment strategy

Data source: Bloomberg.

this is demonstrated in Figure 5.5, where the daily profit and loss changes are widely spread. During the lifetime of the hedge/investment pair, significant profit and loss spikes can arise, although they should be lower than those of a DV01 or notional approach that does not consider the correlation between hedge and investment.

A dynamic hedging approach – where the offsetting investment position is continuously adjusted to a trailing weighting factor which incorporates the most recent moves in correlation – can be considered, but this results in a meaningful turnover from adjusting the offsetting investment position. The total profit and loss from this strategy amounts to €–0.1 mn, which is the lowest absolute value of the four strategies discussed herein, driven by offsetting effects from both value changes and carry costs. However, from Figure 5.6, one can see that while for most of the year the cumulative profit and loss oscillated in a range of €–2 mn to €2 mn, it dropped from €4 mn to €–5 mn in a short period of time.

5.1.4.3 Notional neutral hedge and reinvestment strategy

Portfolio managers often apply a notional, or exposure-outstanding, approach when hedging loans. The structure of this combination is determined by a notional amount of hedge CDSs that is equal to the notional amount of CDS investment. In an extreme case, where both the hedge and investment obligors default, the resulting profit and loss will be determined

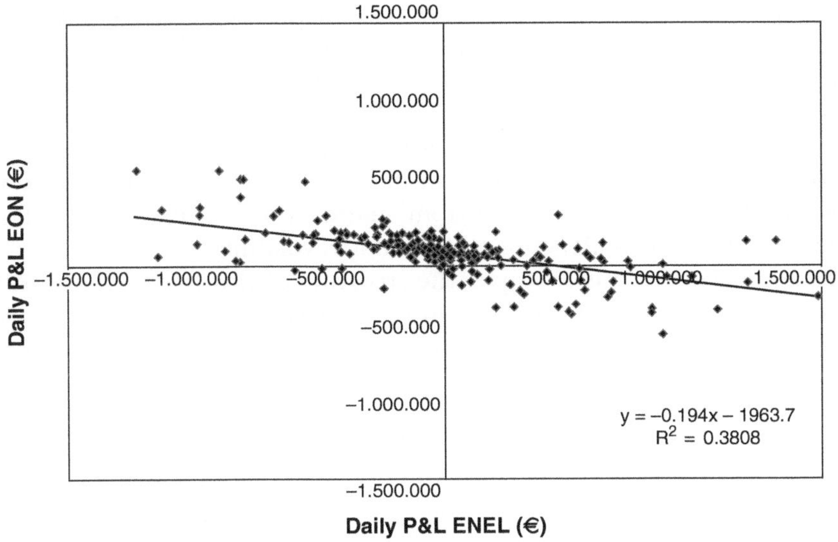

Figure 5.7 Correlation of daily P&L changes from hedge and investment under the notional neutral approach

Data source: Bloomberg.

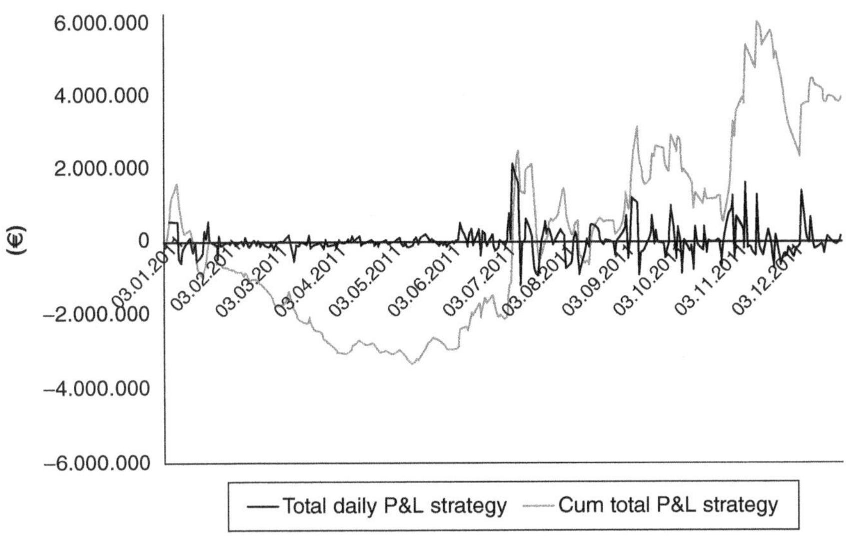

Figure 5.8 Daily and cumulative P&L of the notional neutral hedge and reinvestment strategy

Data source: Bloomberg.

only by the difference in the recovery of each name.[23] Like the DV01 neutral approach, daily profit and loss moves are dispersed due to the higher volatility of the hedge compared to the investment, as shown in Figure 5.7.

The total profit and loss is €3.92 mn because of the positive spread-widening effect from insurance bought on ENEL, which outweighs both the losses from the investment in E.ON and the higher protection costs for ENEL. It becomes clear from Figure 5.8 that this strategy is less effective for counterbalancing profit and loss volatility.

As evidenced by this example, the structure of this trade exposes the bank to mark-to-market gains and losses from spread moves of the hedge and investment, since the DV01s of the two strategies are not equal, nor do the spread changes perfectly offset each other.

5.1.4.4 Cost (cash flow) neutral hedge and reinvestment strategy

If a portfolio manager has been allocated a budget for hedges which cannot be exceeded, a strategy that keeps hedge carry costs as low as possible may be appropriate. In the example of ENEL and E.ON, the costs of protecting against a default of ENEL are 2.14 times higher than

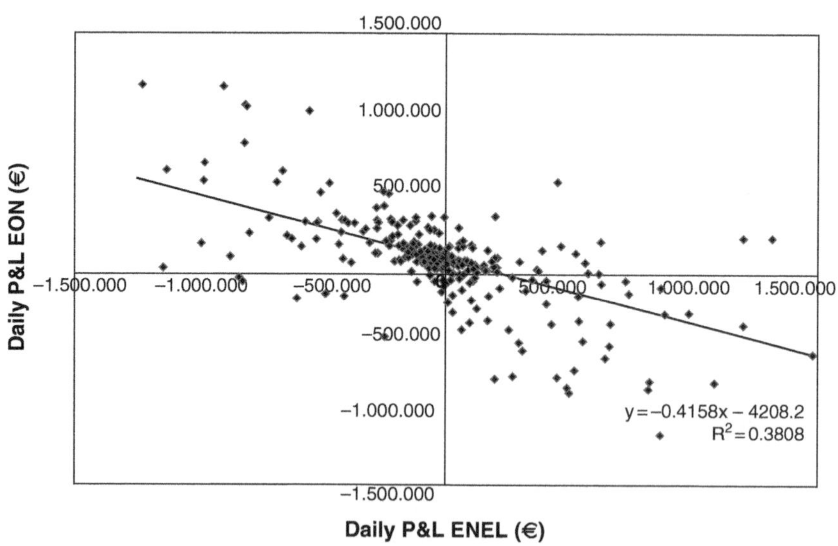

Figure 5.9 Correlation of daily P&L changes from hedge and investment under the cost neutral approach
Data source: Bloomberg.

[23] Assuming the two defaults take place simultaneously and ignoring the time value of the recovery.

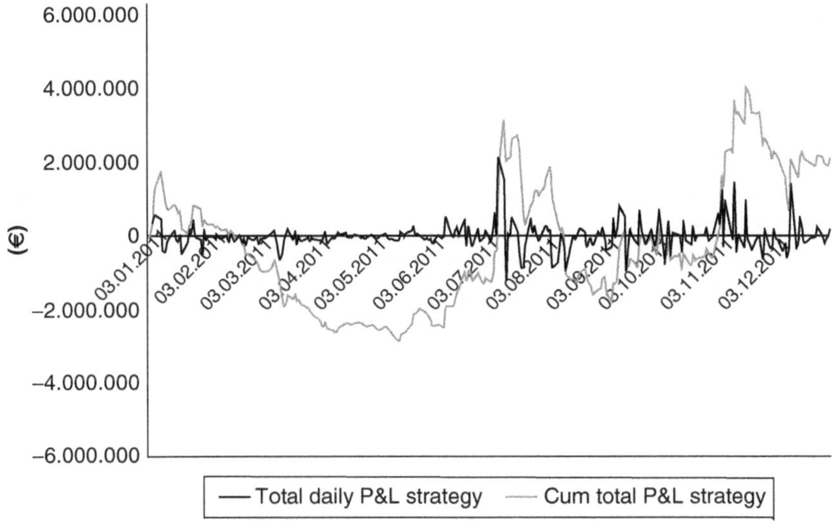

Figure 5.10 Daily and cumulative P&L of the cost neutral hedge and investment strategy
Data source: Bloomberg.

those for E.ON at the trade date. Thus, the portfolio manager would have to sell €214 mn protection for E.ON to match the cost of buying €100 mn protection for ENEL. The cumulative profit and loss is then solely determined by value changes resulting from the spread moves of the hedge and investment, and no longer by the different costs of carry. As shown in Figure 5.9, this strategy yields less daily profit and loss volatility and direction compared to the DV01 neutral and notional neutral strategies, since the ratio of the hedge and investment is determined by the ratio of the their spreads, which already reflects the different degree of idiosyncratic risk. In this case, the cost strategy is also superior to the beta-neutral strategy. In general, while the structure of the trade offsets all running cash flows from the hedge with those of the investments, the cash flow from an exit other than termination at maturity may be non-zero.

Nevertheless, even in this case, where the slope of the linear regression of the daily profit and loss moves from the hedge and investment is –42°, close to the ideal –45°, there are significant dispersions around this line. Also, the cumulative profit and loss over the course of the hedge period exhibits significant distortions, ranging from €–2.83 mn to €4.04 mn, although these are the lowest minimum and maximum values of the four tested strategies.

5.1.4.5 Conclusion

Combining hedges with investments helps to reduce profit and loss volatility arising from value changes in hedges. However, because of diverging spread moves of hedge and investment, the remaining daily profit and loss swings, as well as cumulative profit and loss, can be material. The new Basel 2.5 rules have a detrimental effect on the capital efficiency of these strategies since the capital relief from hedges in the banking book is offset by capital charges on investments in either the banking or trading book. All four strategies are best suited for bulk risk reduction for investment-grade companies, where the hedge can be counterbalanced by liquid investments – for example, the iTraxx index – provided the basis risk of the diverging spread moves of the hedge and index is acceptable to the portfolio manager. Credit indices, however, expose the investor to credit, sector, and country risks of index constituents that may be unwanted. Product-specific basis risk, that is, from CDS hedges offset by investments in corporate bonds, can become a concern. The higher the CDS's share of idiosyncratic risk, the less appropriate a hedge/investment strategy. Here, outright risk reduction should be considered rather than a risk substitution. As a regular portfolio management tool for managing single names, combinations of hedges and investments play only a minor role. On a portfolio level, especially the fair value option is being used for loans, investments can improve the relevant risk metrics through diversification, and can also mitigate the effects of an accounting mismatch.

6
Regulatory Capital Management under Basel II

Under the Basel II international capital framework,[1] banks must maintain a minimum level of capital against the risks taken to ensure capital adequacy. Besides the economic risk transferred by hedging loans or bonds with CDSs, a key and sometimes primary motivation for banks to engage in such risk mitigation is the resulting capital relief, since the Basel capital framework explicitly recognizes credit risk mitigation (CRM) techniques as an effective risk-management tools which can significantly reduce credit risk.[2] Basel II revised the approach to credit risk mitigation, allowing a wider range of credit risk mitigants that achieve regulatory capital relief compared to Basel I. The tight capital situation of banks has been a concern, particularly in the aftermath of the Lehman crisis, but it was also highlighted by the EBA stress tests, which were followed by requests that banks close the gap between their actual capital base and the requested threshold. According, capital management has become a high-priority exercise for most banks. Advanced financial institutions view capital management as a holistic, firm-wide function encouraging both regulatory and economic capital discipline and consistency as opposed to a post-business care, where costly and cumbersome capital optimization initiatives seek to restore the capital base. A centralized approach ensures that capital is coherently allocated throughout all business divisions as part of a common strategical and tactical framework. Improved awareness of the amount of capital deployed, the capital intensity, and the costs attached to it are key to capital0-efficient business operations, not just for the risk-weighted,

[1] See BCBS (2006). The framework is adopted by European law via the capital requirements directive (CRD).

[2] See BCBS (2011b). The BCBS noted that certain credit protection transactions exhibit the potential for regulatory capital arbitrage and thus will be closely scrutinized by the bank's supervisors. While those concerns relate primarily to high-cost credit protection under the securitization framework, it becomes clear that regulators will keep a close eye on how banks optimize their capital in general.

asset-intense units. Increasing the capital flexibility warrants in-depth insights as to how quickly capital can be reallocated across business functions or redeployed within a unit where capital relief has been achieved. Correct anticipation of related effects from an active capital management on liquidity, revenues, and profit and loss is critical in enabling senior management to take informed decisions. Even though profitability hurdle rates which explicitly acknowledge capital efficiency – either regulatory or economic or a combination of both – are introduced at most major banks, the development of the capital base may not always follow the path set out in the risk and business strategy if carried out in a different than expected operating environment. As a consequence, enacting micro level or single name–specific adjustments up to high-level portfolio or whole business-line transactions using risk transfer instruments can help to maximize the risk/return profile of a portfolio while making optimal use of the capital base.

6.1 Capital optimization – key considerations

A bank has two alternatives for improving its capital ratio: either increase the numerator, which is the core capital, or reduce the denominator, that is the risk-weighted assets. Core capital consists, inter alia, of total equity: common stock, retained earnings, and other paid-in capital, minus goodwill. Although a number of banks raised capital by issuing new stocks during recent years, most look first at optimizing the asset load to avoid dilutive effects of the capital increase on the existing shareholder base, in terms of both share of ownership and share of operating profit. Assuming that the risk weight of assets has been – from the regulator's perspective – correctly assessed, leaving no room for further capital relief from optimization, the balance sheet may be further rightsized by transferring risks that are inefficient from a capital perspective while retaining those that are efficient. Figure 6.1 shows non-exhaustive key considerations for any RWA-optimizing transactions, which may also serve as a recipe for suitable capital relief transactions.

In any case, a bank that wants to reduce capital consumption from its assets has to weigh the costs against alternative measures and eventually also against the cost of capital. The return on equity (ROE) will remain constant or improve only if the return on assets selected for reduction is below the weighted average cost of capital (WACC). The efficiency of capital optimization, measured in terms of costs relative to the amount of capital relief achieved, is therefore a key criterion for determining the most appropriate solution. However, even if for capital relief purposes a transaction does not stand out as overly efficient, it may still offer features that make it more attractive than other instruments. For instance, synthetic risk transfer is in most cases less efficient in terms of the costs relative

Building block	Key consideration	Synthetic risk transfer	True sale	Joint venture/ spin off
1 Efficiency	✓ Capital relief relative to costs ✓ Consistency of regulatory and economic capital effects ✓ Coherence to business and risk strategy	• CDS or FG • Structured (tranched) versus unstructured • Counterparty risk capital charges • Medium to high efficiency	• Highly efficient • Maximum capital relief • No further involvement after execution	• Transfer of substantial part or whole portfolio • Capital injection or guarantee • Medium capital efficiency • Applicable to discontinued business/ring-fenced assets
2 Complexity/ timing/ flexibility	✓ Time to implementation/execution ✓ Market timing ✓ Retained upside/downside (P&L implication) ✓ Open/closed form (asset substitution and replenishment)	• Structured transaction generally more complex, time consuming • Highly selective, flexible and short time to execution for standard CDS	• Loan syndication less complex • Selective assets • Discretionary timing (subject to market conditions) • No further upside/downside	• Significant complexity • Substantial lead time • Loss/recovery participation through provided capital
3 Stability/ effectiveness	✓ Rating stability of underlying ✓ Stability of rating methodology applied ✓ Stability of other RWA determinants	• Efficiency dependent on RWA trends of underlying	• No further effects	• No further effects
4 Cross effects	✓ P&L effects ✓ Implications to funding ✓ Legal, accounting, regulatory and tax implications	• Funded? Collateral? • Expected loss vs market spreads? • Valuation of retained tranches • MtM for derivatives	• Strict documentation regarding asset transferability • Funding release • Immediate profit and loss impact	• Substantial legal and tax related requirements • Deconsolidation must be consistent with accounting rules • Significant costs

Figure 6.1 Building blocks of capital optimization

to the amount of capital released compared to true sale transactions, where the assets exit the balance sheet because residual capital charges for remaining risks, such as counterparty risk, apply. Hence, synthetic risk-mitigation never fully neutralizes capital consumption. Nonetheless, the in-principle higher level of standardization which results in a short time to market and discretionary timing of implementation, combined with less administrative burden, argue for synthetic risk transfer as the most flexible solution for tailorized and asset-specific capital reduction. Other effects – such as the stability of capital release efficiency, which is subject to the underlying risk weight and therefore varies with its rating, as well as profit- and loss-related implications – have to be considered in an overall assessment of the suitability of the measures being considered. An in-depth comparison of alternatives to managing bank capital is of particular interest to active credit portfolio management but is outside the scope of this book. In what follows, we concentrate on the aspects of regulatory capital relief achieved by using CDSs for hedging purposes, which has been a major focus point up to now.

6.2 Regulatory capital relief through CDS and guarantees

Credit derivative protection bought[3] with the purpose of mitigating credit risk and booked into the banking book reduces, under certain conditions, the capital requirement of the banking-book asset being hedged. The level of capital relief from CDS hedging depends on various conditions, which are summarized in what follows. However, the use of CRM techniques should not result in higher capital requirements than there would be if no such techniques were applied.[4] If supervisors are satisfied that banks have met certain minimum operational requirements regarding the risk-management process, and where credit derivatives are direct, explicit, irrevocable, and unconditional, banks are permitted to consider the credit risk protection from these instruments when calculating the capital requirements.[5] More

[3] Credit derivatives qualifying as credit risk mitigants under Basel II are CDSs, guarantees and, under certain conditions, 1st- and 2nd-to-default baskets and total return swaps (TRSs).

[4] See BCBS (2006a), ¶113.

[5] See BCBS (2006a), ¶140, and BCBS (2011 b). Paragraph 189 specifies that a guarantee or credit derivative must represent a *direct* claim to the protection provider. *Explicit* means that the protection must reference specific exposure or pool of exposures. Both conditions ensure that the protection is clearly defined and incontrovertible. *Irrevocable* excludes contract clauses that allow the protection provider to unilaterally cancel the contract or clauses that would result in increasing costs due to a deterioration of the credit quality of the hedged asset. The protection provider must not be prevented by any contract clause from being obliged to timely pay out in case of a non-payment by the original counterparty in order to make the protection *unconditional*.

Table 6.1 Hedge eligibility criteria under Basel II

Criteria	Description and Condition
Contract type	CDS, TRS,[a] CLN[b] and 1st- or 2nd-to-default baskets[c]
Credit events	Credit events covered by the CDS contract have to include at least • failure to pay • bankruptcy, insolvency or inability of the obligor to pay its debt when due • restructuring, including forgiveness or postponement of principal, interest or fees resulting in a credit loss event[d]
Credit event determination	The parties responsible for determining whether a credit event has occurred must be specified and must not be solely the protection provider. The protection receiver must have the right to notify the responsible parties of the occurrence of a credit event.
Reference obligation	The underlying obligation must be specified as the reference obligation under the credit derivative. An asset mismatch is permitted if the reference obligation ranks pari passu with or is junior to the protected asset, provided that both hedged asset and reference obligations are obligations of the same obligor and are legally enforceable due to cross-default or cross-acceleration clauses.
Maturity	The maturity of the credit derivative must match the maturity of the underlying asset, including any grace period and term-out or extension option.
Settlement	Cash settlement: a robust valuation method must be in place for a reliable estimation of the credit losses, including a clearly defined period when the post-credit-event valuations of the underlying obligation will be obtained. Physical settlement: if physical settlement has been agreed, any required consent of the delivery of the hedged asset to the protection seller must not be unreasonably withheld by the protection provider.

Notes:

a For a TRS where the net payments received are recorded as net income but as not offsetting the corresponding decline in the value of the asset protected, no recognition of the credit protection is permitted.

b Only cash-funded CLNs issued by the bank and protecting assets in the banking book will be recognized but treated as cash collateralized transactions.

c A first-to-default basket hedge is defined as a basket of names for which the bank receives credit protection and where the first default of the referenced names triggers the credit event and contract termination. The protection-buying bank may receive regulatory capital relief only for the basket asset with the lowest risk-weighted amount and only if the notional amount of the protection is at least equal to the exposure of the protected asset. The calculation of the risk weight follows the treatment of securitization tranches in the case that an external rating for the basket has been obtained. For baskets with no external rating, which has to be assumed as the standard case, the risk weight is calculated as the aggregated risk weights of the assets included in the basket (capped at 1.250%) multiplied by the notional amount of the basket. For second-to-default baskets, the bank will only receive capital relief if it also owns the first-to-default protection of the basket. A second-to-default basket where a credit event has occurred effectively becomes a first-to-default basket. The capital relief for a second-to-default basket follows the treatment of the first-to-default basket, with the exception that when aggregating the risk weights, the asset with the lowest risk weight can be excluded. See BCBS (2006a), ¶¶207–10. Since baskets in general are less frequently used for capital relief by credit portfolio managers due to their lower level of standardization and complexity, the following text will focus on plain vanilla CDSs.

d If 'restructuring' as a credit event is excluded from the CDS contract but all other conditions outlined in Table 6.1 are met, a partial recognition of up to 60% of the hedge is permitted. This is in particular relevant as the Standard North American Contract (SNAC) excludes 'restructuring' from the list of credit events. However, in the U.S. most restructurings fall under chapter 11 of the U.S. Bankruptcy Code, which automatically triggers the Bankruptcy Credit Event.

specifically, banks must demonstrate that they have robust procedures, processes, and a strategy in place to control residual risks[6] which may arise from CRM techniques, namely legal, operational, liquidity, and market risks. Another concern of regulators relates to concentration risk resulting from the bank's CRM activities, a concern which seems to be well founded given the fact that the market for CDSs is largely dominated by a few global players. This is confirmed by an ECB[7] report showing that – based on a survey conducted by Fitch, and DTCC and BIS data – JPMorgan, Goldman Sachs, Citigroup, Morgan Stanley, Bank of America, and Barclays account for a substantial share of the global CDS market. Given that other major dealers, like Bear Stearns, Merrill Lynch[8] and Lehman Brothers, but also natural sellers of protection, such as hedge funds, CDOs, SIVs, bank conduits, and monoliners, discontinued or reduced their involvement in CDS trading and investing with no new actors taking their places, it is quite likely that the level of concentration of this market has increased in recent years. Concentration risks from CRM techniques must be assessed in terms of their interaction with the bank's overall risk profile. If a supervisor views the robustness, suitability, or application of a bank's CRM management policies and procedures as inadequate as to the capital relieved by those CRM measures, the bank may be asked, among other possibilities, to take immediate remedial actions or to hold additional capital against residual risks.[9]

The Basel II capital framework specifies that the operational requirements for guarantees and credit derivatives so that they result in capital reduction.[10] Besides the preconditions described above, credit derivatives are recognized for the assessment of capital based on the following criteria:

Guarantees must be an explicitly documented obligation assumed by the guarantor, covering all payments the debtor is obliged to make under the transaction contract, including principal, margins, fees, and so on.[11] Guarantees are recognized if the bank receives full compensation for the outstanding amount in a timely fashion after a qualifying default

[6] See BCBS (2006a), ¶¶115 and 767–8. Legal risks are further outlined in ¶¶117–18, stressing that contracts must be legally binding and enforceable, thus strictly avoiding the pitfalls of ineffectiveness because of untested documentation.

[7] See ECB (2009). According to a survey conducted by Fitch at the end of the first quarter of 2009, the counterparties to 96% of the credit derivative exposure of the U.S. firms surveyed were only five bulge bracket investment banks.

[8] Both Bear Stearns and Merrill Lynch were taken over in 2008, so they disappeared as an independent market maker for CDSs.

[9] See BCBS (2006a), ¶769.

[10] See BCBS (2006a), ¶¶189–97, 488–9.

[11] See BCBS (2006a), ¶190. In case only the principal is covered by the guarantee, a bank may proceed with the capital reduction but only for the principal amount.

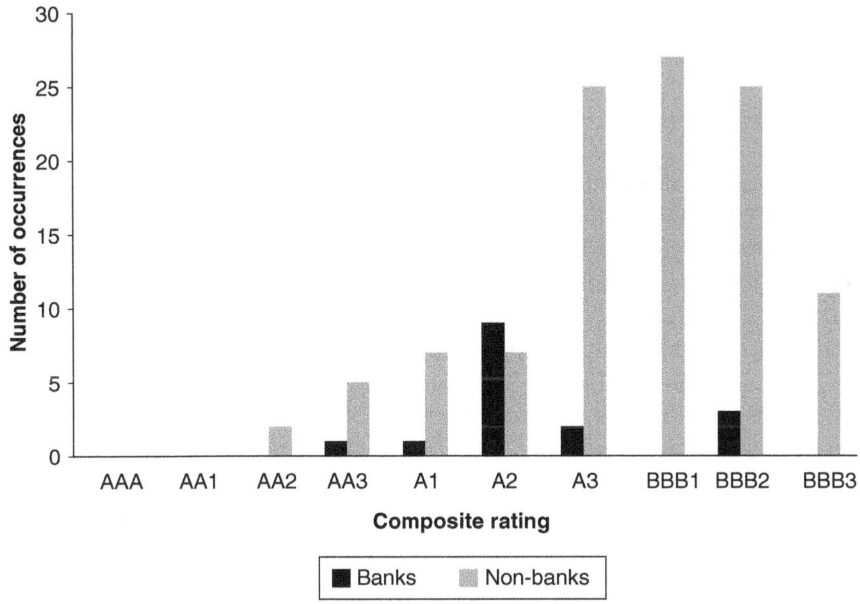

Figure 6.2 Rating distribution of 125 iTraxx constituents (banks and non-banks) as of December 2012

Data source: Bloomberg.

or non-payment by the obligor so that it does not have to take any legal action to enforce the payment from the guarantee provider. The compensation can be in the form of a lump sum. Alternatively, the guarantor can assume all the obligor's future payment obligations. This rule clearly violates the IAS eligibility requirements for financial guarantee accounting, which limit any compensation payment to actual losses incurred by the owner of the guaranteed debt asset. Partial or proportional cover of credit risk by credit derivatives or guarantees when the loan amount exceeds the hedged amount will result in capital relief for the protected part, while the unprotected share will be treated as unsecured.[12]

6.2.1 Determination of capital relief amount

The amount of capital required for an exposure hedged by CDSs or guarantees is determined according to the standardized approach or the internal ratings–based approach (IRB), which is then further split into the

[12] See BCBS (2006a), ¶198.

foundation approach for those banks which are using supervisory values of LGD and the advanced approach for banks using their own internal LGD estimates.

Substitution approach: Within the standardized approach under Basel II, the adjusted risk weight of the hedged asset will be reduced to a level comparable to a direct exposure to the hedge provider, which is unchanged from the 1988 accord. This is called the *substitution approach*. Thus a capital reduction through hedging will be achieved only if the protection provider carries a lower risk weight than the underlying obligor.[13] If this condition is not met, banks may decide not to recognize the credit protection for capital relief purposes. Eligible protection providers include sovereign entities, public sector entities (PSEs), securities firms with a lower risk weight than the counterparty, and other companies rated at least A–. Even though banks experienced significant pressure on their ratings in the aftermath of the financial crisis, their average single-A rating still supports capital relief when serving as a counterpart to hedging corporates rated at the lower end of the investment-grade rating spectrum or below. Economically, corporates weigh the leverage-driven increase return on equity (ROE) against the cost of capital, which disproportionally rises as credit quality deteriorates. For European corporates, the equilibrium is found in the low BBB area, whereas in the U.S. investors tolerate a more pronounced gearing in exchange for a higher ROE. Nonetheless, an increase in leverage leaves less room for error, meaning that a cyclical downturn will exhibit stronger adverse effects for those firms which accept higher leverage and lower debt coverage ratios.

Banks, on the other hand, have to maintain a higher rating, as implicitly required by regulators through the minimum capital ratio. In addition, a BBB rating for financial institutions in general is inconsistent with many business segments, in particular where banks serve as counterparts or receive deposits for funding purposes. Unfortunately, the current distribution of spreads does not conform to the prevailing rating. These days, the credit markets inherently price in a higher probability of default for banks compared to corporates, even within the same rating category.

As a result, capital relief from hedging using CDSs may prove to be too expensive. In general, a business model where the funding costs of financial institutions stay above those of their corporate clients for a prolonged, period of time may prove to be unsustainable. A looming credit crunch induced by banks that become reluctant to lend because of their elevated funding costs will ultimately hit firms with a weaker credit profile. Any restricted access to capital for corporates with immediate

[13] See BCBS (2006a), ¶141.

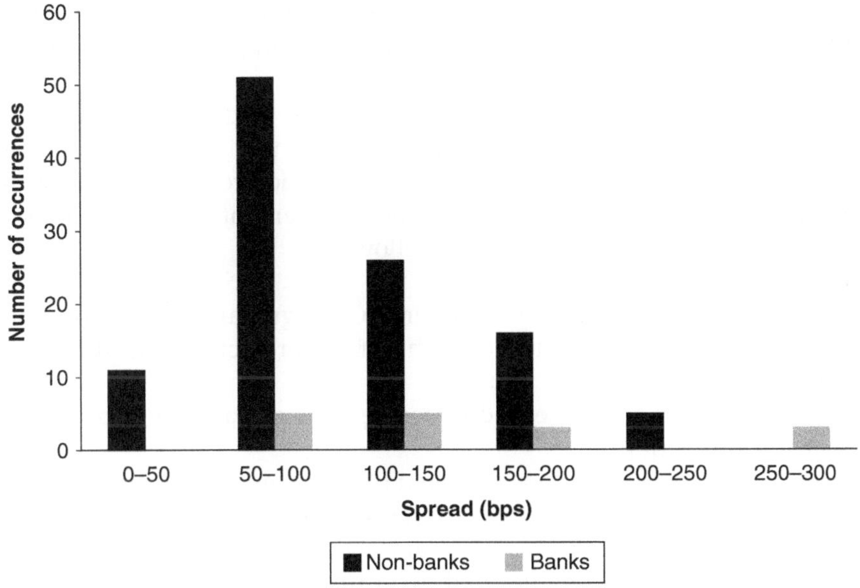

Figure 6.3 Credit spread distribution of 125 iTraxx constituents (banks and non-banks) as of December 2012

Data source: Bloomberg.

funding requirements poses a risk of an accelerated liquidity drain up to insolvency. Consequently, even when costs of capital freed up by hedging are considerably high, the risk-mitigating effect may be worthwhile from a forward-looking perspective.

The **foundation approach** follows closely the standard approach. In addition to the eligible guarantors under the substitution approach, credit risk protection providers that are internally rated equivalent to A– or better also qualify under the foundation approach, while under the advanced approach there are no restrictions on the qualifying protection provider. For banks qualifying under the foundation or advanced IRB approach, the risk weight of the protected share of the transaction is derived from

- the risk weight function of the guarantee provider;
- the internally assessed PD of the guarantor;
- the LGD of the guarantee.

Here, the regulatory treatment differs substantially from the economic risk of the hedged loan. While the substitution approach reflects the fact that the credit risk of the obligor is eventually replaced by the counterparty risk of the hedge or the guarantee provider in case of an obligor default,[14] the two risks cannot be seen in isolation. Hence, under the IRB approach, hedges and guarantees are treated in a more sophisticated way.[15]

Double default approach: Banks qualifying under the foundation or advanced IRB approach have the option to use the double default approach when calculating the capital consumption for a credit risk–protected asset, which is, in addition to the requirements described above, conditional (non-exclusively) on the following:

- the protection instrument is either a CDS, guarantee, first- or nth-to-default basket where the (n–1)th default protection has also been obtained;
- the risk weight of the hedged exposure does not already incorporate the risk protection;
- the hedge provider being a regulated bank, investment firm, or insurance company and regularly active as a protection provider and rated internally at least equivalent to A– at the time of hedge trade inception or at least investment-grade at all other times;
- a hedged obligation that is a corporate (with the exception of specialized lending), a PSE (public sector entity), or a small business exposure;
- an underlying obligor that is not a financial firm described as a hedge provider or associated with the protection seller;
- the full compensation of credit losses from the hedged asset resulting from a credit event specified in the hedge contract;
- the protection provider and the obligor must not exhibit 'excessive' correlation, meaning that they must not be connected beyond the systemic risk drivers.

6.2.2 Adjustments in capital reduction for CRM

Basel II defines haircuts to the degree of capital relief when the loan specifics are not fully matched by the hedge, which creates a form of basis risk or incomplete risk transfer. Examples provided here are of maturity and currency denomination mismatches.

Maturity mismatch: A maturity mismatch occurs when a hedge expires before the underlying credit exposure matures. To assess the expiration date of the loan, extension options have to be taken into account, along with a conservative estimate of a grace period. For the hedge, the shortest

[14] Simplistically, the hedge seller or guarantee provider assumes the obligations of the defaulted borrower and therefore takes the place of the original obligor.

[15] See BCBS (2006a), ¶¶300–4.

effective maturity is assumed, which should consider certain embedded options, such as a right of the protection seller to call the hedge. Because of a maturity mismatch between hedge and the hedged risk, the level of capital relief can be significantly reduced. In some cases, the hedge will not be recognized at all. A maturity mismatch, as defined by Basel II, is less of a concern for credit portfolio managers from a pure risk-mitigation point of view because loans are typically short to medium term and rarely match the standard, mostly liquid, five-year maturity of CDSs, meaning that the standardized five-year tenor of a CDS almost always exceeds the loan maturity. However, a maturity mismatch exposes the bank to the profit and loss of the remaining leg of the hedged pair once either a loan or the hedge matures, which can be significant. Consequently, any maturity mismatch between a loan and a related hedge contrasts sharply with the IAS requirements that hedge accounting for credit risk (HACR) can be applied only if the maturity of the hedge does not exceed the maturity of the hedged asset.[16] In the opposite case, where the hedge expires before the loan, the maturity mismatch will have a detrimental effect on the hedge effectiveness of the pair, which is a condition for applying HACR. Even though the fair value option (FVO) is less restrictive in that respect and tolerates maturity mismatches, the residual profit and loss volatility from value changes in the hedged item, which are only partially offset by those of the hedge, may be a source of concern. While hedging a loan with a CDS of corresponding tenor is advisable from the risk transfer, economic (profit and loss), and accounting perspective, shorter CDS maturities are usually less liquid or even illiquid. As a consequence, small offer sizes result in a significant ramp-up period in which to accumulate the CDS to cover the full loan amount that needs to be hedged, and in higher transaction costs from wider bid-offer spreads, which are also characteristically for lower liquidity. In some cases, particularly for non-frequent issuers, only standard maturities are offered by CDS dealers.

a. **No capital relief**: In a maturity mismatch, a hedge will not be recognized for capital relief if the *original* maturity of the CDS is *less than a year.* The same applies for hedges with a *residual* maturity of *less than three months* and maturing before the underlying credit.
b. **Reduced recognition of capital relief**: According to Basel II, the value of credit protection adjusted for maturity mismatch equals[17]

[16] Hedges expiring on the next standard maturity date (20th of March, June, September, and December) following the maturity of the loan are compliant with IAS rules, and thus eligible for HACR.

[17] See BCBS (2006a), ¶¶204–5.

$$Pa = P \times \frac{t \quad 0.25}{T \quad 0.25}$$

where:

Pa = maturity mismatch–adjusted credit protection value
P = CDS amount (adjusted for any haircuts)
t = min (T, residual maturity of the CDS), in years
T = min (5, residual maturity of hedged asset), in years

Example: Let's assume that a bank wants to fully protect the credit risk of a €100 mn loan exposure (original maturity of 4.5 years with a CDS hedge). A dealer offers 3- and 5-year maturities for the obligor. Since a standard 5-year CDS maturity would not qualify under hedge accounting for credit risk, the bank decides to buy €100 mn of protection on the client with a maturity of 3 years after a prospective test proved the effectiveness of hedged pair. From the Basel II formula, the following maturity mismatch–adjusted credit protection amount can be recognized for the capital relief calculation:

Figure 6.4 shows that even though the maturity mismatch is constant at 1.5 years, the value of the recognized credit protection decreases over-proportionally when the hedge approaches the expiration date. 'When the remaining lifetime of the hedge is down to three months, the hedge no longer meets the rule that hedges with a residual lifetime of three months.'

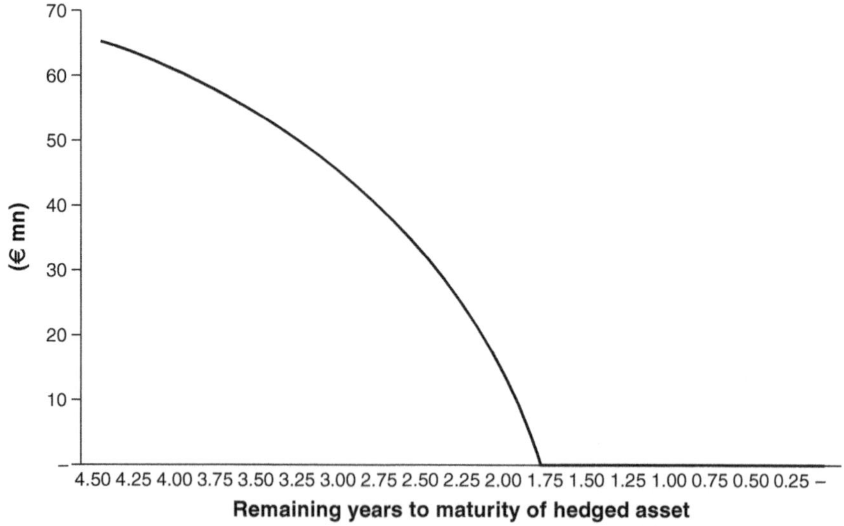

Figure 6.4 Maturity mismatch–adjusted credit protection value

While a maturity mismatch is not a cause for concern in the case of a bankruptcy or failure to pay credit event, it can have some ramifications in a restructuring, which may prevent the loan's or bond's physical delivery to the auction. (For more details, see Chapter 7, §2.2, 'Restructuring credit event'.)

FX mismatch: If the CDS contract is denominated in a different currency than the hedged risk, a haircut based on a 10-business-day holding period to the hedged amount will be applied. The supervisory haircut equals 8 per cent.[18] While CDSs are usually available in all major currencies such as the G-8 and beyond, some loans feature optionalities, such as multicurrency options, which allow the borrower to decide in which currency it will draw under existing loan documentation. Thus a currency mismatch will occur if the CDS is denominated in a different currency than the one drawn by the obligor, unless the CDS is dynamically adjusted in full or partial amounts corresponding to the drawing under the loan contract, which may be difficult and costly.

6.3 Conclusion

In principle, the Basel II rules for capital relief achieved through the hedging of credit risk by a CDS or other instruments are broadly accepted by portfolio managers. Regulatory capital arbitrage, introduced by Basel I capital weightings, has become significantly less attractive under the new rules, and it attracts close scrutiny by the bank's supervisors. However, the financial industry continues to encourage accounting standard setters and global regulators to improve the consistency of the two regimes, which still creates obstacles for an economically sound credit portfolio management. More specifically, the portfolio manager's objective concerning the accounting view of hedges in most cases is to avoid an accounting mismatch – that is, accrual accounting for loans in the banking book, while valuing CDS hedges mark-to-market. Regarding the regulatory view, the purpose of hedges is to achieve a maximum reduction of capital charges from the hedged loan. Under current rules, as discussed in previous chapters, the two views do not fully coincide. A third view relates to the economic risk of credit assets, measured in internal, risk or economic capital. Since economic capital explicitly recognizes the correlation structure of credit assets and the portfolio, again, significant differences may emerge as to the selection of the optimal hedge strategy and asset. Since the Basel rules are constantly evolving, the economic and regulatory perspectives

[18] See BCBS (2006a), ¶200. The scaling up of the haircut according to the square root of time formula is further detailed in ¶168.

are likely to converge at some time in the future. Nevertheless, under certain circumstances, single name hedging efficient for regulatory capital relief purposes may turn out to be significantly less efficient in terms of economic capital, for instance when the portfolio post-hedging exhibits a higher concentration a resulting from hedging only more granular or less correlated assets. Hence, prudent credit portfolio risk-management principles will have to consciously recognize prevailing shortfalls of the regulatory framework. In any case, consistency between tools applied for risk-management purposes, accounting and regulatory requirements and market practices is a key prerequisite to providing banks with the flexibility to adapt to a rapidly changing operating environment. In light of banking's industry-wide need to restore or improve the capital base, capital optimization efforts have become an important and common objective for credit portfolio managers.

Part III
Hedging Techniques and Toolkits

Credit derivatives, underpinned by impressive market growth and ever new applications and related products, represent the financial innovation success story of the last two decades. Although the market is still considerably smaller than the much larger one for interest rate swaps, the notional amount of outstanding credit default swaps (CDSs) nonetheless shows their unparalleled growth since the early 1990s. Accelerated by the introduction of the first CDS-based, broader credit index iTraxx in 2004, the market expanded more than tenfold during the next three years, until 2007, when it surpassed the $50 trn mark for the first time.[1]

However, during the past years, credit derivatives have been intensively discussed in public, and the role those financial instruments played in the demise of such once venerable Wall Street giants as Lehman Brothers

---

[1] One should note that a pure comparison of the notional amount as depicted here refers to the nominal amount of protection sold rather than the market value of the CDS. The rapid fall in notional amounts since the first half of 2007 is attributable to the decreasing number of new trades but is also largely due to the 'termination cycle', during which trades outstanding have been compressed to reduce the overall number of trades and notional outstanding. However, the representation of the market size by notional outstanding has often been criticized as a major reason for misunderstanding. From a risk perspective, the notional amount would only equal the net risk, which a CDS seller owes to the buyer, if the recovery value of the protected debt instruments would be zero. A more appropriate measure for the CDS market size is the replacement value, which describes the current net present value of the CDS contracts. Although this measure is currently not available as a long-term time series for the global CDS market, survey results indicate that the replacement value is only a fraction of the notional amount of existing CDSs. Anyway, the development of the trend shown in Figure III.1 was confirmed by a report of the BIS. Interestingly, the report notes that while in 2009 notional amounts of CDSs between financial institutions continued to decline, the outstanding contracts with non-financial customers more than doubled. See Avdjiev et al. (2009).

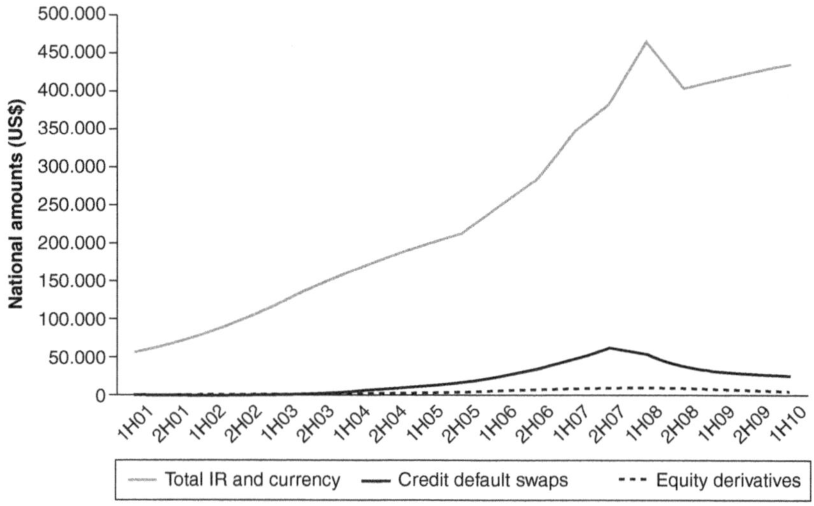

Figure III.1 Size of IRS, CDS and equity derivative markets
Source: ISDA.[2]
Reprinted with permission of International Swaps and Derivatives Association, Inc., © 1987–2010 International Swaps and Derivatives Association, Inc.

has been questioned. Worse, CDSs were suspected of being abused for purely speculative purposes with the unethical objective of profiting from forced corporate and sovereign borrower defaults. In his annual letter to shareholders, Warren Buffet, the CEO of Berkshire Hathaway and 'sage of Omaha', quite outspokenly called derivatives 'financial weapons of mass destruction', which could harm not only the parties involved in such highly complex transactions but the economy as a whole.[3] Clearly, the opaqueness of individual over-the-counter (OTC) trades combined with the perceived low level of transparency of the CDS market as a whole, including regarding its size and importance for financial markets, contributed to the mistrust of credit derivatives. At the same time, the financial industry, which appears to be in the midst of a general overhaul, has not ignored the calls for higher transparency. In 2008 the Depository Trust and Clearing Corporation (DTCC) issued a statement clarifying that the preception of a lack of a central registry for OTC credit derivatives was as unfounded as blaming CDSs for being a driver of the U.S. mortgage

---

[2] See ISDA, www.isda.org.

[3] See www.berkshirehathaway.com, annual letter to shareholders, 2002. Ironically, Berkshire Hathaway ranked eighth in the list of top ten non-sovereign CDS reference entities on the basis of net protection amounts as of July 2009. See ECB (2009).

crisis.[4] Nonetheless, the perception that a few market participants, such as hedge funds or proprietary traders, are solely short-term profit oriented and uninterested in the broader economic repercussions of their activities, has added to the publicly voiced reservations about credit derivatives. The vicious circle of rising CDS spreads, indicative of a deterioration the credit quality of the underlying obligor, and constrained access to capital markets, as observed in the Greek sovereign debt tragedy, has been a prevalent source of unease for government representatives and regulators alike. Although neither the IMF[5] nor the European Commission found compelling evidence that naked[6] CDSs led to an increase in systemic risk and credit defaults, the concern is that this could become the case in times of distress, thereby destabilizing government bond markets. Polleit and Mariano (2011) argue, instead, that '*...sound economic analysis reveals that CDS are fully compatible with the principles of the free market, and that CDS are not to blame for the disintegration of credit markets.... CDS provide investors with an efficient and effective instrument for exposing economically unsound and unsustainable fiat money regimes and the economic production structure it creates – which, in turn, provokes a (n intellectual) counterattack from government officials (and their "court intellectuals"), who argue for regulating or even banning CDS.*' The ban on naked sovereign CDSs and on the short selling of government bonds introduced by the European Commission[7] follows an attempt to distinguish the use of CDSs for (respected) hedging purposes as opposed to (not tolerated) pure speculative trading. As a consequence, the liquidity in sovereign CDS has suffered, thereby underpinning concerns that a proper market functioning will be disrupted by the ban. Being stripped of the perfect instrument to hedge transfer risk arising from governments imposing capital transfer restrictions, such as the one observed in Cyprus in March 2013, it seems that market professionals turned to the second best solution to hedge their risks. As an unintended consequence of the European Commission regulation, hedgers obviously replaced sovereign CDSs by buying protection on those banks domiciled in the weaker countries such as the European periphery. As a result, the bank's CDS spreads trade significantly wider than their bonds, thereby

[4] The DTCC made clear that its automated trade information warehouse was established in 2006 as an electronic central registry for CDSs, registering the vast majority of CDS trades. Moreover, the DTCC clarified that less than 1% of the registered CDSs related to residential mortgage-backed securities. See DTCC public press release, 'DTCC Addresses Misconceptions about the Credit Default Swap Market', October 2011, www.dtcc.com.

[5] See IMF (2010), IMF (2013).

[6] A naked CDS position refers to buying CDS protection on a reference entity without owning a deliverable obligation.

[7] See http://ec.europa.eu/internal_market/securities/short_selling_en.htm.

forming a so-called positive basis, and more in line with their sovereign CDS spreads. This development confirms the view that the sovereign CDS ban is an unnecessary and ineffective restriction that imposes substantial costs to others.

In stark contrast to the fear that CDSs may contribute to an accleration of financial crises, there have been marked doubts about the effectiveness of CDSs as risk-transfer instruments, though. The stated intention of political leaders to avoid at all costs a CDS-relevant credit event in Greece to protect the global economy and the European sovereigns in particular from the fallout of a hitherto unthinkable but de facto failure of a EU member state did spark a lively debate. Even experienced market participants were uncertain whether CDSs will hold or drop dead. The long-running drama in Greece finally came to an end when the ISDA announced the Greece credit event on March 9, 2012. The subsequent payout – as little as $2.89 bn, or 78.5% of the remaining $3.68 bn outstanding CDS – turned out to have no impact on markets, even though this was more by chance rather than by design. And another example of the built-in flaws of CDSs surfaced in context of the nationalization of the Dutch mortgage lender SNS Reaal in February 2013. Because the Minister of Finance of the Netherlands expropriated the holders of subordinated bonds of the failing bank, all of a sudden buyers of CDS protection effectively saw their costly hedges become worthless as there were no assets left to be delivered to the seller of the CDS. To counteract the risk of financial contagion, politicians and regulators alike stepped up their efforts to get a better handle on the market for credit derivatives. Central clearing, counterparty risk management, and margin standards as well as the adjustments to Basel II with respect to the trading book, dubbed Basel 2.5, set the stage for wide-ranging improvements. In addition, the CDS product itself underwent some significant changes. The so-called 'Small Bang' and 'Big Bang' protocol introduced by ISDA in 2009 serves to facilitate the liquidity of the CDS market by increasing its standardization. Another overhaul of the CDS documentation that addresses the identified shortcomings is yet to come but already in discussion. As a result of all these initiatives, CDSs re-emerged as a cleaner and straightforward instrument, with growing acceptance among market participants, regulators, and politicians. The recent events surrounding CDSs confirm that the product in principle passed the test of time but also laid bare persistent criticism and dangerous shortfalls, particularly for hedgers. All that is required for the market professionals as well as decision makers to gain a better knowledge of micro and macro economic benefits of standardized risk-transfer instruments. After all, spreading risk and diversifying risk are two sides of the same coin, and one cannot go without the other.

A central aspect of portfolio management is the active and frequent use of techniques to transfer risk: loan syndication, subparticipations, guarantees, and securitization are as much part of the package as CDSs. However, given their high level of standardization and outstanding liquidity, CDSs provide portfolio managers the ultimate tool, one which allows them to micromanage the portfolio on a single-name basis. The derivative nature of CDSs, which requires the holder to account for them on a mark-to-market basis, makes CDSs suitable to hedge both spread risk, which arises from changes in the valuation of the hedged item, and default risk, which denotes the risk that an obligor will fail to make payments when due. But even though the CDS is regarded as the instrument of choice for risk transfer, the experience of the last years, with an ample number of defaults of CDS reference borrowers, clearly shows that CDS users should obtain in-depth knowledge of the key features of credit derivatives if they want to engage in profound and solution-oriented hedging strategies and to avoid unpleasant surprises. The same holds true for CDS-based instruments such as indices, tranches, and options. This part of the book, therefore, aims to provide a detailed description of CDSs as a hedging tool for credit portfolio managers. While most literature on credit derivatives offers a wealth of information on pricing-related topics, there is little available on such important aspects of CDS hedging as the definition and outcome of credit events or the mechanics of the auction process, which can be quite complex and cumbersome, as in the case of the restructuring credit event. Although sometimes a bit technical by nature, the mechanics of CDSs are deemed relevant if not critical for actively managing a portfolio of credit risk, thus representing a specific point of interest for loan and bond portfolio managers. Other hedge instruments such as loan CDSs and subparticipations are introduced, explaining the key features to be considered when engaging in these products. The following chapter continues with credit derivative indices, which are often used as portfolio proxy hedges benefiting from low transaction costs. Finally, correlation and volatility-sensitive products, such as nth-default baskets and swaptions, which represent a leveraged form of credit portfolio protection, are explained. The chapter concludes with a brief discussion of imperfect or macro hedges, which may become relevant as substitutes for CDSs due to regulatory or market-related restrictions.

7
CDS: Hedging of Issuer and Counterparty Risks

Credit derivatives have a broad range of applications throughout the capital markets, for portfolio managers, traders, and investors alike. The favourably liquid nature of these products, which translates into low transaction costs, contributes to their broad acceptance. CDSs are used for hedging credit risk, managing of economic and regulatory capital, speculative or proprietary trading, synthetic (or unfunded) investments, pricing credit risk assets, and capital-structure arbitrage and as a gauge for credit risk through market implied ratings (MIRs) or Early Warning Systems (EWSs). The single name credit default swap is a widespread form of transferring credit risk from the protection buyer to the protection seller and is often compared to an insurance contract. As with insurance, a premium has to be paid for compensation of potential future losses from a specified event occurring to the insured item. However, there are substantial differences, too. One of the arguments against CDS as insurance points to the fact that any payout under insurance is conditional on the holder owning the insured object or at least experiencing losses caused by the insured event; this is not true for a CDS. Thus, a CDS contract designed as a financial guarantee may actually be a closer match to an insurance contract because it (a) indemnifies the protection buyer only for losses incurred and (b) is subject to accrual accounting, thus no value changes appear over its lifetime. Another view compares CDSs to options where the protection buyer owns a put option on the credit risk of the reference entity. According to this theory, a CDS is in the money if a credit event occurs for the reference borrower; otherwise the cash outflow of the CDS protection bought is limited to the coupons to be paid to the seller of the CDS. However, this applies at only one point in time, namely at the CDS expiration date; whereas both the seller and buyer of CDSs are exposed on a daily basis to gains or losses from mark-to-market valuations, which may exceed coupon payments by far. CDSs are popular with credit portfolio managers and client-relationship managers because they protect a borrower's credit risk, but – unlike loan syndications – do not require the consent of a bank's customer.[1] Even better, the risk transfer takes place without the involvement or notification of the client, thus giving the bank maximum flexibility and discretion when managing credit risk. In a portfolio context, credit derivatives allow banks to[2]

- isolate the credit risk component of assets and manage it separately from other risk types, such as interest-rate risk;
- optimize the risk/return profile of a credit portfolio by replacing risks that exhibit a suboptimal contribution with other assets that allow moving the portfolio closer to the efficient frontier;
- apply a dynamic hedge approach;
- smooth peak exposure, which arises from seasonal patterns of drawings under committed lines, to a target average exposure;
- manage counterparty risk, which arises from market value changes of derivative transactions;
- reduce portfolio concentrations in the form of regional, industry, single name, collateral, or product clusters;
- increase the level of portfolio diversification by way of substituting assets with others that have a significantly lower correlation with the existing risk concentrations;
- balance loan pricing risk, which arises from changing market conditions during the period between final negotiation of loan terms to contract subscription, which at times can take weeks;[3]
- hedge the risk of significant price changes for loans in the syndication phase until the asset has been successfully syndicated or sold into the primary or secondary market. The same applies to underwriting risk from bonds which a bank takes on its books until the securities are fully placed in the market.[4]

[1] Although the borrower's consent to transfer the obligation must be ensured for physical delivery under a CDS in some cases.

[2] See also Banks et al. (2007).

[3] Even though the bank is not legally bound to any agreement on terms and conditions of a loan, including the loan margin, until the loan document is signed by both parties (the borrower and the bank), it may feel morally bound and stick to the negotiated contract. In practice, the bank weighs the pricing risk against the reputational risk, which can be severe if it decides to walk away from a deal due to an adverse change in market conditions.

[4] Assuming that the transaction is fully underwritten, in contrast to an agreement to place the assets on a best-efforts basis, where the risk that a lower-than-targeted amount of proceeds will be raised ultimately remains with the client.

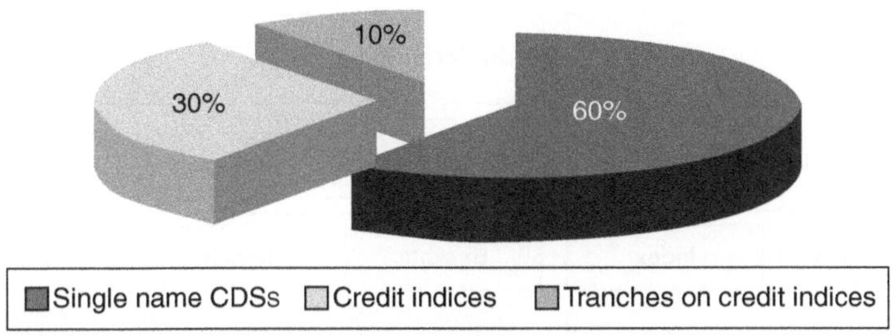

Figure 7.1 Breakdown of credit derivatives by type (as of April 2012)
Source: DTCC.

The tremendous growth of the CDS market – the CDS was originally designed as an individual, bilateral contract for hedging credit exposures of a bank's balance sheet – has been supported by an ever-increasing range of applications, coupled with improved standardization and liquidity provided by market makers and electronic trading platforms.

The growing acceptance of credit derivatives and involvement of diverse market participants and specialists has led to the invention of a variety of CDS-based products. CDS index families and options are the best known; but tranched CDS indices, baskets, CSOs, and recovery swaps have also been created to meet the demand of more sophisticated market participants. Assets referenced by CDSs are unsecured bonds and loans from investment-grade, high yield and emerging market corporates, senior and subordinated bank debt, developed and emerging market sovereign securities, municipal debt, and commercial and residential mortgages. Additionally, loan credit default sawps (LCDSs) have been developed for syndicated secured loans. The 'sweet spot' of trading activity centres on five-year transactions for high-grade single name corporates and indices with sizes of \$10 mn to \$50 mn per trade, whereas high yield typically trades in \$2 mn to \$5 mn lots.

This chapter on CDSs is structured as follows first, an introduction to CDSs and product-specific conventions is provided. Recent initiatives to increase the standardization of credit derivatives, such as the Small and Big Bang, are highlighted. Key elements of a CDS trade that drives both prices and recoveries, that is, deliverable obligations and credit events, are discussed. The standard procedure by which the final price of defaulted debt is determined, and the auction process is described, elaborating on the decisions a hedger must take in that specific context. Since LCDS have become a regular tool to manage secured loans, the essentials of the instrument are outlined. Case studies illustrate real-life examples of the functioning of CDSs. The information contained herein is not exhaustive, nor does it represent legal advice, nor is

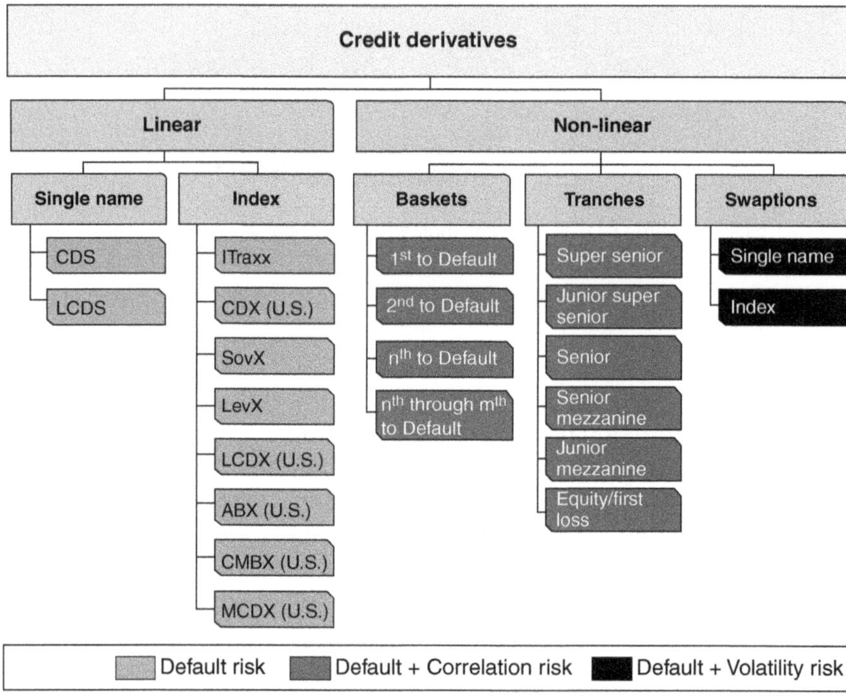

Figure 7.2 Overview of credit derivative products

it intended to be a substitute for reading the original ISDA definitions and supplements.

7.1 Mechanism and conventions of CDSs

All standard CDSs are governed by a set of definitions and provisions – for instance, the 2003 ISDA Credit Derivatives Definitions and Master Agreement (the '*2003 Definitions*') – which detail the relevant credit events leading to a CDS payout. The Small Bang and Big Bang, introduced by ISDA in April and July 2009, respectively, corrected CDS shortfalls, which were identified as a lesson learned during the crisis years, and aimed to facilitate the liquidity and stability of the CDS market. The Big Bang protocol, or the 2009 ISDA Credit Derivatives Determinations Committees and Auction Settlement Supplement (the '*March 2009 Supplement*'), deals with changes related primarily to the determination of a credit event and the subsequent CDS settlement. The protocol became binding for all new CDS transactions and took effect immediately. Market participants were free to choose whether to apply the 2009 Supplement to existing CDS trades for a short period. Following the Big Bang, ISDA published the 2009 ISDA Credit Determinations Committees, Auction Settlement and Restructuring Supplement (the *'July 2009 Supplement'*). The purpose of this Small Bang protocol was to implement a standard auction process for restructuring credit events with particular relevance to the European CDS market. Other efforts to improve contractual standardization, such as the introduction of fixed coupons and upfront payments in the Standard North American Contract (SNAC) or Standard European Contract (STEC), found widespread acceptance. Unlike interest-rate swaps, the bilateral nature of CDSs led to enormous and inflated growth of gross exposure in the past, which exaggerated the 'real' economic risk after netting or offsetting transactions. The introduction of a central clearing substantially reduced counterparty risk. Additionally, portfolio compression aims to reduce notional size and number of contracts without changing the net risk position of the portfolio by replacing existing trades with new trades exhibiting a risk profile and cash flows similar to the original portfolio.[5]

7.1.1 Transaction terms and conditions

A CDS is a financial contract which provides loss protection to the buyer in exchange for periodic payments to the protection seller. A CDS sell position refers to selling protection on the credit risk, which is economically equivalent to a long position in the underlying obligation, buying a corporate bond a loan, and vice versa. CDSs, like other credit risk instruments such as corporate bonds, are predominantly characterized by the underlying credit risk. However, the derivative nature of CDSs requires additional contractual features. The key elements of a CDS trade confirmation are outlined in Figure 7.3.

The following text provides a more detailed description of those CDS components and elaborates on the pitfalls which warrant attention.

7.1.2 Quotation conventions

Standardizing conventions has significantly contributed to smooth functioning of the market for CDS and related credit derivatives products, in particular in volatile times. The introduction of *fixed coupons* proved to be an efficient way to reduce the jump-to-default risk which

[5] According to ISDA, approximately USD74.6 trn in CDS notional in single name, index and tranche contracts, covering the U.S., Europe, Japan, and emerging markets, was eliminated in 2010, mostly through TriOptima, but Creditex and Markit also provided portfolio compression services. See www.isdacdsmarketplace.com.

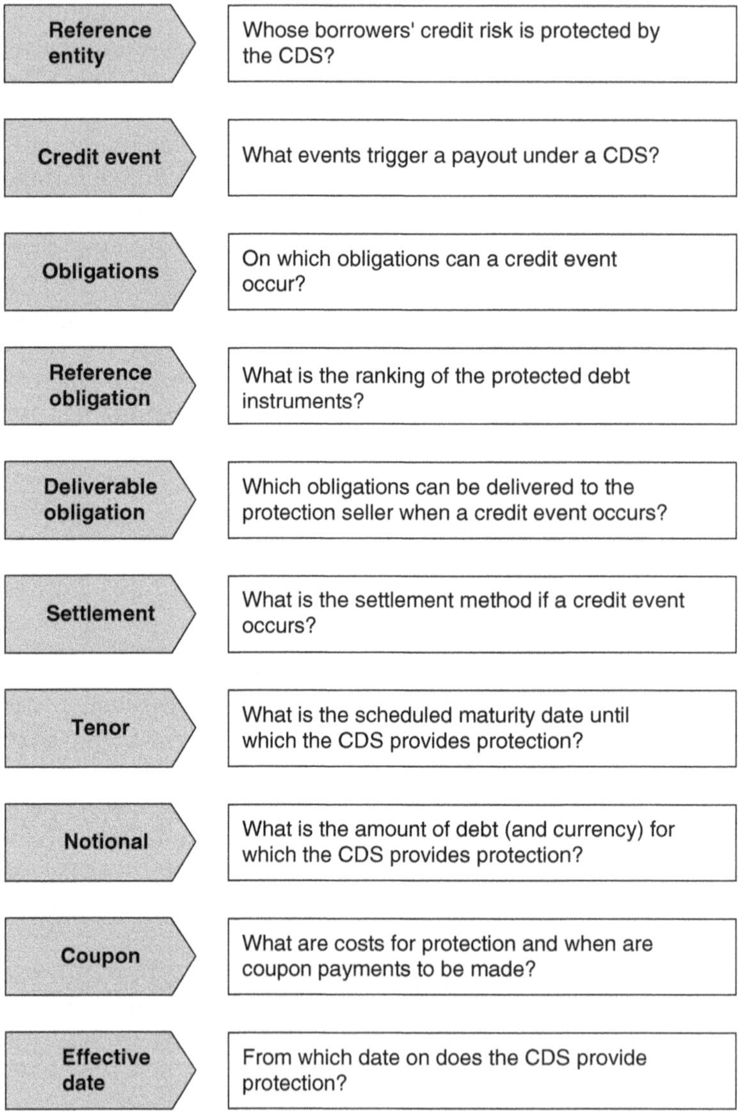

Figure 7.3 Key elements of a CDS trade confirmation

arose from CDSs that were deep in the money and offset by a counter-position with a substantially different coupon that had been set according to the prevailing traded spreads. *Standard maturity dates* have further improved the efficiency of CDSs, but they also matter for regulatory capital relief through CDS hedging, as well as in the context of accounting rules.

Fixed coupon (bps)	European corporates	Western European sovereigns	North American corporates, sovereigns	Japan corporates, sovereigns**	Emerging markets*
25	Yes	Yes	No	Yes	No
100	Yes	Yes	Yes	Yes	Yes
500	Yes	No	Yes	Yes	Yes
1000	Yes	No	No	No	No

*: Latin America, Asia corporates and sovereigns, eastern Europe, Middle East and Africa sovereigns.
**: Likewise for Australia and New Zealand corporates and sovereigns.

Figure 7.4 CDS fixed coupon standards

7.1.2.1 *Spread, fixed coupons, and upfront payments*

Until 2009, most CDSs traded on par with no initial upfront payment. That means that CDSs were quoted as a running spread, which was then fixed as the coupon for a trade, thus resulting in zero net present value at trade inception. When the spread moved, so did the coupon for the next trade. In June 2009, fixed coupons were introduced to achieve a higher level of standardization. Since then, CDSs have been quoted with the fixed coupons as shown in Figure 7.4.

Most common are coupons of 100 and 500 basis points (bps), while 25 bps are also used for sovereigns and European corporates, although to a lesser extent. From 2010 on, North American LCDSs have traded with a fixed coupon of 250 bps, which is an exception, but 100 bps and 500 bps may also be available in selected cases. As a general rule, the coupon will be determined by current and historical spreads and existing trades. Since the fair spread of a CDS transaction rarely matches the fixed coupon, the equivalent of the net present value of the difference between the actual spread and the coupon is paid up front.

Example: A trader wants to buy €10 mn protection on BMW, five-year senior unsecured, at a fair spread of 145 bps. The coupon for a BMW standard contract is 100 bps. To compensate for the 45 bps lower coupon paid during the five years of the contract, the CDS is priced at 97.864 per cent, meaning that the CDS buyer pays the protection seller an upfront amount of 2.14 per cent, or €213,619.[6] Let's assume the coupon for the five-year BMW is 500 bps. Then the upfront payment is equal to the net present value of five years of 365 bps difference between coupon and fair spread, payable by the protection seller. In this case, the upfront payment amounts to 16.85 per cent, or €1,685,217.

[6] *Source*: Bloomberg, using the CDSW function, which is based on the ISDA standard model v1.

The fixed coupon convention also solved an issue which hedgers faced when the asset underlying a CDS hedge became distressed and they wanted to close out the hedge position to monetize the valuation gain. In order to close the CDS buy position and realize the profit, the trade had been balanced by selling CDSs with identical contract specifications – that is, obligor, tenor, and currency. The only difference related to the coupon, since the CDS was initially bought when the issuer spread was tight, whereas the spread for the CDS sell position was significantly higher due to the subsequent deterioration of the issuer credit quality. The two transactions completely eliminate the credit risk of the borrower, and pay a quarterly income stream from the coupon payments received from the CDS selling leg, net of the coupon payments to be paid for the CDS buy leg. However, when an investor closed out a trade where the coupon was far out of the money, a new type of risk emerged. Jump-to-default risk arises because the positive difference between the spreads of the two legs is paid for the remaining lifetime of the contracts *only* if no default of the CDS reference entity occurs before maturity. Otherwise, all payments are terminated, and the CDSs are settled. Although for the combined CDS buy and sell position, the default risk of the borrower is neutralized, the future cash flows related to coupon payments from the two offsetting legs still leave the hedger exposed to the credit risk of the reference entity. Unfortunately for borrowers that trade at elevated spread levels, the probability of default is considerably high, implying that investors are less likely to receive many coupons from the CDS selling leg. Equally probable, not all coupons for the CDS protection buy leg will have to be paid. Because the coupons from the CDS buy position are lower than the coupons received under the CDS protection sell leg, a significant amount of future income is uncertain from the transaction that was considered closed. Alternatively, the portfolio manager may decide to unwind the transaction with the hedge counterparty rather than offset the original hedge with a sell protection position. In that case, the jump-to-default risk attached to the CDS coupons is effectively transferred to the dealer, through it is still not eliminated. The dealer may then hedge that jump-to-default risk by buying additional short-dated protection on the name, which is in most cases very expensive, as high default risk borrowers tend to trade with a higher short-end risk premium compared to medium- or long-term spreads in what is known as an 'inverted curve'. Moreover, funding the higher coupons of the sell protection leg generates additional costs for which the dealer will seek compensation. The dealer will charge the investor with the costs from hedging jump-to-default risk and funding, which will diminish the amount of gains from widened spreads on the hedge position that should compensate the investor for potential losses from a default of the hedged entity. Fixed coupons offer a solution, as the original trade and the offsetting transaction will have identical coupons, while the difference in valuations is paid up front.[7]

Two kinds of quotations became usance in CDS markets: *spread quotation* and *upfront*, or *price, quotation*. Spread quotation applies to CDSs whose reference borrowers are rated investment grade, both for single name CDSs and indices such as iTraxx Europe (Bloomberg: ITRXEBE) or CDX IG North America (Bloomberg: IBOXUMAE). Additionally, indices for European crossover names (XOVER, Bloomberg: ITRXEXE) and sovereigns (i.e. SovX, Bloomberg: ITXSWE) and the index for municipal issuers (MCDX, Bloomberg: MCDNAA5) are quoted in spreads. By contrast, CDSs of North American high yield issuers are quoted in price terms for both single name CDSs and the high yield CDS index (CDX HY, Bloomberg: IBOXHYSE). The same applies for the North American index for a loan-only CDS on syndicated secured first-lien loans LCDX (Bloomberg: LCDXGE) and its European pendant LevX (Bloomberg: ITRXLX5).

7.1.2.2 Termination and coupon payment dates

Maturity dates are set to one of four *roll dates*, which are the 20th of March, June, September, and December. For trade days between the roll dates, the maturity is rounded to the next roll date. For example, a CDS contract traded on August 15 will have a maturity of September 20. This specification is relevant for hedge accounting of credit risk (HACR), since under IAS 39 the maturity of the hedge must not exceed the maturity of the hedged item. The maturity convention implicitly caps the number of days that a standard CDS hedge may exceed the maturity of any underlying at a maximum of 90 days.[8] Since this rule appears to be acceptable under IAS 39, the condition for HACR is respected. Every three months, the standard maturity rolls forward three months. If the maturity falls on a non-business day, then the contract matures on the following business day. Coupons of CDS transactions are paid quarterly, calculated on an actual/360-days basis with a full first coupon. Payment dates coincide with the standardized maturity dates. The first full coupon equates the three-month period between the standard roll dates in which the CDS traded with the protection seller paying the buyer accrued interest for the days between the previous maturity date and the trade date. This is similar to accrued payments for corporate bonds.

[7] Upfront payments are calculated assuming a flat curve. When using pricing models based on non-flat curves derived from observable CDS quotes, i.e. either upward sloping or inverted, the trade spread given upfront payment and fixed coupon will differ from the convention. That effect is more pronounced, as described in the example above, for higher coupons and inverted curves, where the protection seller is exposed to jump-to-default risk for the remaining coupons.

[8] After 90 days, a new roll date would be available, with the difference in days between maturity of underlying and hedge starting again from zero.

Example: An investor buys protection on August 15. The first full coupon is paid by the investor to the protection seller for the time between June 20 and September 20. The protection seller pays the buyer accrued interest for the 55 days between June 20 and August 15.

It should be noted, though, that CDS coupons stop accruing on the date a credit event is determined. This leaves the protection buyer with a mismatch, since by contrast coupons of the underlying likely will be unpaid for the period from after the last coupon payment to the date of the credit event. As a result, the protection buyer faces a cash-flow mismatch, where the costs of hedge coupon payments are not compensated by coupons received from the hedged item during the period of the last coupon payment received to the credit event determination date.

7.1.3 Reference entity

The *reference entity* is the obligor whose credit risk is being transferred by the CDS protection, either a corporate or a sovereign. Although the selection of the reference borrower seems obvious when a hedge strategy has been developed to protect the credit risk of a particular name, it nevertheless warrants close attention, as sometimes different entities within a corporate conglomerate exhibit varying default risks and are disconnected from each other in case of a default of one. Moreover, recoveries within a corporate group can vary, too. Two examples illustrate the importance of being clear and correct about the reference entity. First, in December 2000, the U.S. company Armstrong World Industries filed for reorganization under chapter 11 because of asbestos injury claims which exceeded the value of the company. While the action triggered a credit event for Armstrong World Industries, the parent company, Armstrong Holdings, was unaffected. A similar situation occurred in October 2002, when TXU Europe Ltd. defaulted after a subsidiary failed to make an interest payment on two outstanding bonds. The U.S.-based firm TXU, however, was impacted only on a $500 mn working capital facility which featured a cross-default provision triggered by a default of TXU Europe. Besides the reference entity, the reference obligation also contributes to an exact definition of the credit risk hedged by a CDS.

7.1.4 Reference and deliverable obligations

A critical aspect of CDSs for hedging (and other) purposes concerns the debt which is deliverable in case of a credit event: the *deliverable obligation*. While most of a reference entity's outstanding obligations are relevant for the determination of a credit event, only a subset will be eligible for delivery from the protection buyer to the protection seller following a credit event. Hence, the deliverable obligations are essential for determining the recovery at the auction process. In general, a CDS covers obligations that are issued or unconditionally guaranteed by the reference entity. Contract specifications determine the debt instruments relevant for the settlement of a CDS contract by defining

- the **obligation category** or the type of debt, which could be bonds, loans (or bonds and loans) or borrowed money – in principle, any obligation which the borrower has to repay sometime in the future – or the reference obligation only;
- the **obligation characteristics;** for instance, the maximum maturity, the ranking (i.e. seniority or subordination),[9] the currency, the governing law, and the market of issuance.[10]

The type of debt is important, as there are meaningful differences to be considered when hedging credit risk. Off-balance-sheet credit risk, such as committed lines or revolving credit facilities which have not been drawn at the time of the credit event, are excluded from the range of deliverables – although undrawn lines consume regulatory capital which can be released by buying CDS protection. A partially drawn revolver can be delivered, but the CDS covers the drawn part only; protection for any future drawing under the revolver, as the protection buyer must indemnify the protection seller from any future liability that arises from drawing post the credit event. It should be noted that equity-like instruments such as preference shares are not eligible as deliverable obligations, while perpetuals may or may not be, depending on the conditions of repayment. Besides the obligations that are directly issued by the borrower, guarantees in which the reference entity agrees to assume all payments due on the obligation of another obligor may also be eligible, as long as they are irrevocable, transferable, and non-dischargeable other than by payment. Since banks often provide loans to subsidiaries of their clients, under certain circumstances, hedging can take place at the parent or subsidiary level of a corporate, depending on whether downstream and/or upstream guarantees are in place that qualify under the ISDA rules. For instance, if a parent company guarantees the debt of a subsidiary, hedging the credit risk of the subsidiary is possible with a CDS on both the parent and the subsidiary as a reference entity. This is so because if the subsidiary experiences a credit event, it is obvious that the subsidiary's debt is deliverable into the CDS of the subsidiary, provided it qualifies as a deliverable obligation. However, if the parent that guarantees the debt of the subsidiary does not satisfy the claims of the holders of the

[9] In some cases, subordinated debt is excluded as a deliverable obligation.

[10] For some countries, such as those in Emerging Europe i.e. Eastern Europe, or Latin America, only non-domestic debt, issued under non-domestic law in a non-domestic currency, qualifies as a deliverable. Nevertheless, cross-default clauses must be observed, as they can effectively bridge the gap between domestic and non-domestic debt.

subsidiary's debt as promised in the guarantee, a credit event on the parent occurs, and the subsidiary's obligations become deliverable into the parent's CDS, too. The same holds true if a credit event takes place at the parent; even without a corresponding credit event at the subsidiary, the subsidiary's debt becomes immediately deliverable into the parent's CDS because of the parent's guarantee. From the perspective outside of market participants that are not involved in direct lending through loans, the undisclosed interconnectedness of affiliates by way of guarantees makes it more difficult to anticipate the pool of qualifying deliverable obligations for the auction after a credit event, which is ultimately a key driver of the CDS-determined auction recovery value. Moreover, certain restrictions apply to the obligations of a reference entity in order for them to become deliverable to the CDS auction. The main deliverable obligation characteristics for standard CDS contracts are

- *not subordinated*: the obligation must rank at least pari passu with the most senior reference obligation in priority of payment, or if no reference obligation is specified, the borrowed money obligations of the reference entity that is senior.
- *specified currency*: the currency or currencies in which an obligation or deliverable obligation must be payable. Standard contracts include CAD, JPY, CHF, GBP, USD, and EUR.
- *maximum maturity*: 30 years.
- *not contingent*: any obligation whose repayment of principal exclusively depends on the borrower.
- *assignable loan*: a loan that can be assigned or novated without the consent of the obligor.
- *consent required loan*: a loan that can be assigned or novated with the consent of the obligor.
- *transferable*: loans must be able to be assigned or novated on the delivery date without anyone's consent.
- *not bearer*: the obligation must not be an unregistered security that is payable to its bearer or the person who possesses it.

Even when an obligation does not fulfil the criteria for a deliverable obligation, it may still trigger a credit event, although it will not be deliverable to the auction following the credit event. The protection buyer is entitled to deliver any acceptable delivery obligation to the protection seller after a credit event to settle the CDS contract. Hence, the recovery value will be determined by the value of these deliverable obligations at the auction. From the perspective of the CDS seller, the list of deliverable obligations is a kind of blind pool of which any asset might be delivered in the case of a physical settlement, including, and very likely, the cheapest asset conforming to the criteria of the deliverable obligations. This is called the *cheapest-to-deliver option* a CDS buyer owns and indicates that the protection buyer may source a cheaper deliverable obligation in the secondary market and subsequently deliver the asset to the auction, while the initially hedged asset can be sold at a higher price. Since for both assets, the recovery value will be the same for all credit events except restructuring, a CDS buyer may make a windfall profit by replacing the originally hedged obligation into the cheapest-to-deliver obligation.

Case Study 5. Nationalization of SNS Reaal

SNS Reaal, a Dutch banking and insurance group that is predominantly active in domestic mortgage lending with systemic relevance to country, was nationalized by the finance ministry of the Netherlands in February 2013[11] to avoid a disorderly demise of the bank because of fears of potentially severe disruptions in financial markets and corresponding threats to the economy. The action, that did cost the Dutch tapayer EUR 3.7 bn, included the hitherto unusual step of expropriating all subordinated bonds as well as the shares issued by SNS Reaal.[12] Deposits and senior unsecured bonds were left untouched as Finance Minister Jeroen Dijsselbloem did seek to avoid a run on the local banks. According to the Dutch ministry of finance, the expropriation has saved the state EUR 1 bn of expenses. However, this case exhibited a flaw in the ISDA CDS documentation since nationalization itself does not qualify as a credit event under the 2003 ISDA Credit Derivative Definitions which are the contractual basis for standard CDSs. Thus, buyers of CDSs were left wondering if they were going to receive any pay-out from their hedging as a compensation for the losses from expropriation. On February, 13th 2013 ISDA announced that a restructuring credit event has occured which implied a subsequent credit auction to be held to determine the recovery value of all bonds of SNS Reaal.

[11] See 'State of the Netherlands nationalises SNS Reaal', http://www.government.nl/documents-and-publications/parliamentary-documents/2013/02/01/nationalisation-of-sns-reaal.html.

[12] Interestingly, the aim of the expropriation was clearly communicated to ensure that the private sector was to contribute as much as possible to the rescue of SNS Reaal. While it stopped short of tapping senior unsecured creditors and deposits for bearing the bail out costs, it was also Jeroen Dijsselbloem in his capacity as the new Euro Group chief to call for a more brave approach and to let all creditors rather than taxpayers share the burden of bank failures when Cyprus was requested to impose a haircut on deposits of its domestic banks in March 2013. While this move initially sparked a significant rise in CDS spreads of banks, markets soon afterwards dismissed this as a case on its own. However, one can expect governments to continue on their way towards a 'bail in' of creditors and depositors alike with the risk of substantial losses to these investors in the event of a bank failure.

Because of the expropriation, investors in the subordinated bonds had no assets to deliver into the auction for SNS Bank NV, which took place on April, 4th 2013. As a result, a final price of 95.5 was determined for bucket 1 and 85.5 for bucket 2 with no difference between senior and sub debt. For those owners of subordinated bonds who were hedging the bonds with CDS, the compensation payment for every Euro loss was as low as 4.5 cents, assuming either cash settlement or buying a deliverable bond at the final price of 95.5. The incidence makes clear, that situations may arise where the contractual design of CDSs is insufficient to protect CDS buyers from losses of the hedged item.

7.2 Credit events

One of the key questions a portfolio manager may ask when hedging credit risk is *what am I protected for*? The answer to that question, however, is not as straightforward as for *credit losses incurred*, which would meet the definition of a financial guarantee but not of a CDS. To provide a precise answer, we split the question into two parts: 1) **when** is a payment to be made from a CDS, and 2) **how much** will be paid and how does it relate to credit losses from the hedged instrument? For the first part, we will find the answer in the *credit events*, defined in the 2003 ISDA Credit Derivative Definitions, that trigger a payment under a CDS from the protection seller to the protection buyer. These events, are not simply defined as payments due but not made under the obligation They are much more broadly defined, as will be explained later conditions. The second part of the question deals with the settlement procedure after a credit event and the way the payment amount or recovery is determined. (Detailed information on this subject is provided in §7.3, 'Settlement after a credit event'.) Let's come back to the question of when a payment under a CDS will be made. As was said, a payment from a CDS will be triggered by a credit event. The following six constitute a credit event when they occur:

1. Failure to pay
2. Bankruptcy
3. Restructuring
4. Repudiation or moratorium
5. Obligation acceleration
6. Obligation default

Table 7.1 provides brief definitions of the credit events and indicates the type of the CDS reference entity to which each may apply. By design, credit events are one of the key determinants for CDS valuation and are specified in the CDS trade confirmation.

Table 7.1 Overview of CDS credit events

Credit Event	Definition	Corporate CDS	Sovereign CDS	Municipal CDS
Failure to pay	Failure of payment by the reference entity on one or more obligations when due, after expiration of grace period. Since this credit event results in exactly quantifiable losses (the amount unpaid), it is the only trigger which meets the definition of a financial guarantee.	Yes[13]	Yes[14]	Yes
Bankruptcy	Insolvency, liquidation, administration. Status of borrower that cannot meet its obligations under the debt owed to creditors. The only credit event related to the borrower, not the obligation. CDS may be triggered under this credit event well in advance of any losses occurring.	Yes	No	No
Restructuring	Change in agreement between reference entity and obligation holders due to a deterioration in credit quality or financial condition of the reference entity.	Yes[15]	Yes	Yes
Repudiation/ moratorium	Authorized officer or governmental authority declares or imposes the moratorium or repudiation, and a failure to pay occurs within 60 days (or the next payment date for the relevant obligation).	No[16]	Yes	No
Obligation acceleration	Situation (other than a failure to pay) where one or more obligations become due and payable as a result of a default but before the time it would have been without the default.	No[17]	No[18]	No
Obligation default	Situation (other than a failure to pay) where one or more obligations become capable of being declared due and payable as a result of a default but before the time it would have been without the default.	No	Yes	No

[13] Not applicable to emerging market or Latin American corporates.
[14] Not applicable to emerging market or Latin American sovereigns.
[15] Not applicable to North American corporates, though older contracts may feature the Old R or Mod-R.
[16] Applicable to emerging market or Latin American corporates.
[17] Applicable to emerging market or Latin American corporates.
[18] Applicable to emerging market or Latin American sovereigns.

As part of the ISDA Auction Supplement Protocol, or Big Bang Protocol, introduced in April 2009, a *Determinations Committee* (DC) has been established to formalize the determination and settlement of credit events. Any counterparty to a CDS or eligible market participant can request that that the DC determine the occurrence of a credit event, either in its own name or anonymously, as a general interest question. In order to be recognized, a credit event must have occurred no earlier than within the past 60 calendar days before the date on which a request has been raised to the ISDA Determination Committee to determine whether or not a credit event has occurred (Credit Event resolution Request Date), a date which is known as the *credit event backstop date*. The backward-looking nature has important implications if a credit event has occurred but CDS and related debt still trade, as in the case of Greece. Since a CDS that is initiated after the credit event but within the 60-day period can be immediately triggered, the Greek sovereign CDS market effectively came to a standstill after the post–credit event settlement. The DC determines whether or not a credit event or succession event has taken place and, if so, the corresponding date and type of the event. Once a credit event has been determined, interest stops accruing at the *event determination date*, which is the date at which publicly available information on the potential credit event has been provided to the DC. The DC approves and specifies the deliverable obligations that are eligible for the auction process. The DC is composed of 15 voting members, of which 8 are global dealers, 2 are regional dealers, and 5 are non-dealers. In addition, four non-voting members, composed of two dealer and non-dealer investors, respectively, attend the committee, while the ISDA serves as the secretary and coordinator. Five different DCs cover the geographical regions: Europe (EMEA), the Americas, Japan, Asia (except Japan) and Australia–New Zealand. All relevant information about requests to the DC and related decisions are available on the ISDA website.

7.2.1 Hard credit events

All of the credit events listed in Table 7.1 are so-called hard credit events, restructuring being the only exception. Hence bankruptcy, failure to pay, repudiation/moratorium, obligation acceleration, and obligation default automatically trigger the CDS contract once they are determined to have occurred, with the subsequent settlement of the CDS between buyer and seller. By contrast, a restructuring credit event is considered a soft event because both the protection buyer and the protection seller have the right but not the obligation to trigger the CDS. A trigger by one party to the CDS is sufficient for settlement. However, if no one decides to trigger, the CDS remains in place until another credit event takes place or the CDS matures.

Determining a **failure to pay** is quite straightforward namely, whenever a reference entity fails to make a payment on one or more obligations when due. Further conditions, if applicable, are that the amount unpaid must exceed the payment-requirement threshold and the grace period has passed. **Bankruptcy is** a bit trickier, though. Intuitively one would expect legal proceedings arising from insolvency to be a clear-cut case for bankruptcy, but other actions prior to or leading to an insolvency can equally trigger a CDS under this credit event. While section 4.2 of the ISDA framework specifies the bankruptcy provision in great detail – it is worth a read as the wording matters – the key actions constituting a bankruptcy event are if a reference entity[19]

- is dissolved (other than through a merger, consolidation, etc.);
- becomes insolvent or unable to pay its debts;
- makes a general assignment, arrangement, or composition with or for its creditors;
- faces insolvency or bankruptcy proceedings;
- is wound up or liquidated;
- becomes subject to the appointment of an administrator, liquidator, conservator, receiver, trustee, custodian, or the like, for all or the majority of its assets;
- has a secured party take possession of all or substantially all of its assets;
- causes or is subject to an event which is analogous to any of the above under the applicable laws of any jurisdiction.

The broader definition provided by ISDA conflicts with the Moody's more stringent definition of what it considers to be a default, which is[20]

- any missed or delayed disbursement of interest and/or principal;
- bankruptcy or receivership; and
- distressed exchange where (i) the borrower offers debt holders a new security or package of securities that amount to a diminished financial obligation (such as preferred or common stock or debt with a lower coupon or par amount) or (ii) the exchange has the apparent purpose of helping the borrower avoid default.

In case study 6 it also becomes clear that bankruptcy as defined by ISDA includes events which could take place well in advance of any losses occurred. This violates the requirements of IAS for a financial guarantee, leaving failure to pay as the only undisputed credit event

[19] See Haworth (2011). This report provides a clear and insightful overview of credit events.

[20] See Tolk (2001).

Case Study 6. Fannie Mae and Freddie Mac Bankruptcy Credit Event

The diverging approach of Moody's and ISDA can have far-reaching implications, as observed in the case of Fannie Mae and Freddie Mac. These so-called government-sponsored enterprises (GSE) play a key role in the U.S. housing market, where they are engaged in granting and guaranteeing loans to other banks and mortgage lenders. During the decade ending in 2007, the combined portfolios of the two firms exhibited strong growth in the region of a tenfold increase in terms of volume.[21] As GSEs, the firms had a mission to facilitate the origination of home mortgages and provide liquidity to the U.S. residential mortgage market, thereby making housing affordable. Unsurprisingly, given that Fannie and Freddie were integral to the housing market, the financial turmoil which started with defaults of low-quality or subprime mortgages and ended with house prices slipping across the board hit them hard.[22] After Fannie Mae booked $58 bn of losses and Freddie Mac $50 bn just days before the Lehman demise, they were placed into conservatorship on September 7, 2008, by the Federal Housing Finance Agency. That action met the ISDA definition of bankruptcy. Consequently, CDSs on both names were triggered because of a bankruptcy event. However, Moody's affirmed the AAA senior and Aa2 subordinated debt rating of the two companies with a stable outlook since '*the conservatorship of both firms does not limit in any way their ability to service their senior or subordinated debt obligations*'.[23] The support of the U.S. Treasury for the obligations did not extend to the preferred stock, as the conservator suspended the dividend payments for those securities at both companies. As a result, Moody's downgraded the rating of the preferred stock to Ca and the bank financial strength rating to E\+. Shortly afterwards, on October 6, 2008, ISDA published the auction results for Fannie Mae senior and subordinated debt, which was determined to be 91.51 and 99.9 per cent, respectively. For Freddie Mac, the recovery has been fixed at 94 per cent for senior debt and 98 per cent for subordinated debt. The debt of the firms later traded at par, indicating that the ongoing bailout by the U.S. Treasury was credible to market participants. Hence the credit event did not necessarily did favour the protection buyer. Today, Fannie Mae and Freddie Mac, together with Ginnie Mae, guarantee most of the single-family mortgage issues in the U.S.[24] and still receive taxpayers' money to stay afloat, in total $117.1 bn for Fannie Mae alone, while they remain under government control.

---

[21] See Felsenheimer and Gisdakis (2008).

[22] A very well written and interesting comment on the course and inherent reasons of the Fannie Mae and Freddie Mac collapse is provided by Banks (2011).

[23] See Moody's Investor Service, Rating Action: Moody's affirms Aaa senior and Aa2 subordinated debt of Fannie Mae and Freddie Mac. Global Credit Research, September 7, 2008.

[24] Until the fourth quarter of 2011, Fannie Mae, Freddie Mac and Ginnie Mae accounted for 90% of the single-family mortgage issuance. See Standard and Poor's, *Fannie Mae*, January 24, 2012, on Global Credit Portal.

applicable if a portfolio manager wants to avoid mark-to-market accounting for the hedge.

Repudiation or moratorium replaces bankruptcy for sovereigns and some emerging-market corporates and is not applicable to North American and European corporates. The credit event occurs if

- an authorized officer of the reference entity or a governmental authority either repudiates (disclaims, rejects, challenges) the validity of or imposes a moratorium (standstill, rollover, deferral) on one or more obligations, which is called a *potential repudiation/moratorium*; and
- a *failure to pay* or *restructuring* subsequently takes place.

It should be noted that the repudiation/moratorium credit event triggers a CDS only if both conditions are satisfied. If the failure to pay or restructuring occurs only after the scheduled termination date, whereas the potential repudiation/moratorium happened before, the CDS covers the event even though it took place after the CDS maturity, provided that the contract is extended by a repudiation/moratorium extension notice by one CDS counterparty to the other.

7.2.2 Restructuring credit event

The restructuring credit event has become a focal point for market professionals, not only in the context of bank and sovereign restructurings, but also for the corporate sector. While often met with some reservation because of its vagueness, the restructuring event has played a significant role in the recent past. Well-known names that experienced a restructuring credit event include Anglo-Irish Bank, Allied Irish, Irish Life and Permanent, Xerox, Thomson, Aiful, and SNS Reaal, as well as Ecuador and Greece. Since restructuring differs in many aspects from more common credit events such as bankruptcy and failure to pay, a closer look at its implications for the buyer of CDSs and the seller of protection appears to be worthwhile. In a first step, we examine the actions which constitute a restructuring credit event and highlight the different provisions which emerged in Europe, compared to the U.S. and other countries, driven by local bankruptcy law and regulatory requirements. Moreover, we analyse the implications from a risk and capital management perspective. Finally, a case study sheds some light on the mechanics of the restructuring credit event and related aspects.

The main reason for a CDS restructuring credit event[25] is a change in the documentation in the debt contract (loan or bond) of the reference entity. Contractual changes include

[25] See ISDA 2003 credit derivatives definition, Doctor et al. (2011), Bruyere et al. (2006), Haworth (2011).

- *reduction* in interest rate, interest amount due, or principal;
- *postponement* of interest or principal payments or *extension* of repayment instalments;
- a change in priority ranking, causing contractual *subordination* of the obligation;
- a re-denomination of the currency or composition of interest or principal into any other than a *permitted currency* (G7 or country that is a member of the OECD and rated AAA for its long-term local currency debt by Standard and Poor's, Moody's, or Fitch)[26]

and must bind all holders to one or more obligations (this is a key requirement). A restructuring event is further conditional on

- changes in documentation of the reference obligation, which must not have been introduced at a later of the issuance of the obligation[27] and the credit event backstop date;[28]
- the restructured debt amounting to at least $10 mn or the equivalent in the currency in which the CDS is denominated (default requirement), unless otherwise specified in the CDS confirmation;
- changes in documentation of the reference obligation directly or indirectly arising from a decline in the credit quality or financial condition of the borrower;
- the multiple holder obligation (unless specified as non-applicable in the trade confirmation), which is satisfied if more than three holders hold the obligation that triggers the restructuring credit event, and where at least two-thirds of the holders agree to the event.[29]

The restructuring must be coercive; that is, it must be imposed directly by a borrower or a government by way of announcement or decree, or must result from an agreement between a borrower or government authority and a sufficient number of obligation holders to become binding all the

[26] A currency re-denomination becomes relevant as a restructuring credit event for EMU countries which carry a rating below AAA and re-denominate their debt into a local currency when leaving the EMU. See Mahadevan et al. (2012).

[27] Bruyere et al. (2006) provide an example of step-up coupons of corporate bonds which do not trigger a restructuring credit event given their inclusion in the bond documentation at issuance.

[28] Credit event backstop date: 60 calendar days before the date on which a request has been raised to the ISDA determination committee to determine whether or not a credit event has occurred (credit event resolution request date).

[29] If the obligation in effect is a corporate bond, the two-thirds requirement is automatically fulfilled provided that the bond is held by more than three holders. See Haworth (2011).

holders. There is a fine line between a voluntary debt restructuring which triggers the event and those which do not. If more than the required threshold but not all holders consent to a voluntary restructuring which is then binding on all holders, that is, due to a collective action clause (CAC), then the CDSs are triggered. This happened to Uruguay in 2003 and Greece in 2012. The majority decision under the CAC bound all holders, including those not agreeing to the debt restructuring – which also calls into question the voluntary nature of the restructuring.

CDS trade with different restructuring conventions, namely

- no restructuring (**No R**),
- old restructuring (**Old R**) or full restructuring (Full R),
- modified restructuring (**Mod-R** or MR), and
- modified modified restructuring (**Mod-Mod-R** or MMR).

The modified restructuring was published in May 2001 as the Restructuring Supplement and has been applied to CDS trade confirmations for U.S., Australian, and New Zealand reference entities. However, it was not adopted as a market standard for Europe, Japan, or Asia. The modified modified restructuring was introduced by the 2003 ISDA Credit Derivatives Definitions, which has been the market standard for European reference entities ever since. The background of the modified restructuring is related to the impact of interest rates on long-dated bonds, which can result in deeply discount prices for those bonds. Without any maturity limitations as in the original old restructuring style, a CDS buyer may deliver these bonds rather than the higher-valued loans or bonds for which the hedge was originally intended. This effectively creates a cheapest-to-deliver option for the protection buyer, with an implied sensitivity to interest rates. Examples of a situation where long-dated deep-discount bonds were delivered to the protection seller after a credit event are the cases of U.S. insurance company Conseco, which triggered a restructuring credit event in 2000, and Xerox in 2002. The Mod-R and Mod-Mod-R provisions restrict the maturity of the deliverable obligations to prevent the buyer from delivering those discount obligations, thereby substituting more valuable and expensive (restructured) debt. However, valuing the Mod-R or Mod-Mod-R provision is generally difficult and subject to the specific case, as the restructuring can affect the range of corporate liabilities quite differently. Unlike hard credit events, such as failure to pay or bankruptcy, where there should be no differences in the valuation of the concerned obligations of the same borrower and the ranking, regardless of their maturity and asset type, in a restructuring credit event substantial price discrepancies between loans and bonds with different maturities, margins or coupons, currencies, and governing

Table 7.2 Overview of restructuring credit event conventions

Convention	Details	Corporate CDS[30]	Sovereign CDS[31]
No R	Restructuring is excluded as a credit event	North America	
Old R	Restructuring included as a credit event with settlement like for bankruptcy or failure to pay. Any deliverable obligations with a maturity of less than 30 years are deliverable.	Subordinated European Insurance Emerging Europe Japan Asia Latin America	Western Europe Emerging Europe and Middle East Japan Asia Latin America
Mod-R or MR	Restructuring included as a credit event. Additionally, the following limitations apply for contracts triggered by the CDS buyer: Maturity limitation:[32] CDS buyer is prevented from delivering a deliverable obligation with a final maturity later than the earlier of • 30 months following the date of the restructuring • the latest final maturity of the longest restructured bond or loan[33] Transferability:[34]the deliverable obligation must be transferable on the delivery date without the necessity to obtain any consent.	Australia New Zealand	Australia New Zealand

Mod-Mod-R or MMR	Restructuring included as a credit event. Additionally, the following limitations apply for contracts triggered by the CDS buyer: Maturity limitation:[35] CDS buyer is prevented from delivering a deliverable obligation with a final maturity later than • 60 months following the date of the restructuring for restructured bonds or loans, or • 30 months following the date of the restructuring for all other deliverable obligations • the scheduled termination date Transferability:[36] the deliverable obligation must be transferable on the delivery date without the need to obtain any consent.	Europe

[30] See Haworth (2011).

[31] See Haworth (2011).

[32] Restructuring maturity limitation provision. No limitation date applies if the CDS seller triggers the contract except the general restriction of the maximum of 30-year maturity of the deliverable obligation.

[33] The exception is that debt that matures before the scheduled maturity of the CDS can be delivered even if the maturity is beyond the maximum 30 months time horizon.

[34] Fully transferable obligation provision. Loans must be able to be assigned or novated on the delivery date without anyone's consent.

[35] Modified restructuring maturity limitation provision. No limitation date applies if the CDS seller triggers the contract except the general restriction of the maximum of 30-year maturity of the deliverable obligation.

[36] Conditionally transferable obligation provision. Loans must be able to be assigned or novated on the delivery date without anyone's consent; or, where the consent is required, it may not be unreasonably withheld or delayed to fulfil this requirement.

laws can occur.[37] The different style of provisions has been subject to heated debates among market practitioners, resulting in bifurcated markets when the users of CDSs were unable to agree on a single standard. Nonetheless, names trading with different restructuring conventions are rare because the conventions are consistently applied within the respective countries. Since 2009, when the SNAC and Standard European Contract (STEC) were established, single name CDSs for U.S. corporates trade No R, in line with the CDX indices, which are composed of U.S. firms. In any event, most restructurings in the U.S. fall under chapter 11 of the U.S. Bankruptcy Code, which automatically constitutes a bankruptcy credit event. Therefore, it provides little added value to incorporate the restructuring credit event into the contract for corporates domiciled in the U.S. By contrast, Basel II explicitly reduces the capital relief through CDS hedges if the restructuring event is excluded, which will likely continue to be the key driver for maintaining the Mod-Mod-R convention for European corporate CDSs. In general, the Mod-Mod-R is less restrictive than the Mod-R, which favours the protection buyer. The restructuring conventions are listed in Table 7.2.

Another important aspect of the restructuring credit event concerns the transferability of the loan. Loan documentations typically include a clause which gives the bank the right to terminate the loan if the borrower does not meet its obligations under the loan contract. Hence, in the case of the hard credit events, failure to pay, and bankruptcy, any non-transferability clause becomes ineffective since the bank is factually released from the requirement to obtain the borrower's consent when delivering the loan to the seller of the CDS. However, a restructuring of certain debt does not necessarily mean that the obligor fails in his or her duty on all outstanding debt, and for debt, explicit borrower consent to deliver the loan after the credit event is required. Some loan documentations permit the bank

[37] In the case of Greece, the market correctly anticipated that bonds issued under international law would likely fare better than those bonds governed by domestic law, which were already settled after an auction. Jersey et al. (2007) reported that back in 2004 a spread difference of 10 bps for Shaw Communications quoted as Mod-R and No R, whereas they observed that in general Mod-R contracts tended to trade approximately 5% wider than No R contracts. They concluded that the spread differences reflected the expectation of market participants regarding the probability of a restructuring event. Since the different conventions also differ in relation to the credit grade of a CDS reference entity with a high yield in the U.S. generally trading No R, a situation where more than one convention is applied to the CDS of a particular corporate may occur for names which cross the line, i.e. fallen angels which were originally investment grade but have been downgraded, or rising stars which were born high yield and made their way up to investment grade. Spread differentials for those names may reflect of the valuation impact of not only the different restructuring provisions but also the specific composition of the markets regarding the type of investor for high yield versus investment-grade debt.

to sell or transfer the loan without notification to the borrower, but in many cases the bank's clients want to ensure that their ultimate creditor is known and acceptable to them. Therefore the transferability of the loan has to be ensured – if necessary by means of a separate agreement with the borrower.

This is particularly relevant for loan hedges within the scope of hedge accounting for credit risk (HCAR). Loans selected as hedged items must be deliverable when it comes to a physical settlement. Although the definition of a financial guarantee specifically requires the transferability of the defaulted asset, restructuring is excluded from the applicable credit events. The reason for this is related to the 'soft' nature of the restructuring – even though a restructuring credit event is determined by the DC, it may not directly result in losses for the debt holders of the firm in question. For instance, in the case of the Paris, France–based company Thomson, a payment deferral triggered the restructuring credit event even through on the deferred date, no failure to pay occurred. In the case of a financial guarantee, however, the protection buyer is compensated only for losses incurred. Consequently, it is possible, if not likely, that loan-loss

Case Study 7. Thomson Restructuring Credit Event

Thomson, today known as Technicolor, was seen as the test case of the Mod-Mod-R convention shortly after the implementation of the Small Bang protocol, since it was a member of various (linear and tranched) iTraxx, HiVol and Crossover index series, as well as a reference entity to a range of CDSs, CDS options, and CDOs. Because of that, the notional amount outstanding in Thomson credit derivatives was comparably large and far exceeded the company's debt. Additionally, the widespread consideration meant that various market participants were active in that name – from asset managers, hedge funds, bank portfolio managers, and insurance companies to traders and correlation desks, all of which were following different strategies and motivations.

On July 24, 2009, the French media-components manufacturer Thomson announced that it had signed a restructuring agreement with a majority of its senior creditors.[38] A statement released by the firm on August 9, 2009, indicated that Thomson had deferred principal payments under a private placement, due in June 2009, with the agreement of 'a sufficient number of holders to bind all holders'.[39] The wording of the statement met the definition of a restructuring credit event, which was determined accordingly by the ISDA determination

[38] See www.technicolor.com

[39] See Haworth (2011). Thomson agreed on a waiver and forbearance on the 6.5% notes due on June 17, 2009.

committee.[40] On October 6, 2009, ISDA published a list of deliverables for the Thomson auction which consisted of private placements and revolving credit facilities (RCF), split into three separate tranches. Sellers of CDSs had two days, until October 8, 2009, and CDS buyers; five days, until October 13, 2009, to trigger their CDSs. Before the auction took place on October 22, 2009, CDS holders had to assess the economic implications of triggering the CDS, since it was difficult to anticipate how many buy and sell orders would be submitted to the auction. The ISDA excluded bonds and loans which were subject to the restructuring agreement as deliverable obligations. As a result of Thomson's statement that the restructuring was agreed by a *majority* of holders, only a small amount of the debt outstanding was expected to be delivered into the auction. Three auctions were held, namely for the 0–2.5 year, the 2.5–5 year and the 5–7.5 year bucket. Contracts with maturities matching the scheduled termination dates were allocated to the respective buckets. Since the deliverable obligations for the short-dated auctions were also deliverable into the other, longer-dated buckets, market participants, and research analysts anticipated that the recovery value of the shortest bucket was likely to be the lowest. This assumption turned out to be correct. A strategic positioning of protection buyers, conscious of this consideration, presumably accelerated this effect. The outcome of the three auctions was as follows:[41]

Table 7.3 Recovery values from Thomson restructuring credit event

Bucket	**0–2.5 Years**	**2.5–5 Years**	**5–7.5 Years**
Recovery value (%)	96.25	65.125	63.25

Only a few months after the restructuring credit event, Thomson experienced a bankruptcy credit event. The recovery value of 77.75 per cent determined by the auction on December 10, 2009, closely matched the prices of private placements trading in the secondary market at that time. By contrast, the company offered the note holders 5 per cent of face value for perpetual notes, more in line with their status as equity substitutes. When in October 2009 Thomson released the details of the draft plan for the 'procédure de sauvegarde' which aimed at the going concern of the firm, holders of the perpetual notes who did not accept the offer were threatened with loss of any future coupon payments even if the company opted to distribute cash to shareholders through dividends or by any other means.

The Thomson case uniquely displays not only the various options CDS buyers and sellers have in the context of a restructuring credit event but also the decisions which have to be taken under uncertainty. Moreover, it shows that a company in distress must take into consideration of implications that

[40] Thomson, August 12, 2009, restructuring credit event.
[41] Source: Markit.

CDS hedges (and investments) for the strategic positioning of their creditors. Essentially, a loan portfolio manager has to decide either to agree to a restructuring as proposed by the borrower and not to trigger the CDS contract, or to trigger the CDS and participate in the auction following the credit event. All else being equal, the decision hinges very much on both the soundness of the restructuring plan and the expected outcome of the recovery determined at the auction. However, if and only if the credit asset is perfectly hedged in terms of notional and maturity and further presents a deliverable obligation, then the hedger is indifferent as to whether to trigger or not. In all other cases – for instance, when the hedge matures before the hedged item or the hedged debt does not qualify as a deliverable – the outcome of the alternatives can vary substantially. In general, CDS contracts that include the restructuring credit event provision offer a potential earlier exit option, which nonetheless is complex to value.

provisions have to be built for events described as a restructuring, even though the credit risk is mitigated through a financial guarantee.

According to Big Bang protocol, the DC determines whether or not a restructuring event has occurred. Once a restructuring credit event has been confirmed, both protection buyers and protection sellers have the right (but not the obligation) to trigger their CDS contracts. A major difference between a 'soft' restructuring credit event and a 'hard' credit event, such as bankruptcy or failure to pay, which triggers the CDS automatically, is that in a soft restructuring the credit event trigger is optional for both the buyer and seller of protection. This means that neither party is required to trigger the CDS. When the final list of deliverable obligations is published by ISDA, the protection seller has two business days, and the buyer has five business days, in which to trigger the CDS. There are two considerations to be taken into account when deciding whether or not to trigger a transaction. First, the auction process for restructuring differs from the approach for hard credit events, leaving the protection buyer and seller potentially exposed to significantly diverging prices depending on (a) the maturity of the CDS contract and (b) whether the CDS buyer or seller triggers the contract. Given that the maturity of the contract determines which obligations are deliverable into a particular contract following a restructuring event, it may be required to hold as many auctions as there are CDS maturities in the market. Second, the decision to trigger a CDS will be based on an assessment of the contract value at the auction compared to the expected value of the CDS post the auction. Therefore, some assumptions regarding the outcome of the auction process under the restructuring credit event have to be made – which requires a sound knowledge of the auction process as well as a view on CDS notional outstanding and debt that might serve as a deliverable, by amount, type, currency, and maturity, in order to anticipate certain supply and demand imbalances which drive the recovery rate at the auction. The valuation of the CDS post-auction is by and large determined by the probability of a hard credit event at a later stage. The survival of the restructured firm clearly depends on a variety of factors, but the most striking one for the nearer-term future is whether the proposed restructuring is sufficient to keep the company afloat.

7.3 Settlement after a credit event

The previous chapter described credit events that trigger a CDS and ultimately result in compensation payments from the CDS seller to the CDS buyer for the credit losses of the hedged obligation. Now, the next step is to look at how the recovery amount and the time when payments arrive or are made are determined. A holder of default protection basically has two options. The first option is to transfer the defaulted asset to the protection seller, which makes any further considerations regarding appropriate loss compensation redundant for the hedger as he or she receives the full national amount of the defaulted asset in exchange for the asset. In some cases (for reasons to be explained later) protection buyers continue to own the troubled asset and therefore opt for recoveries paid in cash. In order to better understand the development of the settlement process following a credit event, it is helpful to start with the origins of the physical delivery of the assets before explaining the auction-derived cash settlement.

7.3.1 Physical settlement

Under the 2003 ISDA definitions, CDS contracts were settled physically after a credit event, meaning the CDS protection buyer transferred the defaulted debt to the protection seller for a payment of the notional value of the debt. If the buyer did not own any deliverable obligation, it had to buy one in the secondary market to avoid a termination of the contract without any payment. Naturally, no uncertainty about recovery existed for the protection buyer, as the protection seller had to fully reimburse the holder of the hedged asset for the notional amount of the bond or loan granted. In a first step, either the buyer or seller of the CDS delivered a credit event notice to the CDS counterparty, together with the notice of publicly available information, in which the occurrence of the credit event was documented based on information from a trusted source, including international media news; information provider such as Bloomberg, Dow Jones, or Reuters; or company announcements. Delivery of the credit event notice and notice of publicly

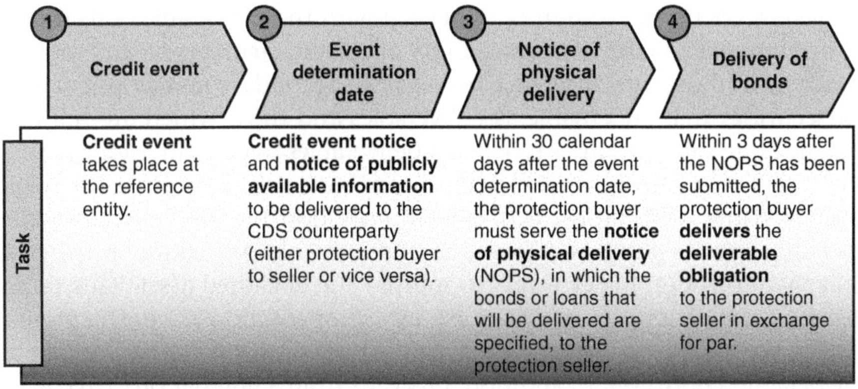

Figure 7.5 Four steps of physical settlement after a credit event under the 2003 ISDA credit definitions

available information constituted the event determination date. The physical delivery of the deliverable obligation had to take place within 30 business days after the event determination date. In order to deliver credit assets to the protection seller, the CDS buyer had to serve the notice of physical settlement (NOPS) within 30 calendar days after the credit event notice. In the NOPS the protection buyer specified the bonds or loans to be delivered to the protection seller. Finally, the protection buyer delivered the bonds or loans which qualified as deliverable obligations to the protection seller within three days of the NOPS submission, in exchange for par or the physical settlement amount. If the principal amount of the delivered debt instruments was less than the CDS notional amount, the buyer received less cash accordingly. Accrued but unpaid interest was excluded from the loss compensation.

However, to resolve operational inefficiencies arising from physical settlement, a new procedure allowing for cash settlement was introduced by ISDA in 2005. The physical delivery as described above represents a substantial amount of work, as each contract has to be managed and settled individually. Moreover, the notional amount of CDS contracts outstanding in many cases significantly exceeds the amount of debt of the reference entity serving as a deliverable to a CDS. As a result, prices of the eligible deliverables can be heavily distorted by a 'run' on relevant debt securities following the credit event in what is known as a 'short squeeze'.[42] This poses a problem, in particular for portfolio managers, when hedging loans which did not satisfy the criteria for deliverable obligations; for instance, loans denominated in a currency other than the standard currencies. Even though the

[42] When Delphi experienced a credit event in 2005, \$2 bn of deliverable obligations were confronted with about \$20 bn of CDS notional amount outstanding. See Jersey et al. (2007).

hedged credit risk may be fully correlated with the deliverable obligations, meaning subject to the same probability of default, credit event, and capital-structure ranking, the difference between the secondary market prices paid for securities that are eligible as deliverables and those which are not can deviate quite substantially – if the non-deliverables trade at all. Hence, using a CDS as a proxy hedge carried a significant basis risk. The cash settlement, known as the 'CDS protocol', provides a solution for this problem while also allowing for physical delivery, as under the old procedure, in the case that the protection buyer wants to transfer the defaulted asset. This point deserves some attention since a pure cash compensation leaves the protection buyer with some uncertainty as to the final outcome of the workout of the defaulted borrower. In addition, proceeds from a liquidation arrive with a considerable time delay and involve significant resources in terms of the work time of dedicated specialists, which may be expensive. On the other hand, a credit event does not indicate the necessity of a liquidation. In some cases, a restructuring and going concern may prove to be a better alternative compared to a gone concern in which the borrower will be dissolved. If a bank opts to preserve the client relationship after a credit event, it is mandatory to continue to hold the respective debt, or even to buy out other lenders, to become the driver of the restructuring. Under these circumstances, a cash settlement is in the best interest of the CDS buyer – as long as it yields *in principal* a result which comes close to the losses from the restructuring or the loss given default in a liquidation scenario.

7.3.2 Cash settlement and auction mechanics

Cash settlement was introduced by the ISDA in 2005. This development of a standardized settlement process for all credit derivatives, including indices and tranches on indices, has significantly contributed to eliminating the basis risk of diverging recoveries between different debt products. The DC decides on the occurrence of the credit event and the eligible deliverable obligations and whether an auction settlement is required,[43] and, if it is, the terms of the auction. ISDA subsequently publishes the list of deliverable obligations. In the case of a hard credit event, meaning everything but a restructuring credit event, all CDSs are automatically triggered. A single auction determines one fixed recovery at which both all single name CDSs and indices, tranches, options, and others are settled. (The somewhat more complex settlement process for a restructuring credit event will be described later.) Through the implementation of the Big Bang and Small Bang protocols in 2009, the cash settlement procedure

[43] If the amount of CDS notional outstanding is insignificant, the DC may decide not to conduct an auction.

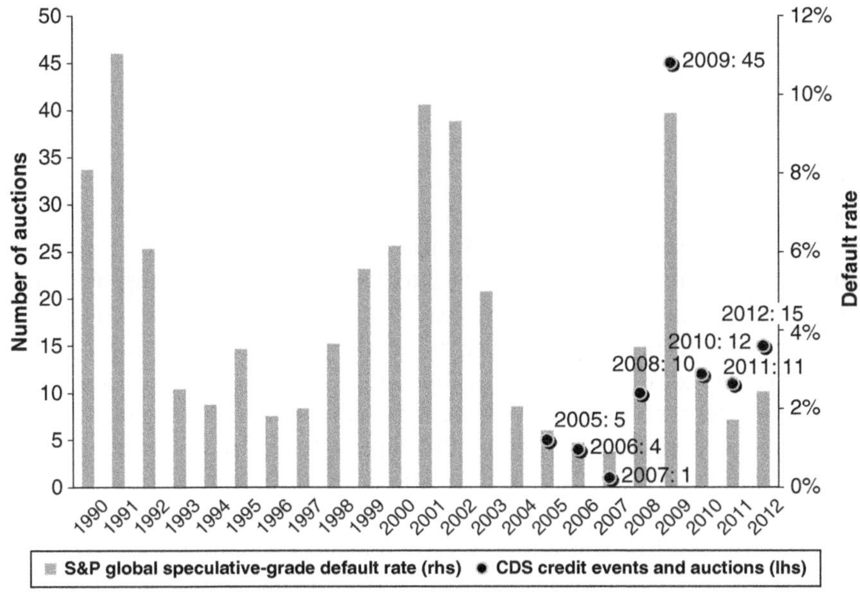

Figure 7.6 Standard and Poor's global speculative-grade default rate versus CDS credit events and auctions

Source: Own, Markit, Standard and Poor's (2010 Annual Global Corporate Default Study and Rating Transitions, March 30, 2011).

was hard-wired into the CDS contracts, meaning the hitherto optional application of the protocol was replaced by the auction as the new standard. This is binding for all contracts, which now enter the auction process following a credit event, the only exception being the restructuring credit event, where both protection buyer and protection seller have the option to trigger the CDS contract. CDS protocols for defaulted firms and sovereigns are published by ISDA, while auctions are administered by Markit and CreditEx.[44] As one might intuit, the number of auctions held in recent years has been fairly significant, reflecting the spike in default rates to record levels in the U.S. and Europe. In total, more than 100 auctions have been conducted since the introduction of the CDS auction procedure in 2005, with a peak of 45 credit events in 2009.

The auction process is composed of two steps to derive the final cash settlement or recovery. In the first stage, an indicative recovery rate, called *inside market midpoint* (IMM), is determined, together with the outstanding notional of bonds and loans to be settled physically. The IMM is a

[44] See www.isda.org for CDS protocols and www.creditfixings.com for auction results.

kind of preliminary recovery rate. In order to derive the IMM, participating dealers establish indicative two-way markets (bid and offer, at which they would be prepared to buy and sell) for the deliverable obligations in a predefined size and predefined bid-offer spread. These are known as the *initial market quotation amount* and *maximum initial market bid-offer spread,* respectively. Depending on the liquidity and range of defaulted assets eligible as deliverables, the size restriction is usually set between \$2 mn and \$5 mn for senior and up to \$2 mn for subordinated debt, while the bid-offer is submitted at a spread of 2 to 3 points, both varying by credit. Additionally, dealers send in physical settlement requests which express their aggregated interest in buying or selling defaulted assets through the auction on behalf of themself and their clients. Note that for senior CDSs, only senior debt is deliverable, whereas for subordinated CDSs, both senior and subordinated debt is eligible. Bids and offers which can be crossed, meaning that the bid is higher than the offer, or vice versa, are matched and eliminated by the auction administrator. The remaining quotes are ranked in descending order for bids and in ascending order for offers. The inside bid is then the average of the best 50 per cent of the remaining bids, whereas the inside offer is the average of the best 50 per cent of the remaining offers. The inside market midpoint is simply the average of these two, rounded to the nearest 1/8. Dealers who quote offside the market have to pay a penalty. Once stage 1 is finalized, dealers have two to three hours to evaluate the amount and direction of the *net open interest,* which arises when the protection buyers want to settle physically whereas the protection seller does not, or vice versa. If the net open interest is zero, the IMM becomes the final price and the auction ends.[45] In stage 2, the participants submit limit orders to buy or sell bonds through participating bidders in order to close the open interest of the first round (Dutch auction). The auction administrator will match market orders until the open interest is cleared. The final price or recovery rate is then the price of the last limit order used to fill the open interest. This final recovery rate is then applied to all bonds, loans, and CDSs entered in the auction. Now that the recovery is determined through the auction, the protection seller pays the notional amount of the CDS contract minus the recovery to the protection buyer. If the protection buyer submitted the physical delivery notice to the protection buyer, the deliverable will be sold at the recovery rate, independent of the type or maturity of the asset. Hence, the CDS

---

[45] Alternatively, if the net open interest is selling bonds or loans but limit bids are insufficient to fill the net open interest, the final price is set at zero. In the opposite direction, if the net open interest is to buy bonds or loans but limit offers do not fill the net open interest, the final price is par. In any case the final price cannot go above par for obvious reasons.

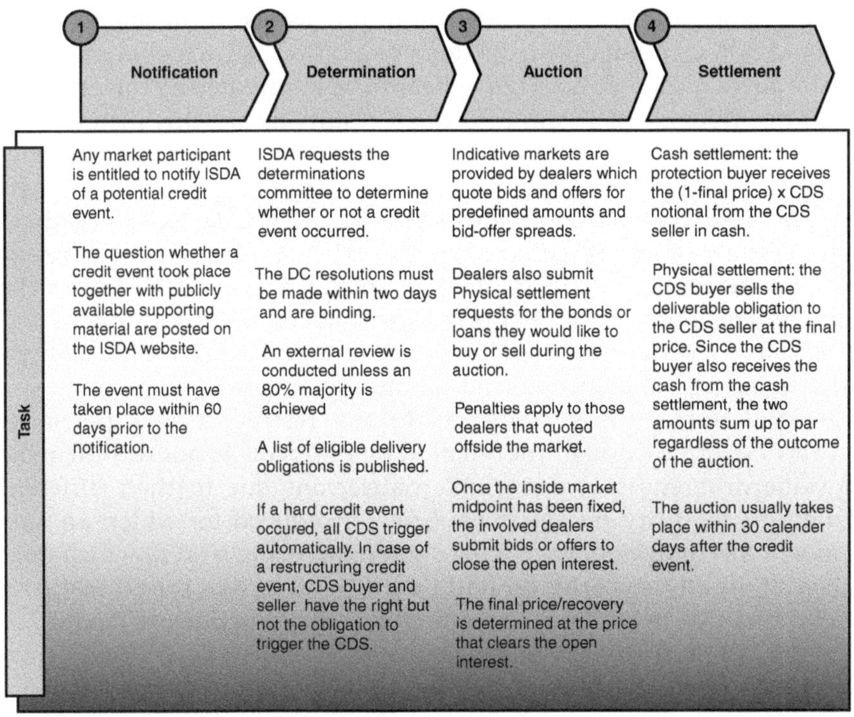

Figure 7.7 CDS auction process after a credit event

buyer will always receive in total the notional amount of the CDS, no matter the auction-determined final price.

The design of the auction preserves the economics of the physical settlement, which included the inherent cheapest-to-deliver option that the CDS buyer owns. However, the process has been criticized as producing systematically biased results, with price distortions in the opposite direction to the open interest; that is CDS auctions tend to overprice bonds or loans when the net open interest shows an oversupply of bonds or loans, and vice versa.[46] For instance, protection sellers have an interest in reducing the payout as much as possible, and therefore aggressively bid for an overhang of bonds in stage 2 of the auction process to drive up the price and the final recovery, which minimizes the cash settlement amount. Protection buyers are not in a position to counteract, since they are excluded from submitting sell orders when the net open interest is to sell bonds. The same holds true for the other way around; that is, protection buyers submit offers that are as low as

[46] See Du and Zhu (2011).

possible when there is open demand to buy assets in the auction. The rational but manipulative behaviour of auction participants provoked by the auction scheme does not appear to be eliminated by the price cap and price floors, which aim to prevent results from being distorted by large limit orders submitted off-market, in particular when there is only a small net open interest. Even though the current approach may not be optimal, there is a common sense that the auction-derived final prices appropriately reflect the market view on the value of defaulted assets. If no auction is held – that is, due to a limited number of CDSs – or the auction does not yield a final price, the fallback settlement method as specified in the CDS trade confirmation applies. This is usually a physical settlement, but cash settlement is also possible.

For the restructuring credit event, the restructuring supplement became effective through the Small Bang protocol. To address the issue of value differences of deliverable obligations due to their different durations, maturity buckets have been introduced for which an auction will be conducted. Except for old restructuring (Old R) which does not contain any maturity limitation, a single auction for all maturity buckets will be held. Possible auction maturity buckets are 2.5, 5, 7.5, 10, 12.5, 15, and 20 years. Deliverable obligations and CDSs are then allocated to these buckets. In general, an obligation is assigned to those maturity buckets whose date is after the maturity date of the obligation. The DC publishes a list of deliverable obligations for each bucket. Once the final list arrives, a CDS buyer has two business days and a CDS seller, five business days to trigger the CDS. CDSs triggered by the protection buyer are allocated to the maturity buckets in a way that ensures that at least one deliverable obligation matures before the CDS contract expires. Otherwise, CDSs assigned to a bucket with only longer-dated deliverables fall into the next earlier bucket, in what is known as the *rounding down convention*. An exception to the rule is the 2.5-year bucket, since there is no earlier bucket. If the CDS seller triggers the contract, the CDS is allocated to the longest-maturity bucket, which enables the protection buyer to deliver any deliverable obligation. This may turn out to be a risk for investors who have offset a CDS short position by a CDS long position with equal notional and maturity, since the CDS may be allocated to different buckets. Furthermore, as the auction per each maturity bucket is likely to yield different results, a basis risk may be created. If both the CDS buyer and seller trigger, the rule for the protection seller–triggered CDS applies. Unlike hard credit events, where the transactions are automatically triggered, the information about the trigger has to be provided to the DTCC by the CDS seller or buyer. If there is an insufficient number of triggered CDSs for a maturity bucket, the DC may decide not to hold an auction. In this case, the movement option allows a CDS buyer and CDS seller to move the CDS within three days to a bucket for which an auction is conducted. Again, it matters whether protection buyer or protection seller moves the CDS. If the latter moves, the CDS will be allocated to the latest bucket for which an auction takes place. If the protection buyer or both exercise the movement option, the CDS falls to the next earlier bucket with an auction. Although the auction process for a restructuring credit event looks complicated, the overarching aim – that the procedure should respect and reflect the peculiarities of the restructuring itself – seems to

Case Study 8. Greece Restructuring Credit Event

The European sovereign crisis, like no other debt restructuring, made visible the diverging and sometimes conflicting objects and constraints of stakeholders, investors, regulators, politicians and, in this particular case, the central banks, some of which played more than just one role. In the interest of financial stability, the ECB exerted pressure to avoid a restructuring or rescheduling but also held a significant amount of Greek government bonds where both rescheduling by way of duration extension and restructuring in the form of a significant debt haircut would have led to meaningful losses if not exempted. Politicians at the same time had to consider any action's knock-on effects to other European countries plagued by unsustainable debt loads – namely Ireland, Portugal and, more worryingly, Spain and Italy, given the huge numbers of their bonds which have to be refinanced in the coming years. Capital markets therefore had to weigh the most likely outcome of the numerous options and their effects on investments. However, unlike corporate debt, a large amount of Greek debt does not feature cross-default or negative pledge clauses. This in turn gave room to a number of restructuring alternatives which had to be taken into account when assessing the probability of a CDS trigger event. Since Greek sovereign bonds issued under Greek law had no collective action clauses, to avoid triggering a default would have required 100 per cent of investor consent to any voluntary restructuring proposal. In contrast, Greek government bond debt issued under English law has collective action clauses which need either 66 or 75 per cent bondholder consent[47] to binding modification of terms and conditions of the respective bonds. In principle, any unilateral or mandatory changes to the terms of bonds, including haircuts and maturity extensions, meet the definition of a restructuring credit event and therefore trigger a CDS credit event. With most of the Greek government bonds requiring the consent of all bondholders, a

[47] 66% of bondholder consent is required for bonds issued before 2004, with 75% thereafter.

voluntary debt exchange for all debt was highly unlikely. However, voluntary acceptance of a write-down does not constitute a credit event, meaning no credit event will be declared by the determinations committee, and consequently CDS will not indemnify the protection holders for the loss. The announcement by the Greek government on February 21, 2012, regarding the key terms of the proposed private sector initiative (PSI) as part of its economic reform program did not in itself constitute a credit event, which further heated up the public discussion about the effectiveness of the CDS as a hedging tool.

After a period of significant uncertainty about the possibility that a payout on Greek CDSs would be circumvented, on March 9, 2012, the ISDA Credit Derivatives Determinations Committee unanimously decided that a restructuring credit event on the Hellenic Republic resulted from the successful Greek debt restructuring. The press release issued by the Greek finance ministry contained a phrase that legally bound investors who opposed the proposed amendments to the bond documentations, thereby exactly matching the ISDA definition of actions which lead to a restructuring event.[48] Most market participants took this as an encouraging sign that governments ultimately move beyond the point of criticizing and blaming the CDS as a source of financial repression to an acceptance and collaboration with financial markets. According to the statement, Greece secured an 85.8 per cent participation rate in the PSI and completed an exchange of €177 bn of domestic law bonds into a series of 20 new bonds, which started trading soon afterwards. The Greek event was the largest sovereign restructuring in the history of the CDS, and the first for a Western European country. Since most market participants adhere to the Big Bang and Small Bang protocols, they were bound to the auction settlement and the final price derived at the auction. Ultimately, the payout from the Greek auction conducted on March 19, 2012, matched the losses from equivalent bond positions. The final payout from the CDS and index positions amounted to $2.89 bn, or 78.5 per cent of $3.68 bn net notional outstanding,[49] indicating that the vast majority of all Greek CDSs have been triggered. Since the credit event was a restructuring, triggering the CDS was optional. In order to facilitate an orderly settlement of the transaction concerned, ISDA published a uniform settlement agreement following the credit event. CDS holders signing the agreement confirmed the decision to trigger all

[48] See www.minfin.gr, press release PSI of March 9, 2012, for further details. ISDA announced that the exercise of 'collective action clauses to amend the terms of Greek law governed bond issues by The Hellenic Republic such that the right of all holders of the Affected Bonds to receive payments has been reduced' conformed to the definition of a restructuring credit event as set out under §4.7(a) of the ISDA 2003 Credit Derivatives Definitions, amended by the July 2009 Supplement. See www2.isda.org.

[49] The gross notional of CDS on Greek amounted to approximately $69 bn as of March 2, 2012. Source: www.dtcc.com.

its contracts. The recovery of 21.5 was very close to the prices at which the Greek CDS and domestic law bonds were trading prior to and post the restructuring. Other assets eligible as a deliverable obligation – for instance, Greek international bonds; state-guaranteed debt; or bonds of state-owned institutions, such as Hellenic Railway; and short-dated T-bills – were trading at comparably higher levels, since their owners were holding out for better terms than those offered for the restructuring of the domestic bonds. Hence, the PSI bonds were the cheapest-to-deliver obligation and consequently drove the final price. The IMM, which resulted from the first stage of the auction process in which 15 dealers bid on the approved Greek deliverable obligations, was derived at 21.75. A smaller-than-expected net open interest of €291.6 mn to sell marginally lowered the IMM to the final price of 21.5. However, this outcome was achieved more by chance than by design. Unlike the case of Thomson, the use of the collective action clause (CAC) by the Greek government triggered the CDS and resulted in an immediate haircut on the old bonds, so that ISDA was not able to conduct the auction before the bonds were restructured. If the new debt had traded significantly higher, the payout of the CDS would have been correspondingly lower, e leaving losses partially uncovered on initially perfectly hedged assets that were deliverable into the CDS. In particular, basis investors[50] with long credit positions in Greek domestic law bonds were exposed to this kind of recovery risk, which arose from the potential difference between the economic recovery of the bonds and the final CDS price. It should be noted that the market did not perfectly anticipate this issue, since it was possible to unwind a basis package near par prior to the credit event. To complicate the matter further, holders of Greek domestic law bonds that were restructured through the PSI received $31.5 for each $100 of unrestructured bonds, which effectively created an imbalance between the initial CDS hedge position of par equivalent and the bonds, assuming a full hedge. Thus CDS buyers that agreed to the restructuring were short bonds going into the auction and had either to buy additional bonds to cover the short, unwind CDS amounts exceeding the new bond notionals, or accept the cash settlement, which could have been significantly different from the losses from the bond haircut.

The Greek credit event also highlighted the importance of considering the difference between bonds issued under domestic and foreign law. For instance, it is quite likely that holders of Greek foreign law bonds will realize lower losses compared to the PSI debt swap offer, which imposed

[50] A basis investor buys a package consisting of (a) CDS protection on a reference obligation with a lower spread and (b) the higher-yielding reference obligation in identical notional amounts and maturity to receive periodic income from the yield difference of the two (the basis) or to benefit from a decrease of the yield difference. In the latter case, a basis package shows a positive mark-to-market since the gains on one leg exceed the losses on the other.

an effective 75 per cent haircut on the net present value of bonds issued under domestic law. A prominent case is the European Central Bank, which announced that its €4.27 bn holding of the €14.4 bn non-PSI eligible bond issue that matured at the end of March 2012 has been fully repaid. Moreover, on May 16 the Greek government decided to repay €435 mn of bonds due the day before to avoid a hard credit default event, which would have triggered cross-default clauses on other bonds remaining outstanding after the March 2012 restructuring. Approximately €3.3 bn of €6 bn outstanding debt appears to have such cross-default clauses. Greece's decision will make it very difficult to achieve an agreement similar to the PSI in future restructurings. The two-tiered approach for international versus domestic bonds weighed heavily on the new bonds offered as part of the restructuring, with 10-year notes trading below €0.14 after the announcement to redeem the debt maturing in May in full. This price compared to the value of €0.2878 for those bonds the day after the auction had been conducted in March, implying a more than 50 per cent loss for investors who stuck to the exchanged debt. It is clear that the decline in prices of the new securities reflected concerns that Greece would have to leave the Eurozone eventually, with unpredictable consequences for the country. Although the prices for the Greek government bonds recovered significantly after the ECB's pledge 'to do whatever it takes to save the euro', the various stages of the Greek drama highlight the important aspects and strategic choices for both the debtor and the lender in the context of sovereign restructurings.

The outcome of the SNS Reaal nationalization and Greek credit event is taken by market experts as a call to the ISDA Credit Steering Committee to revise the concept of the corporate and sovereign CDS to maintain its status as a suitable risk-management product. Concerns are well founded that future restructuring credit events, which could become more common for sovereigns, could leave the holders of credit protection with severe losses. Ensuring that the payout under a CDS matches the losses or haircuts on the hedged asset, therefore, is key to the survival of sovereign CDSs. The problems arising from the 60-day look-back period that is a standard clause in CDS contracts warrants equal attention. Dealers were confronted with a completely closed market for the 60 days following the credit event determination date, since CDS buyers and the sellers of new CDSs were entitled to trigger immediately after trade inception during this period. The lack of CDS trading has been blamed in part for dislocations not only at the long end of the new Greek sovereign bond curve but also at shorter maturities during that time. This issue was also new to the market, since trading in a name typically does not pick up this soon after a credit event emerges. By contrast, the debate about whether the concept of CDS is waterproof if all debt owners consent to an unfavourable loan amendment or bond documentation appears to be missing the point. No derivative, whatever its design, will alter the decision of its owner to deliberately forgo any loss compensation.

be achieved. This comes at the expense of a significantly more involved process, as several additional steps have to be taken into account and each auction bucket is kind of a settlement on its own, separate for senior and subordinated CDSs.

The case studies provided in this chapter emphasize the well-thought-through design of the CDS as an instrument, but they also highlight the pitfalls likely to be addressed near-term in order to reflect market practice and preserve the relevance of the product. Within the current process, there are several activities and corresponding decisions to be taken by a portfolio manager who hedged an obligation on whose borrower a credit event occurred. While Figure 7.8 is a simplified illustration of the steps in the process, the point here is that the hedger has various options until the final price or recovery is determined by the auction. First, the CDS can be unwound prior to the auction if there is an expectation that the gains on the CDS plus the recovery on the hedged asset at a later point in time add up to more than par. In other words, the actual mark-to-market profit of the hedge overcompensates for potential losses from liquidation. Unwinding the CDS is a superior

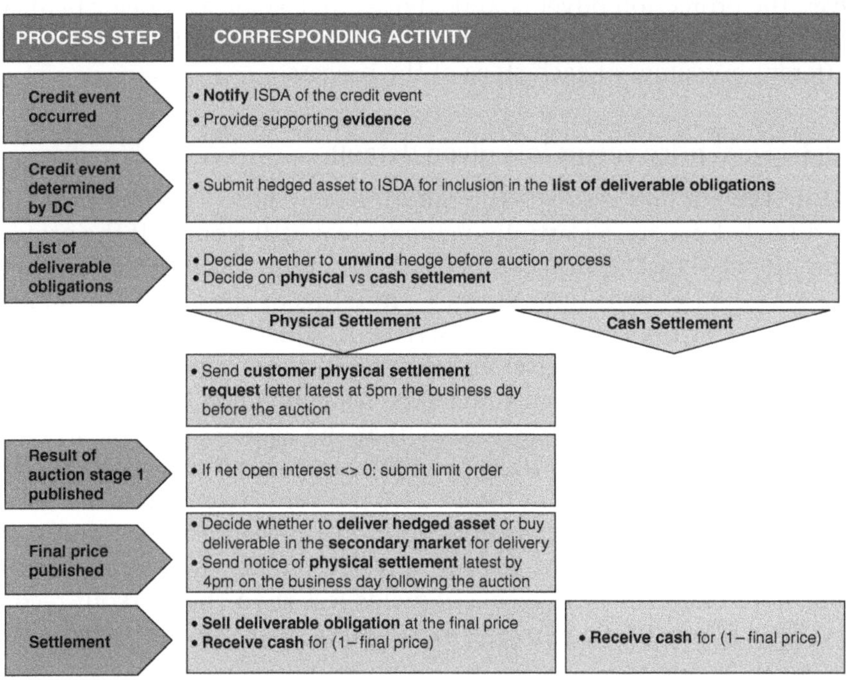

Figure 7.8 Activities and decisions to be taken after a credit event

strategy if the final price derived at the auction is expected to be lower than current gains and the hedger is prepared to keep the asset on the book. Alternatively, the CDS buyer can submit the hedged obligation to ISDA to ensure that physical delivery is an option. Once the list of deliverable obligations has been published, a decision has to be taken as to whether a physical delivery is preferred. At this stage, no decision has to be made on the deliverable itself; it may be the hedged asset or a cheaper asset that is bought in the secondary market. If it is clear that the asset should remain on the books because of other client-driven considerations, the protection buyer likely will opt for a cash settlement. If physical delivery has been chosen, another important measure is the submission of a limit order after the IMM has been determined, provided that the net open interest does not equal zero. Here the auction result can be influenced to achieve a higher recovery, which may be valuable if the hedger did decide to deliver an asset bought in the market in exchange for the originally hedged asset. It makes no difference if no asset but the originally hedged one will be delivered, though – the compensation payment will in any case be the notional amount of the CDS independent of the final price. Since CDSs offer these alternatives, the protection buyer is well advised to develop a strategic plan, as soon as the credit event becomes public, to be prepared to react to the different outcomes of each stage of the process.

7.3.3 Final price versus loss given default

While the auction resolves the question how much will be paid if a credit event occurs, a portfolio manager may still wonder if the protection provided by the CDS compensates for credit risk–related losses on the defaulted or restructured asset – in terms of the amount paid *and* the timing of the compensation payment. This is particularly important when the aim is to offset loan-loss provisions by gains from hedges while keeping the asset on the books. A comparison of final recoveries and final auction prices reveals that the average CDS recovery at 20.6 per cent is significantly below the average final recovery after the workout process, which is around 24.6 per cent.[51] Although the numbers are based on a small sample point-in-time observation and thus should serve as a rough guide only, it is nevertheless noticeable that in almost all cases the CDS recovery yields less than the workout recovery. This is consistent with the expectation that the additional costs

[51] See Musfeldt et al. (2012).

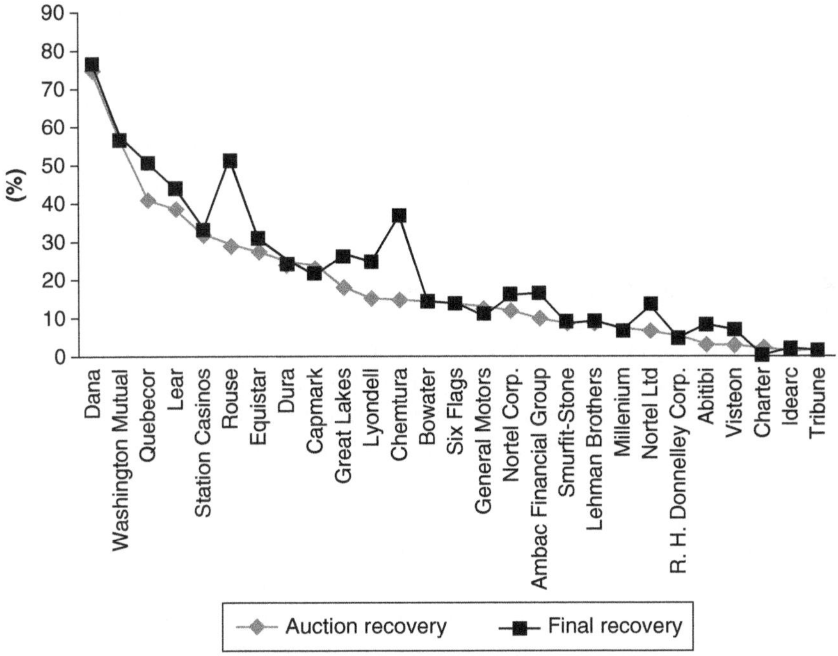

Figure 7.9 Auction recoveries versus final recoveries for a sample set of senior unsecured bonds

Source: Morgan Stanley Research, Musfeldt et al. (2012).

arising from legal advice, the involvement of specialists, and the later arrival of liquidation proceeds should be discounted in the CDS final auction price, provided efficient markets that correctly anticipate the workout results. Another way to look at the different recoveries is that the value added by the workout department equals the net present value of the amount of the proceeds from liquidation that exceeds the CDS auction recovery. If no reputational risks or client-specific strategy has to be taken into account, a bank maximizes the rate of return on defaulted assets via cash settlement if the costs of workout are anticipated to be below 4 per cent, whereas it would likely opt for a physical settlement if costs are higher. Since the average recovery statistically inversely correlates to default rates, meaning that a rise in default rates implies a higher loss given default (LGD), the uncertainty regarding the time value of money from the liquidation proceeds must be considered.

For CDS pricing purposes, the assumptions on recovery rates or final prices resulting from the auction appear to have a minor impact on CDS spreads.[50] It should be noted that pricing models provided by ISDA or Bloomberg usually assume deterministic recovery rates; that is, 40 per cent for senior unsecured debt, 20 per cent for subordinated debt, and 70 per cent for a CDS on first-lien leveraged finance loans. On the other hand, existing literature on CDS pricing often mistakes recovery rates as a stochastic quantity and equivalent to recoveries from workout. This is clearly not the case.

7.4 Succession events

An important aspect of CDSs and other debt instruments deals with corporate events in which one entity assumes the obligations of another entity – mergers, takeovers, leveraged buyouts (LBOs), amalgamation, consolidation, transfer of assets or liabilities, divestitures, demergers, spin-offs, and the like. The determinations committee decides whether a succession event has occurred. In general, CDSs are tied to the debt of a company; thus a succession event will likely change the CDS reference entity. Even a split of the CDS is possible, in which case the CDS may reference more than one entity, depending on the outcome of the corporate event. Unlike loans and bonds, where the decision of a company to relocate or buy back the debt is subject to the approval of the debt holders, a CDS will be mechanically allocated to the original or succeeding corporates, or both, according to the waterfall decision structure, as outlined in Figure 7.10.

To determine the successors of corporates, the relevant obligations have to be identified. They are defined as bonds or loans of the reference entity that are outstanding prior to the effective date of the succession event, excluding intracompany loans. It is necessary to interpret the scope of loans qualifying as relevant obligations with respect to to whether leasing, factoring, and other financing specialties and undrawn commitments are excluded. Introduced through the Big Bang protocol, market participants raise the resolution request directly to the ISDA determinations committee, which in turn decides whether an action constituted a succession event and, if so, the date it occurred and the successors. The determinations committee will us *best available information* to take an informed decision. Information must be made available within 14 calendar days after the effective date of the succession event; otherwise it will be dismissed. To be considered, a succession event must have occurred within 90 calendar days before the succession event resolution request date (succession event backstop

[50] See Schmidt (2007).

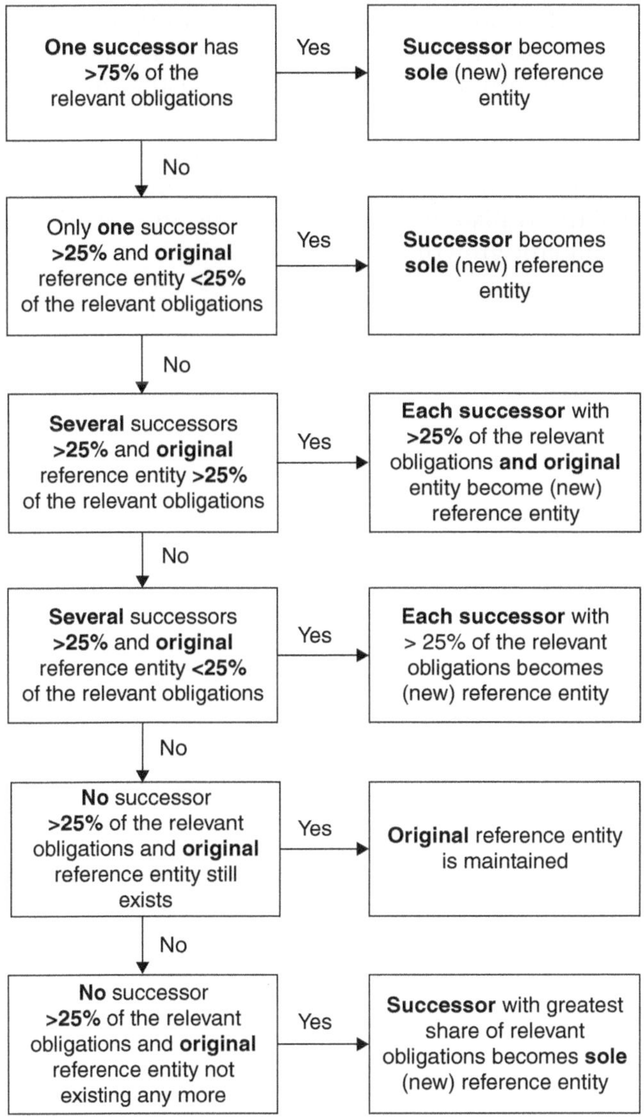

Figure 7.10 Cascading approach to determine a CDS successor
Source: Credit Suisse, Fixed Income Research, Schwarz et al. (2010).

date), the date at which the determinations committee is requested to determine whether or not a succession event occurred. Determining a succession event can be a tricky business, since not all corporate actions are fully outlined or even in the preliminary phase of planning when announced. Missing details relevant to decision making often include the distribution of debt after the action, information about the drawn and undrawn parts of the debt, the amount of guaranteed obligations, or the timing of the changes and the information about the changes.

The number of succession events is driven by the global M&A activity of larger, multinationally operating and listed companies, which in turn is reflective of the availability and cost of funds, stock market conditions, and global economic growth.

8
Loan Credit Derivatives, Subparticipations and Credit Indices

While CDSs represent the standard for micro level hedging, a new CDS subfamily has emerged to reference senior secured loans. These loans typically feature prepayment options and specify ranking and collateral in their documentation. Even though LCDSs never caught up with standard CDSs regarding tradeable sizes, they nonetheless provide an important hedging instrument for leveraged finance assets, which are characterized by higher default risk and lower loss given default due to their secured nature. We highlight the main product specifications and the rationale behind the distinct developments of LCDSs in Europe and the U.S. Since CDSs are mostly available for large, listed firms only, bank portfolio managers are increasingly assessing alternatives such as subparticipations to protect the risk of illiquid assets. This chapter continues with a discussion of the important aspects that arise when an investor remote to the borrower takes the default risk as well as the correspondent implications for the hedger. The last part of this chapter deals with credit indices, which are commonly used as highly liquid proxies for credit portfolio hedges. Although they do not cover obligor non-payment risks as specific, as do CDSs, LCDSs, or subparticipations, credit indices allow the management of spread risks in portfolios of a decent size.

8.1 Loan only credit derivatives – LCDSs

Loan credit default swaps, or LCDSs, are an innovation derived from vanilla CDSs. The underlying is a specific syndicated secured loan. Thus no other obligation category, that is, senior unsecured loan or bond obligation, qualifies as a deliverable (for more details, see §7.1.4, 'Reference and deliverable obligations'). LCDSs allow market participants to pursue strategies similar to those in which standard CDSs are used – namely, hedging, trading, and synthetically investing. Investment managers appreciate LCDS as a liquid, transaction cost–efficient and transparent alternative to funded cash positions such as the referenced loans themselves. At the same time, the LCDS structure includes features which, although derived from syndicated loan characteristics, may create significant differences compared to the underlying cash instrument. Those differences relate in particular to cash flows, return, and pricing. Differences also emerged within the LCDS contract specifications used in the U.S. and Europe. In Europe banks traditionally active in loan syndication apply LCDSs, to achieve regulatory capital relief from hedging; hence, they prefer a risk transfer instrument which is tied as closely as possible to the hedged underlying. By contrast, the contract standard developed in the U.S. mirrors the demand of institutional investors, which are the dominant users of LCDSs, and for this reason it puts an emphasis on tradability to facilitate market liquidity. The rapid growth of the syndicated loan market, in part driven by a surge in M&A activity and met by an equally strong demand from the new investor base of hedge funds and collateralized loan obligation (CLO) managers, contributed to accelerated efforts in 2006 to establish a new LCDS standard documentation. Corresponding indices were launched; for instance, the iTraxx LevX index (2006), which today trades as a senior index referencing to 75 first-lien loans and a subordinated index

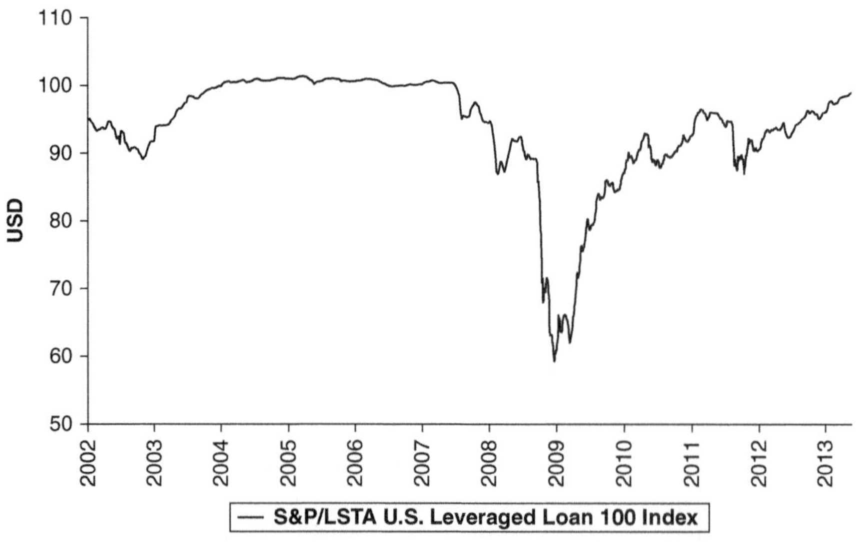

Figure 8.1 S&P/LSTA U.S. Leveraged Loan 100 Index
Data Source: Bloomberg.

composed of 45 second- and third-lien loans, and the LCDX in the U.S. (2007), which contains 100 names. However, the brewing financial crisis and other LCDS-specific issues, such as the early termination feature, prevented the product from exploiting its full potential. Consequently, ISDA published a new documentation for credit default swap contracts referencing North American loans, the 'Bullet LCDS', on April 5, 2010. While the documentation supersedes the *Syndicated Secured Loan Credit Default Swap Standard Terms Supplement* issued on May 22, 2007, the new contract does not constitute an industry-wide protocol that modifies existing contracts, as did the Small Bang and the Big Bang of 2009. The changes follow the feedback of market participants and aim to increase product liquidity and tap new investors. Although existing single contracts will be supported, which is particularly in the interest of portfolio managers hedging loans, it is expected that liquidity in contracts that do not conform to the new supplement will eventually diminish.

8.1.1 LCDS deliverables

One major difference between an LCDS and a CDS concerns the reference and deliverable obligation. Generally, LBO transactions are referenced by an LCDS, and so the peculiarities of those debt instruments are recognized. LCDS-eligible obligations typically include term loans and multicurrency loans or revolvers, but no bonds. For a European LCDS the reference obligation refers to all tranches or facilities of a syndicated loan of the reference entity if not otherwise stated in the trade confirmation. A partially or fully undrawn credit facility qualifies as a deliverable as long as it is not permanently reduced to the part drawn or cancelled and not excluded by 'Delivery of Undrawn Commitments' in the supplement. The total commitment, consisting of funded and unfunded parts, must be specified in the notice of physical delivery (NOPS). The LCDS contract specifies the seniority of liens; that is, first- or second-lien loans. First-lien refers to the line's seniority over other parts of a firm's capital structure and is usually collateralized or secured. Still high in the capital structure but subordinate in priority to claims and collateralization of first-lien loans are second or third liens, which are called 'junior' or 'mezzanine'. While LBOs – as the 'leveraged' in LBO indicates – exhibit a higher credit risk, the debt benefits from collateralization, with a comparably lower loss given default in the event of a failure. Hence, deliverable obligations are obligations that rank at least equal to the reference obligation and are secured by the same assets as the reference obligation. The protection buyer may deliver loans which rank higher than the reference obligation, even though this may not be the cheapest-to-deliver obligation. For U.S. LCDSs, deliverables include loans on the secured list or syndicated loans of equal or higher priority. (Sub)participations or assignments of participations are eligible as deliverables, provided the protection buyer is in a position to grant the protection seller contractual payment rights.

8.1.2 Information advantage

As a general rule, CDS protection sellers suffer from comparatively more restrictive access to debtor information. A loan portfolio manager who owns the loan and seeks to hedge the credit risk for capital relief or other reasons usually enjoys very detailed and timely borrower information. Banks perform at least a yearly credit review on latest available data provided by the client or other sources. In some cases, non-public information contributes to a superior assessment of the borrower's credit quality, provided the rating tools in place to distil the default probability out of the firm's data are sufficiently capable. While CDS typically refers to larger, often multinational and stock exchange–listed corporates that operate worldwide and routinely deal with a global investor base, information on borrowers of syndicated loans underlying LCDSs are more difficult to source and are most of the time private, with access given to the syndicate members and other direct holders of the debt. Since investors in an LCDS will have limited or no access to that information, they are at an information disadvantage. This is mitigated by the disclosure requirements of listed debt, which becomes relevant when a firm chooses to issue high yield debt as a complementary part of the capital structure, as is quite common.

8.1.3 Early termination

Unlike the standard CDS, which continues to exist even if there is no deliverable obligation outstanding, orphaned LCDS contracts are cancelled automatically when all the reference loans are called and not replaced within 30 days. Callable loans are loans where the obligor is entitled to repay, prepay, redeem, or otherwise discharge a loan prior to the final maturity in accordance with the terms of the loan documentation. Since loans relevant for LCDSs generally, and in Europe specifically, contain certain optionalities, such as the prepayment option, the upside potential of LCDSs for investors assuming risk is limited in comparison and should be priced in – in particular for those names where there are only few loans or short-term loans outstanding with a low probability of renewal. While the callability or cancellability feature of LCDS is economically sensible given the nature of the underlying credit product, it creates a problem for many market participants and hinders the LCDS product from closing the lines with its bigger sister, the standard single name CDS. The optionality makes it difficult for investors and hedgers alike to value the risky future coupon payments, especially for contracts with higher par spreads. The probability of early repayment is an additional factor to be considered when valuing the risky annuities, since present value and DV01 of an LCDS are both affected by the expectation regarding prepayments. To put it simply, the cancellation of the LCDS due to loan repayment is comparable to a default-driven contract termination but with a recovery of par; both are early contract terminations prior to maturity. Some traders assume that default and cancellation are highly negatively correlated. The rationale is that an improvement of borrower credit quality decreases the probability of default but increases the ability of the obligor to renegotiate or repay the debt ahead of schedule. This caps the upside potential for the LCDS investor, who will no longer receive coupon payments under the contract once it is cancelled. Additionally, an upgrade to investment grade sometimes releases an obligor from posting collateral since higher-rated loans are usually unsecured. As a consequence, the LCDS-referenced loans would no longer satisfy the ISDA definition of a syndicated secured loan, which would result in an early termination of the LCDS contract, as in the case of Allegheny Energy Supply Company in 2009. While this relationship between borrower credit quality and prepayment probability appears to be unstable and largely dependent on various, not strictly coordinated, criteria such as the refinancing conditions and strategy of the firm, the opposite is more likely to hold: a borrower in financial stress will almost certainly not repay debt early, without having secured the refinancing, to avoid insolvency. However, for an LCDS where the spread indicates a moderate probability of default of the underlying borrower, the assumptions about cancellation can be quite subjective. In general, market participants will adopt a view that by definition will be consistent with their positioning, but may turn out to be quite different from that of a trade counterparty. If a loan documentation includes several prepayment dates, the valuation difference can become significant. Foux and Roy (2008) estimate that, using a Bloomberg function to value LCDSs under different assumptions regarding prepayment options and default versus prepayment correlation, the impact of probability of cancellation to the LCDS present value amounts to 10 to 15 per cent. For borrowers where both LCDSs and standard CDSs exist, the implied probabilities of embedded options can be estimated, although assumptions have to be made regarding the recovery value of loans versus bonds, which are expected to be the respective cheapest-to-deliver obligations. As a rule of thumb, loan recoveries are usually set at 70 per cent, whereas for bonds the standard recovery is 40 per cent. In principle, the spread for an LCDS should trade at tighter levels compared to the CDS to reflect the higher recovery in the event of a default. However, for names with lower credit spreads, in particular in times of improving credit and economic conditions, the value of the prepayment option will lead to wider LCDS spreads relative to CDS. As a consequence of the differing assumptions taken for valuation purposes, an investment or hedge strategy which correctly anticipated the development of the loan borrower's credit quality may turn out to be ineffective if the position cannot be unwound because of a disagreement with the counterpart over valuation. Although the standardization of LCDS confirmation documents in 2006 has contributed to renewed interest in this market, the looming illiquidity of deep-in-the-money contracts has dampened the market participants' initial euphoria.

8.1.4 The new North American Bullet LCDS

To address this problem, the new documentation for the North American LCDS eliminates the cancellability of the LCDS contracts, a provision under which the transactions were automatically accelerated if the reference entity no longer had outstanding loans which matched the reference obligation criteria. The new Bullet LCDS documentation will stipulate that the LCDS contract remain outstanding until maturity (or until a credit event occurs), even if the reference obligation ceases to exist. Of course, in this case the LCDS will be orphaned, which may aid the protection seller but may not necessarily be in the interest of a loan hedger. While the phenomena of an orphaned LCDS are consistent with the plain vanilla CDS, changes to continuity procedures and definitions aim at minimizing that risk. To develop the new Bullet LCDS contract, a fit for purpose *refinancing event* was introduced, which in a certain way extends the existing definition of the succession and refinancing events, thereby responding to typical loan refinancing and succession situations.

8.1.4.1 Refinancing event

Under the 'Continuity Procedures for Bullet LCDS', as published by ISDA, succession provisions have been developed for the first time by defining a refinancing event as one of the following actions:

Repayment through new loans or bonds: a situation where all or parts of the relevant obligations[1] are repaid from the proceeds of the new bonds or loans of at least one obligor that is not the reference entity;

---

[1] *Relevant obligation* denoted an obligation of the reference entity that meets the syndicated secured loan characteristics.

Repayment and asset acquisition: a situation where all or parts of the relevant obligations are repaid, and all or parts of the assets securing the relevant obligations were acquired from the proceeds of new bonds or loans of at least one obligor that is not the reference entity;

Repayment and assets securing new loans: a situation where all or parts of the relevant obligations are repaid, and all or parts of the assets securing the relevant obligations subsequently secure new bonds or loans of at least one obligor that is not the reference entity;

Amendment or restructuring: a situation where, in connection with an amendment or a restructuring event, all or parts of the relevant obligations cease to be the obligations of the original reference entity, and another entity becomes a borrower;

Other event: a situation where another event has substantially a similar effect to those described above.

For categorizing an action as a succession or refinancing event, a designated law firm rather than the determinations committee will be responsible and, just in case, will identify any potential successors. Similar to the changes in the standard CDS contract in 2009, the backstop date of 60 days during which a credit event must be recognized was incorporated into the new framework. Additionally, a backstop date of 90 days for a succession or refinancing event has been implemented.

8.1.4.2 Convention changes

Bringing the North American LCDS into line with other single name CDSs, the new Bullet LCDS will trade with fixed coupons and upfront payments. The 250 bps fixed coupon continues to be standard, with quotes expressed both in conventional spreads and points up front whereas the 100 bps fixed coupon will be quoted in spreads, and the 500 bps fixed coupon quoted in points up front; In addition, a 'zero coupon' has been introduced to accommodate some market participants who prefer to trade in points up front without any coupon. Regarding the conversion of conventional spreads into points up front, the ISDA CDS Standard Model[2], assuming a standard recovery rate of 70 per cent, will be used. Because the terms of the 'March 2009 Supplement' have been incorporated into the new Bullet LCDS, other convention changes of standard CDS apply too. In particular, the determinations committee deciding on a credit event, the auction process following a credit event, and the payment of a full first-quarterly coupon should be noted.

[2] The converter is available on www.markit.com and on the ISDA website, www.cdsmodel.com/cdsmodel/.

8.1.5 Settlement after a credit event

LCDSs, similar to standard CDS contracts, are likely to cash settle following a credit event, although for European LCDSs, only the protection seller can elect cash settlement. If no firm quotes are available for the deliverable obligations subject to the cash settlement, physical settlement will serve as a fallback method. In any case, a protection buyer will not have to make a payment to the protection seller if the loan trades above par following a credit event, thus adhering to the intention of credit protection. However, compared to corporate bonds, the physical delivery for loans is a bit more involved, as loans are governed by documentations which most often require the borrower's consent for a transfer. In general, the physical settlement takes place via assignment or silent (sub) participation. When a borrower gives the protection buyer its consent to assign a loan, the protection seller replaces the erstwhile creditor as a direct signatory to the loan. If the borrower consent is missing, a silent (sub)participation may be an alternative. Under a participation, the original lender keeps the loan on its books and maintains the loan servicing to the client but transfers the credit risk in exchange for the periodic income from the underlying loan. Participations are less desirable since the participant does not become a direct creditor of the borrower, and is thereby exposed not only to the credit risk of the underlying credit but also to the credit risk of the lead bank. Additionally, a silent (i.e. undisclosed) transfer of the credit risk of the loan must respect relevant legal restrictions of the loan documentation.

8.2 Subparticipations

A participation or subparticipation refers to an agreement under which a lender subcontracts a granted loan in parts or as a whole to another financial investor. The subparticipation, either openly disclosed to the borrower of the loan or silent, is a traditional and frequently used measure to distribute credit risks among banks and other non-bank investors. Participations exist in a funded or unfunded format. Funded subparticipations are loans from the participant to the grantor, and the loan repayment is conditional on the ability of the borrower of the loan underlying the participation to perform its obligation. The participant will provide the loan grantor with the funds to allow the grantor to satisfy its obligations under the terms of the underlying loan, in particular regarding drawdowns. Unfunded participations are similar to financial guarantees but lack the contract standardization which the guarantees derived from credit default swaps. In both cases, funded and unfunded, the original lender of the loan will pass on the income received under the loan to the participant as per the agreement. Loan income transferred from the grantor to the participation buyer includes periodic interest payments, one-time fees, and other items the bank charges to the borrower. In return, the participant will reimburse the grantor for all amounts unpaid by the borrower in violation of the loan agreement by paying the full amount due to the grantor while receiving the proportionate share of recovery under the loan from the grantor. The participant has no direct contractual relationship with the borrower and becomes a creditor of the grantor but not of the borrower, although she or he assumes credit risks related both to the borrower and the grantor.

8.2.1 Participations from the perspective of the grantor and the investor

A participation provides a credit portfolio manager with a highly individual and tailored instrument that in general is applicable to all credit products, including bilateral loans and revolving or undrawn facilities. Like CDSs or guarantees, participations allow transfer of the borrower's credit risk without disclosure to the obligor or the requirement to obtain the borrower's consent, hence preserving the client relationship. While the flexibility of this risk transfer tool is favourable, it comes at the expense of complexity and effort intensity due to the lower level of standardization. From the investor's perspective, participations offer access to credit risks in loan format which would otherwise be difficult to acquire when no relationship to the borrower exists. Moreover, loan documentations often include contractual restrictions concerning eligible lenders and on distribution of the loan via loan syndication. Direct lending is generally reserved for regulated and authorized financial institutions, thus excluding non-financial investors from granting loans to borrowers. Other reasons why market participants may prefer participations over a loan assignment are related to tax inefficiencies arising from unfavourable tax treatment for the interest income of the risk assumed by an investor, or simply the lack of willingness of the selling bank to take losses from a loan sale below par.

However, in the wake of the financial crisis and a series of notable bank failures, buyers of participations are in the process of reassessing their positions towards the providers of participations. Sellers and buyers of participations should take into consideration some product-specific features which are specific to participations when they enter into this instrument for risk-mitigation purposes.

8.2.1.1 Loan administration

The seller of a participation is exclusively responsible for the management and administration of the loan. While a grantor has to perform its obligations to administer a loan in compliance with sound and prudent standards, any amendments or changes to the loan documentation are solely in the hand of the original lender and usually do not require the consent of the participant. Unfortunately, in the case of a disagreement, a participant does not acquire any rights to take direct legal action against the borrower, as it does not stand in a direct lender-borrower relationship and hence has to fully rely on the lead bank to represent its interests. Nevertheless, the lead bank is obliged to notify the participant of any changes in the status of the borrower's financial condition or the ranking or collateralization of the loan.

8.2.1.2 Alignment of interest and recourse to grantor

Participants should not take it for granted that the loan orginator shares their interests. This is particularly noteworthy since intercreditor disputes often arise when the borrower of a loan subject to a participation experiences financial stress. Actions that the original lender undertakes to prevent write-downs or to minimize losses from a default are the result of a strategic decision which takes into account the entire client relationship and exposure, not just the economic reasons related to the loan or share of the loan subject to the participation. Additionally, loss provisions are determined by regulatory and political directives and guidance. Other factors to be considered include the ability of a bank to withstand further loan losses, the operating environment and the bank's comfort level in communicating additional provisions to its shareholder base, tax reasons, and so on. Notwithstanding a different view that a participating bank may take on the appropriateness of the lead bank's actions taken to secure a loan, by it is bound to those decisions. As long as the grantor pursues a collection approach consistent with its normal procedures, the participant has no recourse to make claims against the lead bank if it does not agree with the approach taken. Consequently, it remains with the grantor to decide if a workout, forbearance agreements, liquidation, or another alternative is most suitable, and it is irrelevant whether this is acceptable to the participant. Although the original lender is not legally obliged to obtain the participant's consent to any measures taken to recover losses, it may seek an agreement in advance to satisfy its fiduciary duties.

8.2.1.3 Grantor credit risk and insolvency

Moreover, the investor is exposed to the credit risk of the participation seller. Even if the loan borrower continues to make scheduled payments to the grantor, in the event of an insolvency of the grantor those payments would become part of the assets of the grantor, which will be used by an administrator or liquidator to satisfy the claims of all creditors, but not the specific claim of the participant. Subparticipants who are concerned about the grantor's ability or willingness to meet its obligation may request an elevation of its interest in the loan and enter into a direct relationship with the borrower. Alternatively, under predefined circumstances, the grantor may assign all rights and obligations under the loan to a third party or trust, so that the participant enters into a new participation with the third party. As a general rule, the subparticipation contract with the insolvent grantor will terminate on the day the participation is elevated to either the participant or to a third party that becomes the new lender.

8.2.2 Default event

From the perspective of the original lender, a participation is a useful instrument since it retains all discretionary managerial decision-making ability. In contrast to a CDS, where credit events are described in great detail and the decision of whether or not the borrower of the loan experienced a credit event is taken by a neutral party, the determinations committee, there is no such standard for participations. That is to say, the contractual arrangements for loss compensation are subject to an agreement between the grantor and the participant. Moreover, since the participant is not in a position to observe the occurrence of the predefined event, it has to fully rely on the original lender to receive correct, complete, and timely information about losses that occur and when and how much of those losses will be recovered through actions taken by the lead bank. As much as with a CDS, the lender becomes implicitly exposed to counterparty risk when entering into a participation. If a borrower whose loan has been transferred by way of participation defaults, and at the same time, the participant defaults, too, then the lender has a claim against the participant ranking pari passu with other unsecured creditors. Additional costs may arise from replacing the participations with a new risk-transfer transaction that is more expensive. Collateralization is another way to mitigate the inherent counterparty risk – for both sides.

8.2.3 Comparison of subparticipations to standardized CDS

Like a guarantee, a subparticipation is a direct instrument for transferring credit risk from the originator of a loan to another lender. While participations also share certain features with the CDS, there are significant differences which make the instrument comparably appealing, for instance their largely tailored nature, which in principle allows transference of the risk of almost any credit product of all borrowers to other

Table 8.1 Comparison of subparticipations and CDSs

Feature	Subparticipation	CDS
Standardization	+ High degree of individualization + Terms and conditions subject to agreement between grantor and participant, no industry standard – Complex transaction, time and resource intense, longer time to market	+ Terms and conditions standardized (ISDA framework) + High degree of efficiency + Short time to market, immediate execution
Eligible assets	+ In principle, all assets eligible (syndication clause to be observed)	– Only liquid names trading – Restrictions for deliverable obligations apply (although most assets are eligible)
Counterparts	+ In principle, all counterparts eligible – Confidentiality agreement to be signed by both counterparties	– Active dealers only
Liquidity	– No early termination or unwind	+ Ongoing active markets
Accounting	+ Collateral, at cost	– Mark-to-market
Loss coverage	– Losses up to amount realized, when occurred	+ Par minus final price, immediately after auction, independent from losses incurred
Capital relief	+ Risk participation: double default/substitution approach + Funded participation: full recognition	+ Double default/ substitution approach
Settlement	– No physical delivery, cash compensation	+ Physical delivery or cash settlement

investors. At the same time, the lower level of standardization results in operative burdens and, to a certain extent, legal risks as outlined above.

8.2.4 Conclusion

If a bank wants to make participations a regular tool for managing credit risk, it must take into consideration these legitimate interests of the participants. A clear description of default events and the conditions that trigger any payments under the agreement from the participant to the grantor can be derived to a certain extent from CDS contracts, thereby diminishing legal uncertainties around the instrument. The necessity of obtaining the participant's consent to changes and amendments to the loan documentation – such as payment date reschedulings, a change in interest rates, waiver to covenants, release, and pledge of collateral – should be expressly addressed, notwithstanding the fiduciary and agency responsibility of the participation seller. In any case, even though the original lender serves as the loan administrator, which from the investor's perspective makes participations a convenient instrument to acquire credit risks, an in-depth and comprehensive independent credit due diligence is a must before entering into a subparticipation. As a general rule, investors in participations should perform a credit review equal to those performed when engaging in direct lending and thus receive from the originating bank all documents and credit-assessment-relevant information necessary to perform the review. In order to do so, confidentiality agreements between loan originator and investor have to be put in place.

8.3 Linear credit indices

Credit indices go back to the year 2004 when CDX in North America and iTraxx in Europe and Asia were introduced. Since then, indices have become the most liquid instrument within the world of credit derivatives and are traded actively across the globe, accounting for a dominant share of the global CDS turnover.

8.3.1 Index family and composition

The family of indices offered by Markit is widespread, allowing portfolio managers to synthetically acquire or hedge credit exposure for a broad range of underlyings, maturities, and currencies with comparatively small transaction costs.

Additionally, indices for sovereign debt are available, including western Europe; Central and Eastern Europe, the Middle East, Africa (CEEMEA), the Asia Pacific region, Latin America, the G7, Brazil/Russia/India/China (BRIC) and a sovereign index consisting of the most liquid high-grade entities. The sovereign indices trade with five-year and ten-year maturities. All indices are rolled over every six months into new series to keep constant the standard maturity of the current or on-the-run series and to offset the roll-down effect which arises from an index that continuously gets closer to expiration in combination with lower credit spreads for shorter maturities. When a new index is launched, the index composition may

Region	Indices	Sub index	Underlying	Member	Years
Europe	iTraxx	Main	Top 125 high grade CDS	125	3/5/7/10
		Non financial	High-grade industrials	100	5/10
		Sub financial	Fin. institutions, sen. rank	25	5/10
		Sub financial	Fin. institutions, sub. rank	25	5/10
		Crossover/XO	Sub-investment grade	50	3/5/7/10
		High volatility	Highest spread CDS of main	30	3/5/7/10
	LevX	Senior	1st lien syndicated loans	75	5
		Subordinated	2nd/3rd lien syn. loans	45	5
North America	CDX	IG	Top 125 high grade CDS	125	3/5/7/10
		HY	High-yield industrials	100	5/10
		XO	Crossover CDS	35	5/10
		EM	Emerging market sovereigns	varying	5/10
		EM div	EM sov. + corporates	40	3/5/7/10
	LCDX	LCDX	NA 1st lien sen sec. loans	100	3/5/7/10
	MCDX	MCDX	U.S. municipal bonds	50	3/5/7/10

Figure 8.2 Overview of European and North American CDS indices

change. Index members that become ineligible due to default, downgrade, corporate action, sector change or illiquidity are replaced by new names. depending on the rules for the respective indices. For instance, new names to be included are determined through a liquidity poll for iTraxx and a dealer poll for CDX, LCDX, and MCDX. The procedure aims at identifying the single name CDS with the highest turnover or importance in the CDS market in order to support the trading liquidity of the new index series. The on-the-run five-year series is the standard maturity traded in the CDS space and thus the centre spot of the market activity. Unlike the single name CDS underlying the CDS indices, the effective date of indices is the index roll date rather than 60 calendar days prior to the actual date.

The individual composition of the indices by country, industry, rating, and spread provides the credit portfolio manager with a choice of hedge and investment instruments representative of the credit market. The indices are composed of liquid names which are mostly multinational and globally active corporates. Therefore they serve only to a lesser extent as a proxy for smaller and domestically oriented corporates highly sensitive to the credit and operating environment in the region where they are domiciled. Nonetheless, the indices are used as a gauge for credit risk priced by financial markets; hence they reveal the risk-aversion sentiment of market participants and as such have direct and indirect effects on the pricing of other credit and equity products. Although the correlation between a credit portfolio that an investor manages and a corresponding credit derivative index should be carefully assessed before entering into

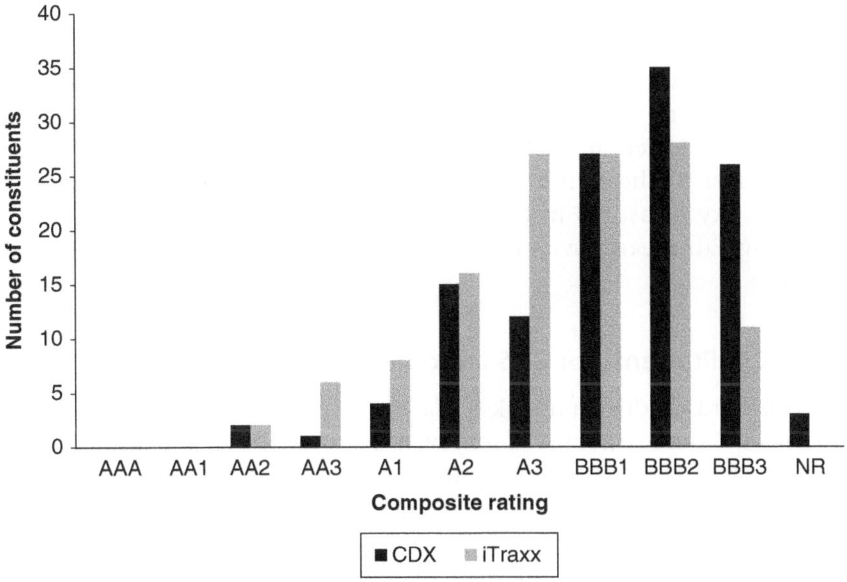

Figure 8.3 Rating distribution of iTraxx Investmentgrade CDS Index (Europe) and CDX Investmentgrade CDS Index (North America), as of December 2012
Data source: Bloomberg.

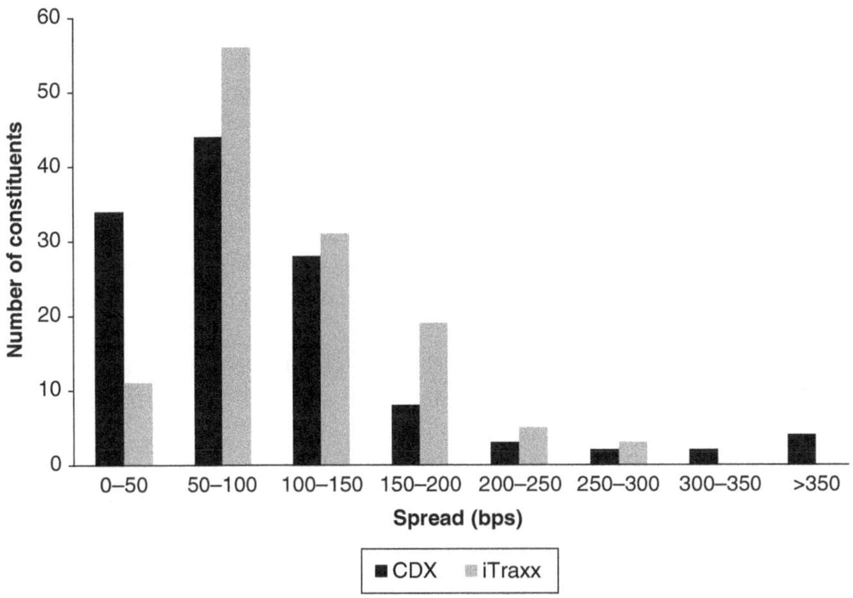

Figure 8.4 Spread distribution of iTraxx Investmentgrade CDS Index (Europe) and CDX Investmentgrade CDS Index (North America), as of December 2012
Data source: Bloomberg.

any index-based hedge strategy, the indices are, not least because of their outstanding liquidity, a popular instrument for credit default, and even more so for credit spread risk management. In general, the rating distribution for North American high-grade names is, compared to Europe, skewed to the lower end of the investment-grade rating scale.

In contrast to the rating distribution, the European index appears to be more risky measured in terms of spreads; this presumably reflects the prevailing European sovereign debt concerns, which add to corporate spreads.

8.3.2 Credit events for CDS indices

When a hard credit event takes place at a credit derivative index constituent, the name affected is removed from the index and settled at the auction. Once the settlement is finalized, a new version, usually named v2 of the index without the defaulted name, starts to trade. The new index consequently consists of n–1 index members compared to the n index constituents for the original series. The index protection buyer receives 1 – recovery for the notional of the index multiplied with share of the defaulted name of the index:

$$P = N \cdot \frac{1}{C} \cdot (1 - R) = \frac{N}{C} \cdot (1 - R) \cdot$$

where

P = compensation payment
N = trade notional
C = number of Index constituents
R = auction-determined recovery

Example 1. The buyer of \$100 mn protection on CDX.NA.HY.17,[3] consisting of 100 members, including Eastman Kodak, received a compensation payment for the default of Eastman Kodak[4] of \$100 mn ÷ 100 × (1 – 0.23875) = \$761,250.

Once the defaulted name has been removed from the new index version, the notional of that index is corrected by 1/n and trades accordingly as

$$N_{New} = N_{old} \cdot \frac{n-1}{n}$$

[3] CDX North American High Yield Index Series 17.

[4] The final price of Eastman Kodak, derived at the auction dated February 22, 2012, was 23.875. Source: www.creditfixings.com.

Example 2. The CDX.NA.HY.17 index originally consisted of 100 names, of which three index members, Dynegy, Eastman Kodak, and the PMI Group, defaulted. Hence, the factor for the index is 0.97, derived from (100 – 3)/100, or $9.7 mn, for a $10 mn ticket.

However, if a restructuring credit event occurs, then the affected index will be split into two parts: one without the restructured name, or (n–1)/n of the index, and the restructured name itself, or 1/n of the index. The different treatment, which lets the restructured name become a single name CDS on its own, relates to the unique nature of the restructuring credit event. In contrast to the automatic triggering in case of a hard credit event, a restructuring requires the CDS buyer and seller to take a decision about whether or not to trigger the contract. Assuming the contract has been triggered, the standard settlement procedure for restructuring applies. If untriggered, the CDS will continue to trade until it terminates at the maturity date or another credit event happens. Hence, while the choice of investors may differ with respect to the triggering, there will be only one index trading: the one adjusted for the restructured name.

9 Hedge Strategies for Baskets, Swaptions, and Macro Hedges

Managing a credit portfolio through an economic cycle necessitates a view on credit-related developments and related consequences for the specific portfolio. Most of the time, a portfolio manager faces considerable uncertainty when forecasting risk drivers and macroeconomic factors, and even more importantly potential interventions by policymakers – which have become a rule rather than an exception these days. In light of the prevailing fallout from the financial crisis, which is still in the process of filtering through the various layers of the monetary transmission mechanism, governments are engaged in far-reaching crisis mitigation measures that are difficult to predict but rapidly change the tune in financial markets, thereby having the potential to make any forecasts redundant. Hence, to be in a position to respond to different and often fast-changing conditions in credit markets, a portfolio manager needs to be equipped with a range of hedging tools which provide suitable and effective solutions to shield the credit portfolio from any adverse impact. A complete toolbox consists of instruments which address

- **asset coverage:** financial markets, although they are the most efficient because of the high level of standardization, mostly provide instruments for the largest corporates and plain vanilla credit products, i.e. term loans and bonds. However, a typical credit portfolio of a universal bank is composed of small businesses, medium enterprises and a broad spectrum of loan products, from current accounts to trade finance, and guarantees which call for bespoke rather than standard solutions offered by capital market.
- **short time to market portfolio protection:** fast-changing market conditions make it necessary to respond quickly by entering into hedges that are quick and easy to execute, with sufficient liquidity in terms of tradable size and acceptable transaction costs. Ideally, such a hedge is applied on the portfolio level rather than on multiple single names.

- **portfolio correlation:** in times of financial stress, the dependency structure of credit risks within a portfolio tends to intensify. A rising correlation, both for credit migration and default risk, increases the probability of large-scale losses or tail risks due to portfolio concentrations, which have been identified as the major reason for failures of financial institutions.
- **volatility risk:** more often than not, a rise in asset correlation is accompanied by an increase in volatility. Although the risk profile of the credit portfolio stock may not be directly impacted by volatility, it has some implications for the credit value chain and active management of the portfolio.
- **hedging restrictions:** sometimes a perfect hedge which references to the single credit asset that a portfolio manager wants to protect is not at hand, for instance due to the illiquid nature of the asset or because of regulatory restrictions. Consequently, imperfect or macro hedges with an acceptable hedge error or basis risk have to be developed.

This chapter discusses hedge instruments, which allow creation of a cash-flow profile to counterbalance the scenario anticipated by the portfolio manager while corresponding to all the requirements listed above. The focus is again, as it is throughout the book, on hedging strategies as opposed to trading. While we acknowledge that there is often not a clear distinction between value preservation and value generation or profit making, the objective of any portfolio management activity must be fully transparent from the beginning and should not become confused subsequently. The rest of this chapter explains risk mitigation approaches using CDS product variations, such as nth-to-default baskets, which address asset correlation and portfolio concentration. The chapter continues with a discussion of swaptions, which are short-term dated and allow one to take a view on volatility, and outlines how specific strategies can be employed to achieve full-cycle active credit portfolio management. The chapter concludes with a discussion of the cross-asset hedging strategies that have become increasingly more important in the context of regulatory restrictions, such as the ban on sovereign CDSs by the EU commission.

9.1 Nth-to-default baskets: Combining default risk with correlation

Nth-to-default baskets on CDSs, introduced in the early days of credit derivatives, can be seen as a kind of 'CSO light', since nth-to-default baskets have much in common with their larger sister but are less complex by nature and closer to the single name CDS. Both instruments share the sensitivity to correlation risk which arises from a cash flow or default hierarchy. In principle any kind of basket can be constructed, although there are some standard applications which benefit from better market liquidity. Most common are 1st-to-default (FtD) baskets on five to a maximum of ten names with a five-year term; 2nd-to-default or 2nd-to-last-to-default baskets have become popular, too. As the name suggests, a portfolio of CDSs arranged as an nth-to-default basket exhibits a default hierarchy. For instance, the protection buyer of an nth-to-default basket pays coupon payments on the basket notional to the protection seller until the nth default occurs among the constituents; then the contract compensates for the loss resulting from the default and terminates. The default hierarchy means that an element of leverage is introduced which is comparable to the structure of the balance sheet of a firm consisting of equity and debt. All losses are initially absorbed by the equity, while the debt starts to suffer only if losses exceed the amount of equity. An FtD basket where the first credit event will terminate the instrument, is therefore the equivalent of equity in a capital structure. A 2nd-to-default basket is more remote from default and loss in that it will become an FtD basket only after the first credit event at one of the names included in the basket occurs. Hence it terminates only once the second credit event takes place. As a result, the structure of a basket is comparable to synthetic CDOs, so-called CSOs, and to tranches on credit indices.

Even though there are similarities, there are differences too. For example, unlike CSOs and tranches of credit indices, which continue to exist even after the equity tranche has been wiped out, the first name out of an FtD experiencing a credit event settles through the ISDA auction process and leaves the protection seller with a loss amounting to

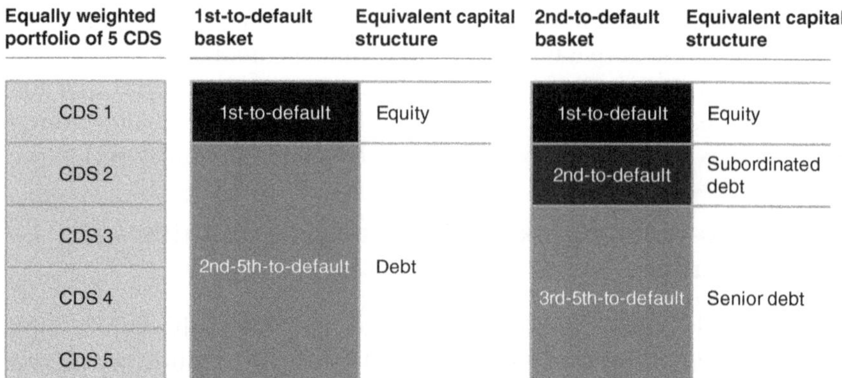

Figure 9.1 Portfolio of equally weighted CDS versus nth-to-default basket structure

$$L = N \cdot (1 - R)$$

where

L = loss

N = notional of the basket

R = auction-determined recovery of the first name of the basket experiencing a credit event

The leverage of nth-to-default baskets becomes apparent when we consider that the seller of an FtD is exposed to the default risk of all basket constituents, with each having the potential to create losses up to the full investment notional amount, assuming a zero recovery – in contrast to a portfolio of an identical notional that is composed of the same names as the basket but each name carrying an equally weighted amount, where a loss would cost the investor no more than the share of the portfolio notional allocated to the defaulted name.

9.1.1 Pricing the correlation factor

Obviously, the pricing of a basket must reflect its different risk profile. Intuitively, one would expect the seller of an FtD to be compensated for the default risk of all its underlying CDSs; thus, the premium would be the sum of the spreads of CDSs 1 to n. However, a clever investor would then choose to sell an FtD basket consisting of names with an almost identical risk behaviour, meaning either they all default at the same time for the same reason or none of them defaults. Let's assume individual CDSs trade at exactly the same spread, which seems logical given that they have the same risk profile. The seller of the basket would then receive n times the spread of the underlying, while he could buy CDS protection for one basket constituent with a notional equal to the basket in order to be perfectly hedged, thus paying only 1/n of the coupon. Hence, the trade would give the seller of an FtD n–1 coupons for free. On the other hand, if all the names in an FtD are fully uncorrelated, a seller of an FtD would have to buy protection on each name to hedge the default risk, thus spending n coupons on a notional of n times the basket notional. Neither case, 0 or 100 per cent correlation, is likely, but it becomes clear that correlation matters. The way correlation impacts pricing is the coupon of the basket, which is determined through the percentage of the sum of spreads. In general, FtDs pay between 70 and 85 per cent of the sum of spreads for a well-diversified portfolio. A 2nd-to-nth-to-default basket enjoys a coupon of 100 per cent of the sum of spreads minus the coupon of the FtD since the costs of the 3rd-to-nth-to-default basket to the nth-to-default basket are quite low. This offers cheap protection provided the hedger can withstand a default of one of the basket constituents since the protection becomes 'activated' only after the first default. Of course, pricing nth-to-default baskets is a lot more complex, since CDS spreads are dynamic and the valuation of correlation products incorporates the impact, unstable over time, that a default of one of the n CDSs has on the remaining names. Hence, a model must not only recognize the interdependence or the correlation between the names within the basket, which is observable at one point in time, but must also elaborate on a richer correlation structure. Pricing is then simulated using a copula distribution and a Monte-Carlo simulation.[1]

9.1.2 Hedging strategies using nth-to-default baskets

Hedging credit portfolios using CDS baskets is particularly helpful when a portfolio manager explicitly considers correlation aspects. As a general rule, the buyer of FtD protection is short the correlation between the names included in the basket, while the seller of protection goes long correlation. Because the pricing of nth-to-default baskets unveils implied correlation of the basket constituents, it also allows for cross-checking for the correlation assumptions taken in developing a scenario against which a hedger wants to protect the credit portfolio. Moreover, an FtD hedge releases regulatory capital of the asset out of the basket that carries the lowest risk weighting.

9.1.3 Hedging concentration risk

A 2nd-to-nth-to-default basket is an effective way to buy cheap protection on a portfolio of concentrated names. Assuming the underlying names are perfectly correlated (thus would default altogether), the hedger pays considerably less than he would have to pay for hedging each name separately, while receiving superior protection, except for the losses arising from the first-name defaulting, which remains unprotected. This is so because the loss compensation for the second default includes losses from the 3rd-to-nth default which has not yet occurred. Thus an unfavourable development of those risk drivers would have massive consequences for the portfolio risk profile, since a range of debtors would be affected. While a portfolio manager would be prepared to accept some defaults, a series of correlated defaults would probably exceed risk appetite and the capacity to absorb losses.

---

[1] See Schmidt (2007) and Zhiyong and Glasserman (2006).

9.1.4 Hedging tail risks

Tail-risk hedging has become a core element of meaningful portfolio protection in the face of repeated significantly negative events which have resulted in large-scale losses for financial institutions. Persistent uncertainties about the quality of sovereign debt in Europe and the future of the euro have had measurable repercussions on the funding costs of industrials and of the financial institutions domiciled in peripheral countries that are perceived to be comparably weak, given their huge indebtedness and rather bleak economic prospects. The knock-on effects from the sovereign debt crisis have the potential, a large-scale derailing of the financial system and, to cause ultimately, also the global economy – a situation that meets the definition of a tail risk. Being at the heart of any stress test, tail risks are defined as an unlikely but severe events. Fundamental concerns related to the economy as a whole or to idiosyncratic events with extreme consequences, such as a sudden collapse of a major systemically relevant financial institution, as happened with Lehman, are likely to translate into intense pressure on valuations across the spectrum of asset classes, pressure partly attributable to an increase in correlation of these assets. Moreover, knock-on effects or second- and third-round effects become hedgeable using the 2nd-to-nth-to-default basket construction. For instance, in the aftermath of the 2011 Japanese earthquake which led to the explosion of the Fukushima nuclear reactor, the global automotive and electronic-equipment industries were hit by a shortage of certain electronic components, those where Japan has a dominant share of the worldwide production. These two industries, which exhibit a moderate correlation based on the common risk driver of consumer demand, were simultaneously affected by this shock event.

9.1.5 Hedging idiosyncratic risk in a benign credit environment

While corporate defaults are rare in a benign economic environment, they nevertheless occur. This is partly due to time lag effects, where a firm had struggled in adverse operating conditions in the past but managed to stay afloat for some time before throwing in the towel, or due to event risk, such as litigation, fraud, M&A, or the like. In order to fully protect for that risk, a portfolio manager would need to buy protection on each and every name, which is clearly unfeasible. However, an FtD basket would hedge exactly this scenario, where only one name experiences a default, while all other borrowers within the credit portfolio remain unaffected. The hedge strategy carries a considerably lower cost, although the costs are still significant, and therefore are sustainable for selected names only. Hence, hedging event risk with FtD baskets is quite popular with portfolio managers. However, because the upside of an FtD basket is limited to the compensation of the loss from a default of one of the n names in the basket, the instrument is less suitable to hedge systemic risks, which denote correlated effects. For sellers of protection, an FtD basket offers a less capital-intense way to collect coupons of multiple names, hence leveraging the amount disposable for an investment.

9.2 Swaptions: Adding a volatility risk component to default protection

Besides the correlation factor that affects the loss distribution of a credit portfolio, there is another concern that relates to volatility in the valuation of financial assets. For instance, a recurring pattern in global stock markets is sudden risk aversion amongst investors, which results in a sharp decline of stock prices coupled with a significant increase of credit spreads. Generally, tail-risk hedges should not only protect against large losses in an extreme event but also offset the effects of a rise in the volatility of risky assets, as is typically observed in times of stress. The massive and market-dislocating impact of probable shock events makes options a suitable tool to counterbalance corresponding portfolio effects. CDS options or default swaptions complement CDSs and CDS-based indices in that swaptions offer cheap protection for credit-market risk, while linear products are more expensive and appropriate for hedging default and migration risk. Unless credit assets are booked into a banking book where no market valuations apply, financial market volatility may be a concern for the investor. But even in a world where banks continue to maintain accrual accounting on loans or bonds, there are reasons to balance larger moves of credit spreads, although they may not become immediately visible in daily profit and loss. For instance, derivative hedges that are measured at fair value introduce credit volatility to credit portfolios. The

Table 9.1 Expressing credit views with swaptions

	Payer		Receiver	
	Buy/Long	**Sell/Short**	**Buy/Long**	**Sell/Short**
Credit risk position	short	long	long	short
CDS pendant	buy protection	sell protection	sell protection	buy protection
Expected spread move	bearish	neutral/ bullish	bullish	neutral/ bearish

Table 9.2 Overview of default swaption characteristics

Component	Description
Underlying	CDS indices (i.e. on-the-run iTraxx or CDX IG series) and to a lesser extent single name CDSs.
Strike	Predefined spread level at which the holder can exercise the option, typically ATM ± 20 per cent.
Exercise	All credit options are European style and can be exercised only at the expiration date, from 9 a.m. to 4 p.m. LDN and 9 a.m. to 11 a.m. EST. Options not exercised terminate at expiration date.
Expiration date	Expiration dates are usually set to the third Wednesday of the expiration month or the standard roll dates of CDSs and indices (20 March, June, September or December of each year) for single name CDS options. Most liquid durations are 1–6 months for index options and 1–12 months for single name CDS options.
Settlement	To monetize the value changes of the option during its lifetime, the option can be assigned or unwound. At expiration date, options physically settle into the underlying, although cash settlement is a possibility.
Credit event	For options on indices, the option notional reduces in line with the underlying. Any loss is compensated analogous to CDS indices. Single name CDS options terminate in case a credit event occurs within the underlying (knockout).
Premium/ quotation	The option premium is the cost of the option and is paid upfront. The quotation convention for options is to express the premium in bps.[2] Furthermore, swaptions trade with delta, which denotes the simultaneous offsetting of the option with a delta equivalent position in the underlying at the reference price that corresponds to the option quote.

timing component of loan origination, where the margin is negotiated a long time before the loan is finally signed by the bank and its client, exposes the bank to the risk of a significant widening in credit spreads, which could make a hedge for the newly originated loan uneconomic. The same applies to debt capital markets' underwriting, where the bank takes the risk of placing certain debt securities at a pre-agreed price, independent of market conditions prevailing at the time of syndication. At the same time, many loans carry prepayment or early amortization provisions, which generally become a concern for loan portfolio managers

[2] An exception to the rule is the CDX High Yield index, for which swaptions are quoted in price terms rather than spread premiums, in line with the usance for the index itself. The terminology for those swaptions also differs from the others in that options are referred to as call and put as opposed to receiver and payer.

when credit conditions improve. Hedging loan portfolio convexity is the objective for another swaption strategy. Other trading strategies, in particular those that are non-directional regarding credit market risk but express a view on volatility, extend the scope of portfolio applications for swaptions. It is important to consider that option strategies generally target mark-to-market gains, unlike CDS hedging strategies, which, from a credit portfolio manager's perspective, are intended to counterbalance default risk and ideally do not show any mark-to-market volatility otherwise.

Swaptions are offered on single name CDS and credit indices, although options on CDS indices are the most liquid. They were introduced in 2003, when CDS indices on U.S. corporates started to trade. After the financial crisis in 2008, the trading activity in swaptions substantially increased and continues to do so. CDS options provide credit portfolio managers with a low-cost alternative for hedging against tail risks or unexpected market developments, for instance, large spread moves. On the other hand, investors such as hedge funds or asset managers make regular use of default swaptions to enhance the returns on their portfolios. Other market participants, like correlation desks, manage convexity or gamma exposure through options. Swaptions are by and large similar to other OTC options but feature some unique characteristics which are described in more detail later. While we provide a sample of applicable hedging strategies for credit portfolio managers, the focus is on downside protection rather than trading or income generation.

9.2.1 Conventions

Default swaptions are referred to as receivers and payers, derived from the usances for interest-rate derivatives.

A receiver is the equivalent of selling CDS protection/buy risk and thus receives the CDS coupon when exercised. Accordingly, a payer has the right to buy CDS protection and therefore has to pay coupons. Buying receivers expresses a bullish view on credit spreads, whereas buying payers conforms to a bearish stance. Table 9.2 details the features of CDS options.

The spot level for the index indicated in a trader run is usually close to actual index levels and serves as the level where the delta exchange takes place. A delta exchange denotes the corresponding index amount to be traded simultaneously with the option trade to neutralize market moves of that index. As for many OTC options, swaptions usually trade with delta to ensure a smooth trading even in volatile environments. To trade swaptions without delta, an investor may trade with delta and subsequently

Underlying: iTraxx Main S19. Expiration: Sep13. Forward at 98.621. Delta at 93

Strike	Receiver	Delta	Vol	Strike	Payer	Delta	Vol
70	3–7	5.5%	41%	90	70.3–74.3	–71.6%	41%
75	5.7–9.7	9.4%	41%	95	58–62	–63.6%	42%
80	9.8–13.8	14.7%	41%	100	47.8–51.8	–55.9%	43%
85	15.6–19.6	21.1%	41%	105	39.4–43.4	–48.7%	44%
90	23.2–27.2	28.4%	41%	110	32.6–36.6	–42.2%	45%
95	33.9–37.9	36.3%	42%	115	27.1–31.1	–36.5%	46%
100	46.5–50.5	44.1%	43%	120	22.6–26.6	–31.5%	47%
105	–	–	–	125	19–23	–27.3%	48%
110	–	–	–	130	16.2–20.2	–23.7%	49%
115	–	–	–	140	11.9–15.9	–18%	51%
120	–	–	–	150	9.1–13.1	–14%	53%

Figure 9.2 Quotes for iTraxx Main S19 September 2013 options, as of May 13,2013

offset the delta by selling or buying an equal amount of the index opposite to the delta[3]. For CDS, the quotes have to be refreshed on an ongoing basis to indicate tradable spreads, whereas swaption spreads are relative to a reference level of the underlying index so that moves in the index are mirrored by an equivalent move in the swaption quote. The forward DV01 of the underlying is the DV01 or mark-to-market valuation for a 1 bps change in the theoretical index underlying used in pricing models to evaluate payoff calculations. The forward does not trade; it is the spread of the index at the option expiry date. The strike, quoted in spread terms for all indices except the CDX HY, is the predefined level at which an option buyer can buy (payer) or sell (receiver) the index protection at expiration. Options trade at-the-money (ATM), meaning that the strike is set close to actual index spread levels; out-of-the-money (OTM), where the option exhibits time value only; and in-the-money (ITM), when the index trades above or below the option strike for a long payer and a long receiver, respectively. Trader quotes, called runs, detail the price, delta, and volatility for a range of strikes of payers and receivers.

For example, an investor would buy an iTraxx Series 19 payer swaption with a strike of 100 at an offer of 51.8, meaning that the option costs a premium of 0.518 per cent of the notional, or €518,000 for €100 mn notional. The delta of -55.9 per cent for this swaption indicates that the sensitivity of buying €100 mn of the receiver option equates to buying €55.9 mn protection of the underlying iTraxx index, quoted at 93 bps for reference. Markit provides standard confirmations for swaptions on its website. The swaption confirmation references a standard terms supplement in addition to the single name CDS documentation framework.

[3] Many traders also agree to trade without delta. Option strategies aimed at hedging an existing portfolio usually trade without delta exchange.

9.2.2 Default event

Fortunately, a credit event for swaptions on indices is fairly straightforward. As described in §8.3.2, 'Credit events for CDS indices', a new index version is created when a credit event takes place for one of the index constituents. In the case of a hard credit event, the swaption automatically refers to the new index version without the defaulted name, and the buyer of an exercised payer swaption receives par minus recovery for the defaulted name, as determined by the auction process – provided that the auction takes place prior to the option expiry. If the auction is held after the swaption expiration date, the option has to be exercised first, and then the trade becomes an index trade that goes through the auction mechanics. From the perspective of the payer option buyer, the decision to exercise will be taken on the option strike versus the spread of the old index as the option underlying, which is equivalent to the spread of the adjusted index version 2, without the defaulted name, plus the compensation payment from the defaulted name. For buyers of receiver options, the approach is similar.

A restructuring credit event, as usual, is a bit more complex. To retain the ability of the index protection seller and buyer to decide whether to trigger the contract or not, the underlying index will be split into a new index with n–1 constituents and a CDS referencing to the restructured single name. However, to be in a position to trigger the contract at the auction, an index option must expire before the auction, since CDS options are European style, meaning they can be exercised only at the expiration date. If the expiration date is post the restructuring credit event auction, the single name CDS that is split from the index remains untriggered, as the window of opportunity for triggering the contract has passed.

9.2.3 CDS option strategies

The similarities between CDS index options and the much larger market for options on equity indices allow for conclusions to be drawn from the diverse literature on stock options. In particular, more complex strategies – for instance, risk reversals, ladders, calendar spreads, butterflies – are standard in other option markets, but in credit markets by and large are actively pursued only by market professionals specializing in those instruments. A detailed and complete discussion of sophisticated trading strategies which express outright or relative value views and volatility positioning are beyond the hedging intention and exceeds the scope of this book. Although CDS options have a lot in common with stock options, there are some significant differences, too. First of all, stock options do not have to deal with defaults; this risk is unique to credit.

Hence, standard option pricing models have to be modified to account for defaults. Nevertheless, the short-dated nature of CDS index options mitigates this risk to a certain, although not a full, extent. Since the impact of a default on an index, and therefore also on an index option, can be significant, investors in CDS options should bear this risk in mind. Additionally, the pull-to-par price effect of bonds for which the full principle will be paid back at maturity unless a default happens – regardless of the price at which the bond trades prior to maturity – makes options on bonds difficult to compare to options on stocks. The pull-to-par effect of bonds translates into a push-to-zero spread effect for the corresponding CDS. By definition, if no credit event happens, any CDS spread will decrease to zero at the termination date. Stock prices, in contrast, tend to exhibit trends but not any of the effects described above, which are particular to credit instruments. Although credit spreads react to both the trend and the volatility of stocks, a direct comparison of stock and credit options price moves may be misleading.

CDS options mainly settle physically. If the option is exercised at expiry date, the holder will enter into a contract in the underlying index at the strike, with the option seller as the counterpart. To monetize any gains from the option, the option holder can then unwind the index position at current market spreads. Assuming no default occurs within the option underlying, the value of an option at expiration date is simplistically represented by[4]

Table 9.3 Stylized value at expiration and risk positioning of CDS swaptions

Option type	Option Value at expiration	Credit risk position	Credit view
Buy payer	$Max(0,(S-K)) \cdot DV01_{Fwd} \cdot N - P$	short	bearish
Sell payer	$-1 \cdot Max(0,(s-k)) \cdot DV01_{Fwd} \cdot N + P$	long	moderate bullish
Buy receiver	$Max(0,(K-S)) \cdot DV01_{Fwd} \cdot N - P$	long	bullish
Sell receiver	$-1 \cdot Max(0,(K-S)) \cdot DV01_{Fwd} \cdot N + P$	short	moderate bearish

4 The representation in Table 9.3 serves as a 'rule of thumb' approximation only; it works better for ATM options, less well the more spot-at-expiration and strike diverge from the forward. The valuation of CDS swaptions is more complex and is formally described in Brigo and El-Bachir (2010) and Rutkowski and Armstrong (2009).

where
S = spot of the option underlying at expiry date of the option
K = strike of the option
$DV01_{Fwd}$ = forward DV01 of the underlying
N = notional
P = premium

For **buyers of** payer and receiver options, the maximum loss is limited to the premium paid, while the maximum gain is constrained only by the spread's widening/tightening potential. By contrast, the net payoff at expiration date is the opposite for sellers of payer and receiver options and can be significantly negative, whereas profits are capped at maximum of the premium payments received, as shown in Figure 9.3.

Value changes of options are sensitive to the price volatility of the underlying, although to a varying degree, depending on the remaining time to expiry and spot to strike level. A higher volatility in general increases the chance that an OTM option may end up ITM at expiration. As a result, an increase in volatility will lead to a rising option premium, and vice versa. Since option pricing models allow isolation of the contribution

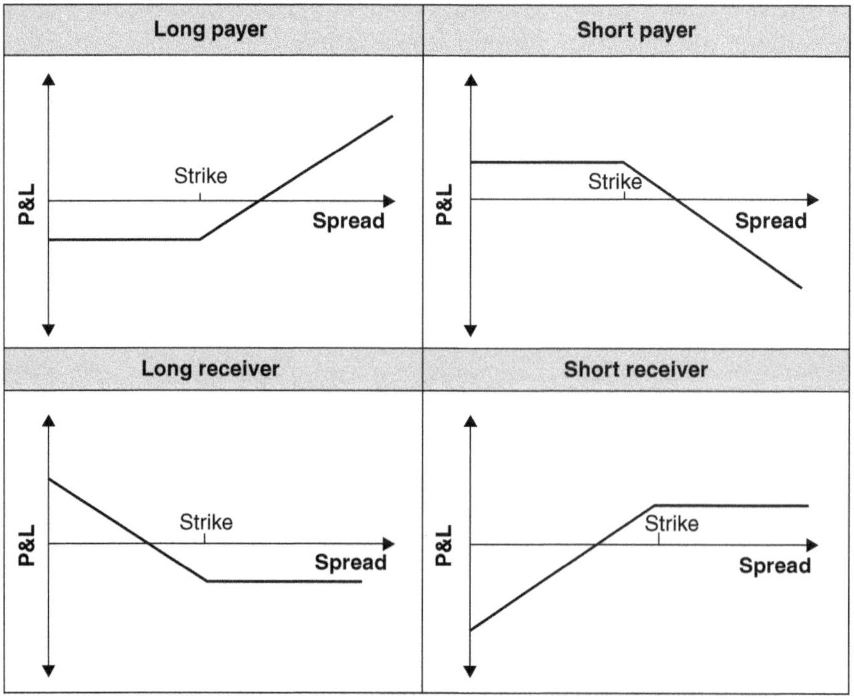

Figure 9.3 Payoffs at expiration date for payer and receiver swaptions

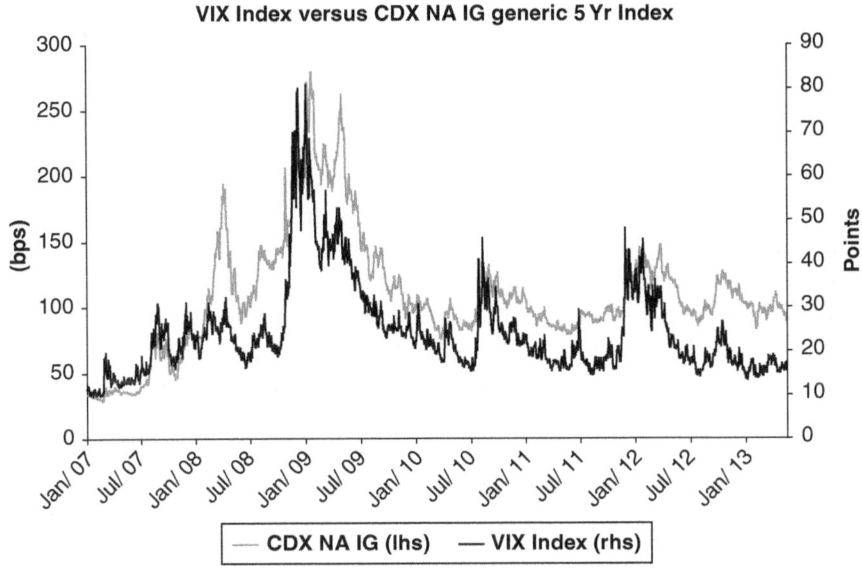

Figure 9.4 VIX Index versus CDX Investmentgrade CDS Index (North America), as of December 2012

Data source: Bloomberg, as of May 2013.

of volatility to the value of an option, option prices reveal an implied volatility which, most of the time, differs from realized volatility of the underlying. The difference reflects supply and demand imbalances, as well as expectations regarding volatility trends for which option traders may be prepared to pay a premium. For swaptions, there is an overlapping effect, since the spreads of CDS indices that serve as the underlying for those options exhibit a notable sensitivity to changes in stock prices **and** to the amplitude of those changes. A measure mostly used for observation of U.S. stock volatility is the VIX or CBOE volatility index, which reflects the market estimate of future volatility based on the weighted average of the implied volatilities for a wide range of option strikes. See Figure 9.4.

9.2.3.1 Development of a hedge strategy using swaptions

Developing a hedge strategy using CDS options follows five steps:

1. **Describing the scenario** for which an investor seeks protection, including the probability of the event(s) materializing;
2. **Translating the scenario** into a potential impact on relevant measures, such as profit and loss;

3. **Determining the hedge strategy** most suitable to counterbalancing the scenario because it has a payoff profile that most closely neutralizes the loss distribution;
4. **Defining the hedge budget** in terms of hedge costs and a maximum loss acceptable resulting from the hedge;
5. Subsequent **timely monitoring** of the hedge strategy, in particular regarding the effectiveness or the hedge error arising from residual unprotected risk (basis risk).

When describing a view of potential trends or events in credit markets, the historical distribution of spread changes serves as a reference for the scenario. Isolating a period of market dislocations helps to identify realistic frequency distributions as a basis for determining potential stress outcomes. For example, the frequency distribution of daily spread changes for the European investment-grade CDS index iTraxx is divided into two periods: prior to the Lehman failure,[5] where spreads mostly moved between +5 bps and –5 bps a day, and post–Lehman default, with significantly more pronounced volatility.

Developing a hedge strategy using swaptions requires a scenario-derived impact on the distribution of spread changes and spread trends. For instance, widening spreads combined with a rise in volatility can be formulated in terms of impact on profit and loss on the credit portfolio to be hedged. Based on that loss profile, it is possible to identify the option strategy that responds to the scenario in a way which matches as closely

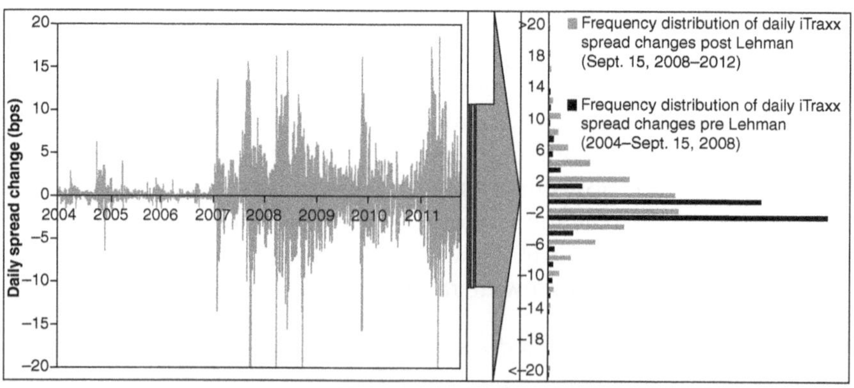

Figure 9.5 Daily spread changes of European iTraxx and frequency distribution
Data source: Bloomberg.

[5] Lehman Brothers collapsed on September 15, 2008. It was the largest bankruptcy filing in U.S. history.

as possible the loss distribution of the hedged portfolio. It should be noted that the most suitable hedging strategy is determined by a variety of factors – that is, volatility and skew and the term structure of the underlying index. Skew denotes the difference in implied volatility exhibited by options with the same underlying and expiry but different strikes. In particular, OTM options trade with higher implied volatilities, since investors prefer OTM payers to ATM options for hedgeing tail risks, which increase the relative expensiveness of those options compared to ATM options. Consequently, the skew is inherently a measure of the risk aversion of financial market participants.

9.2.3.2 Long-payer option

The predominant option strategy to hedge credit portfolios or counterparty risk is to buy OTM payers, or puts.

Example: An investor expects a spread move in European high-grade assets from 150 bps to 200 bps due to a deterioration of the economic environment within the next two months. In that case, losses in the investor's credit portfolio of €100 mn notional with an average maturity of five years will amount to approximately €2.5 mn.[6] To compensate for the potential losses, the investor engages in a delta equivalent of the money long-payer option, with a strike of 150 bps and an expiration date in two months. The

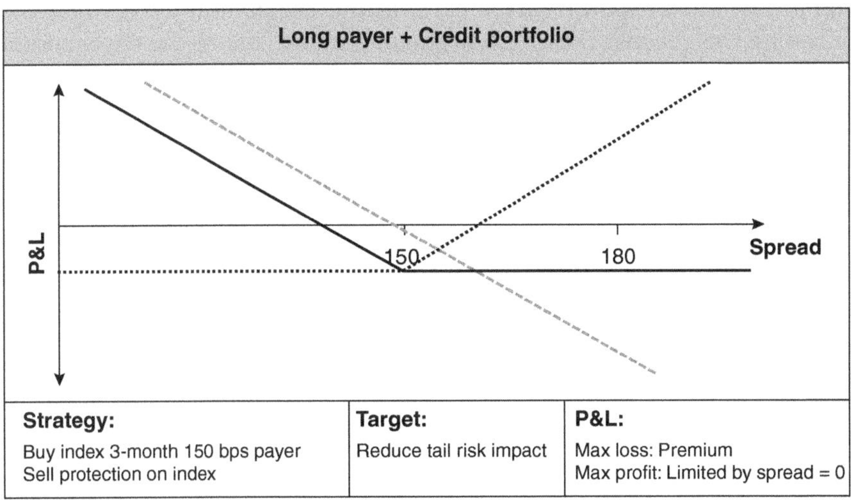

Strategy:	Target:	P&L:
Buy index 3-month 150 bps payer Sell protection on index	Reduce tail risk impact	Max loss: Premium Max profit: Limited by spread = 0

Figure 9.6 Profit and loss of long-payer option and credit portfolio

[6] Assuming a DV01 of €46,506 of the credit portfolio for an average five-year maturity, which is identical to the current on the run five-year iTraxx series.

maximum loss from the combined position if the expected spread widening materializes as expected is capped at the premium payment for the option, which amounts to 15.5 per cent in the example. However, if the concerns turn out to be unfounded, the portfolio manager preserves the upside potential of portfolio value gains from tightening credit spreads net of costs for the protection from the CDS option.

Swaptions offer various strikes and maturities which can be combined in different ways to achieve an optimal cash-flow pattern for a predefined scenario. Besides the correct anticipation of market moves, the time frame in which the expectations materialize is also a major contributor to the success of any option strategy, since both the swaption maturities are rather short and the costs or swaptions premiums include a time value; hence longer-dated options are more costly.

9.2.3.3 Payer spread

Hedging a potential credit-spread widening in times of elevated volatility often combines options which retain a bearish view of spreads while reducing total costs and exposure to changes in the implied volatility. For instance, a payer spread is constructed by buying a payer option with a low strike, and selling a payer option with a higher strike. This combination reduces of the costs of protection against spread widening while also capping the downside either way. The net costs are simply the premium to be paid for the more expensive ATM payer minus the premium to be received for selling the cheaper OTM payer. The maximum loss of the payer spread

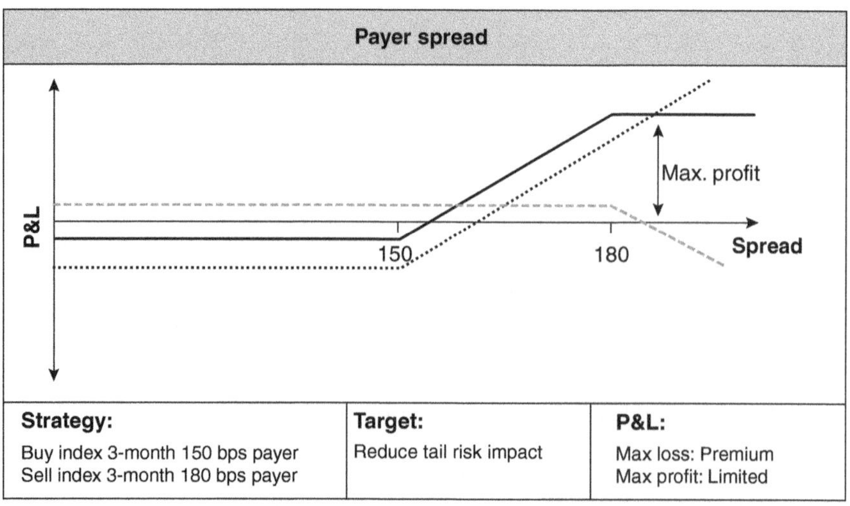

Strategy:	**Target:**	**P&L:**
Buy index 3-month 150 bps payer Sell index 3-month 180 bps payer	Reduce tail risk impact	Max loss: Premium Max profit: Limited

Figure 9.7 CDS swaption payer spread

is the net premium paid at trade inception. The trade gains the most when spreads are at or slightly below the strike of the OTM payer sold. If spreads widen beyond the strike of the short payer position, 180 bps in Figure 9.8, there will be no further gains. On the other hand, if spreads tighten below 150 bps, the strike for the long-payer position, the costs of the strategy are limited by the premium paid. Hence, the strategy works well for a moderate-spread widening, at a significantly lower cost than for buying an outright payer, but misses on the upside of a more substantial spread move.

In general, an at-the-money payer spread virtually replicates the underlying index, but caps the up- and downside. Investors in payer spreads are exposed to skew and volatility which determine the break-even and the costs of the strategy. A positive skew allows the investor to sell the payer with the wider strike at a higher implied volatility, hence at a higher premium, which increases the income received, while the payer with the lower strike is bought at a lower implied volatility, which makes the option cheaper for the investor. As a consequence, any decrease of the skew will add to the gains of the payer spread, while a rise in skew will decrease the profit. Unfortunately, the short skew position makes the strategy less attractive for hedging an event that is extremely negative event against credit spreads since in this scenario the skew is likely to rise. Nonetheless, payer spreads are a good way to express the view of moderate-spread widening while concerns exist about a potential large-spread widening and tightening.

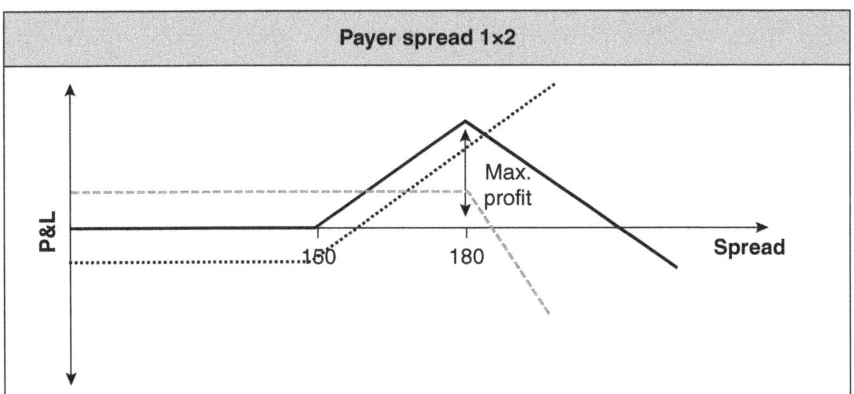

Strategy:	Target:	P&L:
Buy 1 index 3-month 150 bps payer Sell 2 index 3-month 180 bps payer	Reduce negative impact from credit deterioration	Max loss: Unlimited for tail risk Max profit: Limited low cost

Figure 9.8 CDS swaption payer spread 1 × 2

9.2.3.4 Payer spread 1×2

A 1×2 payer spread reduces the costs of protection while preserving the protection for an immediate and pronounced spread widening. However, the investor is exposed to losses from a severe widening beyond the point of protection, which will add to losses from an underlying credit portfolio when the options are used as an overlay. Therefore, the strategy is less suitable for a shock event–driven collapse in the prices of risky assets; but it may be appropriate for hedging out the risk of an adverse development of credit spreads in the foreseeable future.

9.2.3.5 Long butterfly

There are several ways to construct a butterfly. We use four payer options, buying one ATM, selling two OTMs, and buying one OTM with a higher strike than that of the payer sold. In any case, a butterfly always consists of as many options bought as options sold. The result is a profit triangle which benefits from a moderate-spread widening, while the more severe the market conditions become, the less profit remains. Finally, in an extreme event, where spreads widen massively, the value of the butterfly at expiration date becomes a flat line resulting from the sum of premiums received net of premiums paid, which is slightly negative. Again, the strategy offers cheap protection for spread volatility and uncertainty, through it does not perfectly fit tail risks, where spreads blow out. The net premium is determined by the selection of the strikes: the most expensive costs of the ATM payer bought must be compensated by the two payers

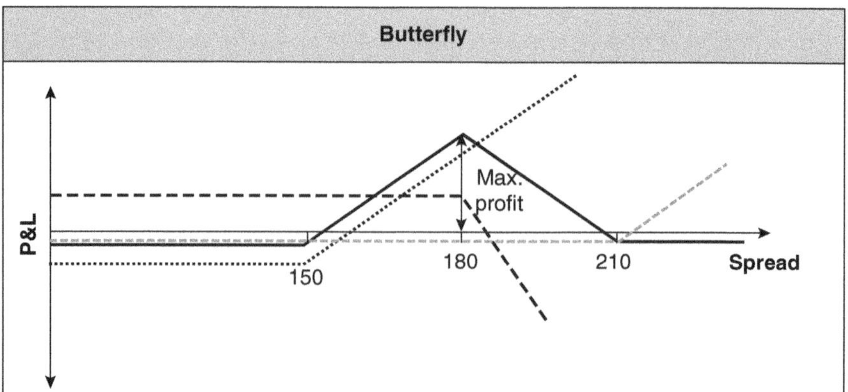

Strategy:	Target:	P&L:
Buy 1 index 3-month 150 bps payer Sell 2 index 3-month 180 bps payer Buy 1 index 3-month 210 bps payer	Range-bound credit deterioration protection	Max loss: Premium Max profit: Limited

Figure 9.9 CDS swaption butterfly

sold, since the costs for OTM payer bought with a high strike are comparably low. Different strikes can also be used to modify the profit triangle. For example, adding low-cost OTM payers extends the range in which the strategy is in the money. The flexibility to shape the payoff profile to match the view on credit spreads by choosing corresponding strikes makes the butterfly a popular instrument for portfolio managers.

9.2.4 Option Greeks

Managing option positions makes use of some key metrics, often called the Greeks, to evaluate risks. The most common measures are the Delta, Gamma, Vega, and Theta.

Delta (δ). The delta denotes the ratio of the change in the value of the option to that of the underlying index. A positive delta indicates that the value of the option increases when the spread of the underlying widens. In general, the delta ranges from 90 per cent for deep ITM payers to 50 per cent for ATM payers and 30 per cent for OTM payers, depending on the spread of the underlying. Shorter maturities exhibit a lower delta of OTM

Table 9.4 Change in market value of swaptions for a widening in the spread of the option underlying

	Payer		Receiver	
	Long	**Short**	**Long**	**Short**
Spread of the underlying (spot) ▲	▲	▼	▼	▲

Table 9.5 Change in market value of swaptions for an increase in volatility of the underlying spread

	Payer		Receiver	
	Long	**Short**	**Long**	**Short**
Volatility ▲	▲	▲	▼	▼

Table 9.6 Change in market value of swaptions for a decrease in the residual time to expiry of the swaption

	Payer		Receiver	
	Long	**Short**	**Long**	**Short**
Residual time to expiry ▼	▼	▼	▲	▲

options compared to longer maturities. Delta hedging describes the replication of an option by the corresponding delta amount of the underlying in a continuous process.

Gamma (γ). The gamma, also called 'spread convexity', describes the rate of change in the option delta for a change of 1 bps in the curve of the underlying index. Buying a receiver exposes the investor to positive gamma, meaning that when the spread of the underlying tightens, the delta of the option becomes more negative. Option gamma decreases with rising volatility. Short-dated ATM options trade with the highest gamma.

Vega.[7] The vega expresses the change in the option value induced by a 1 per cent change in volatility. Vega falls when volatility decreases; the longer dated the option, the more pronounced the effect. The sensitivity of an option to volatility can be a key driver of the option profit and loss.

Theta (θ). The theta of an option denotes the time value or time decay by changing the option value for a 1-day-shorter remaining lifetime. The theta decreases significantly for short-dated options which run out-of-the-money as the probability for a jump in spreads large enough to bring the option back into the money diminishes. Options with high gamma also exhibit high theta.

9.2.5 Conclusion

A major disadvantage of tail-risk hedges, and particularly CDS options, is the fact that in large systemic crises, the liquidity of less well-known and non-plain-vanilla instruments falters. This in turn increases transaction costs to the detriment of gains from hedging positions being realized. Worse, in some cases it might be difficult or impossible to close larger hedges because of traders' unwillingness to enter into deals which cannot be neutralized immediately in the market, leaving them exposed to significant mark-to-market risk from sudden market moves. Additionally, in times of stress, the internal limits banks apply for these mark-to-markets risks are scaled back as a measure of caution. Furthermore, increased market volatility leads to a rise in the internally calculated VaR with a rising limit consumption for existing trades, leaving less or sometimes no room for traders to add new positions without breaching limits. Even when a portfolio manager correctly anticipates credit negative events, there is no assurance that the positions meant to protect against such events can be monetized accordingly. Default swaptions have emerged post-crisis as a

[7] Vega is not a Greek letter. It is often referred to as lambda (λ) or kappa (κ). Sigma (σ) denotes the standard deviation, which is replaced by volatility to value swaptions.

popular and comparably liquid instrument. Hence, they serve well for hedging credit market risk for a shorter period of time. However, the short expiration dates (typically 3–6 months) do not allow for a medium- to long-term view, which is more relevant for the credit risk of a portfolio. Since option values are determined by a variety of factors, including volatility, a precise and complete formulation of the hedge scenario is a prerequisite for a tailorized option overlay strategy that creates the intended cash-flow profile.

9.3 Cross-asset hedging strategies

Portfolio managers apply macro or correlation hedges when perfect hedges of sufficient size and liquidity are not available or where regulatory or other restrictions prevent a direct hedge. For instance, the large ticket loan hedging of weaker corporates by their core banks can create a misperception within the financial community: it might assume that those banks have better information due to their closeness to the customer, and therefore access to more timely and better (inside) information. In that case, a portfolio manager may want to consider other approaches in order to avoid sending misleading signals to the market, even though they represent only a second-best alternative to a perfect hedge. A perfect credit risk hedge denotes an instrument such as a CDS, guarantee, or subparticipation that provides full protection for losses arising from a default of the borrower of the hedged underlying. By contrast, an imperfect hedge exhibits a close but not full correlation in the valuation of the hedge and the hedged item, meaning that credit losses from the portfolio will be compensated to a large extent but not completely. The degree of mismatch between macro hedge and debt security (the basis risk) acceptable to the risk manager clearly depends on the alternatives at hand.

9.3.1 Selection criteria for macro hedges

When engaging in macro hedges, assessing the following criteria can help develop optimal hedge strategies:

- *correlation*: closeness of hedge to hedged item, the maximum variance, the basis risk or hedge error
- *hedge ratio stability*: steadiness of the correlation over time, in particular under stress
- *hedge instrument*: in some cases a portfolio manager might identify a closely correlated security but be prevented from buying protection on it in whatever form. For example, some portfolio management units

are not allowed to engage in stock or index options or to go outright short stocks or bonds.
- *liquidity*: the correlation hedge must trade in decent liquidity to avoid getting stuck with the hedge position when trying to monetize the gains which should compensate for losses on the hedged item.
- *protection costs*: even though a reasonable correlation hedge may be available, its costs must be acceptable and below the expected loss from the hedged underlying. Hedge costs include the running costs, which can be seen as an insurance premium, and transaction costs – that is, bid/offer.

Correlation hedges are useful both on the single name and the portfolio level. For example, some hedge funds run a debt/equity or capital structure arbitrage, where they explore the relative value or cheapness of a firm's debt to equity, and then go long on the debt and short equity, or vice versa, depending on the result of the analysis. For a credit portfolio of European multinational or large corporates, the iTraxx European index, composed of 125 investment-grade names, may serve as a good proxy for hedging purposes because of its presumably high correlation.

9.3.2 Isolating sovereign risk

Macro hedges also make it possible to hedge isolated risks out of a portfolio. Buying protection on Spain sovereign CDSs will mitigate spread and credit risks for firms associated with Spain because of the location of their domicile or due to their economic dependence on the country. The inherent sovereign risk premium is currently observable within most Spanish, Portuguese, and Italian corporates, and even more so for domestic financial institutions. A portfolio manager who wants to hedge out country risk but is prohibited from buying Spain sovereign CDSs by EU regulations[8] may consider buying put options on the Spanish stock index instead. An analysis of the trends of Spain's stock index, IBEX, and five-year CDSs for Spain since 2010, when the sovereign crisis began to dominate the headlines, exhibits a close correlation.

Surprisingly, the correlation is more pronounced than those of Spain sovereign CDSs to the relative performance of IBEX versus the broader European stock market index, Euro Stoxx 50. Hence, credit market participants take the absolute development of the stocks of the largest listed corporates within the equity index of a country as a better approximation for the country's

[8] See Regulation (EU) No. 236/2012 of the European Parliament and of the Council of March 14, 2012, on short selling and certain aspects of credit default swaps.

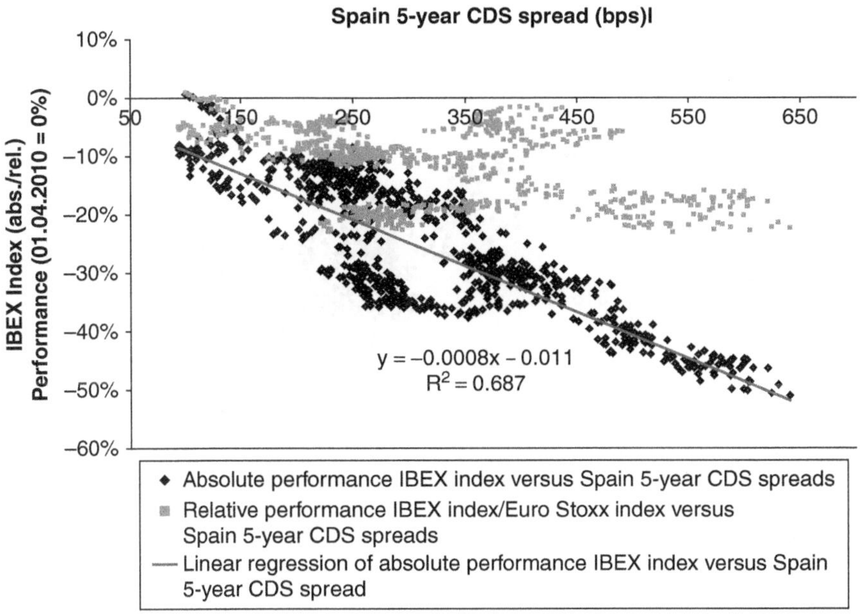

Figure 9.10 Spain five-year CDS spreads versus IBEX performance (2010–12)
Data source: Bloomberg.

sovereign risk than the out- or underperformance of those stocks compared to a broader and regionally more diversified index such as Euro Stoxx 50.

9.3.3 Equity versus debt hedge

The connectivity of equity and debt, which is the foundation of the Merton theory that is applied by risk managers to measure credit risk, also offers cross-asset hedging opportunities. The Merton asset value, or structural credit risk, model – originally proposed by Black and Scholes in their 1973[9] paper on option pricing and discussed in more detail by Merton in 1974[10] – was already anticipated in 1970.[11] In simplified terms, the model assumes that a firm will default on its debt if the value of the firm's assets at the time the debt matures is lower than the value of the debt repayment. Thus, the formula is similar to the payoff of a call option on the firm's value, with the stockholders as buyers of the call option who will not exercise the option or walk away from the company if the value of the firm is below the debt value, which therefore serves as the option strike. In that case, bondholders

[9] See Black and Scholes (1973).
[10] See Merton (1974).
[11] See Merton (1970).

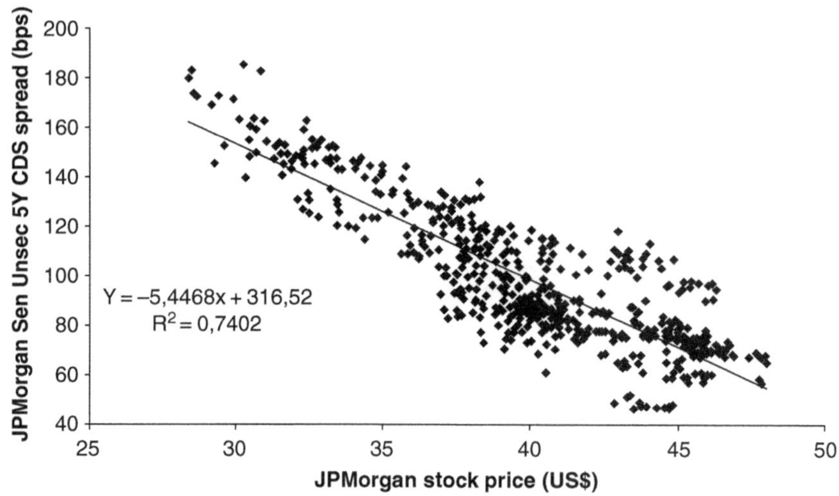

Figure 9.11 JPMorgan stock price versus CDS spread
Data source: Bloomberg.

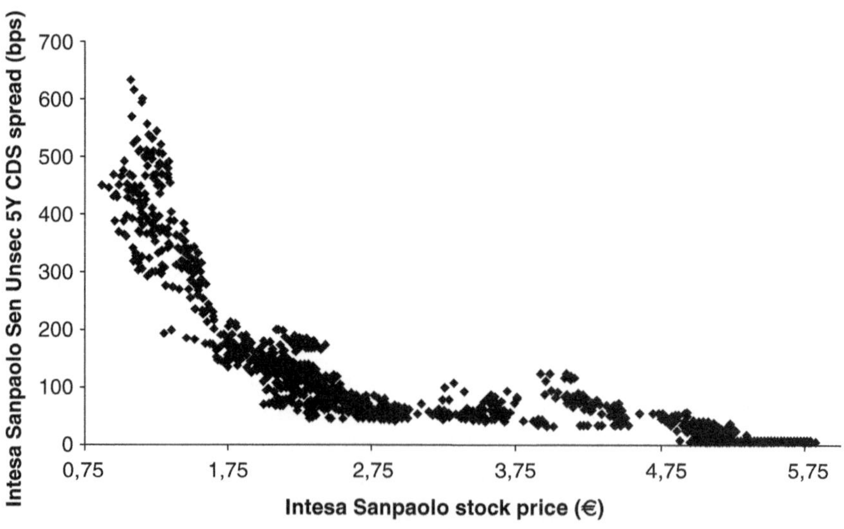

Figure 9.12 Intesa Sanpaolo stock price versus CDS spread
Data source: Bloomberg.

will receive the remaining asset values of the corporation while stockholders receive nothing. Economically, the probability of default is precisely equal to the probability that of the equity holders' call option will expire worthless; that is, out-of-the-money or below the strike level.

Even though there are some shortcomings in the model – for example, reliance on the Black-Scholes approach, to which corporate debt assumptions do not fit well, and the overly simplistic assumption of a one-year zero bond as the only financing source for a firm – Merton's approach is widely accepted by financial market participants. Its use has been promoted by KMV, which started as a service provider for credit quality assessments that are non-judgmental and based purely on market information and prices, and is now owned by the rating agency Moody's. For credit risk managers, the debt-equity relationship, which becomes visible through the correlation of stock prices to bond prices and CDS spreads, allows hedging of credit risk through the purchase of put options on the borrower's stock or by going short on the stock outright. This view is supported by an analysis performed by Domian and Reichenstein (2007), who found that high-yield bonds are sensitive to both high-grade bond returns and stock returns, with the stock component increasing when the rating deteriorates.

For example, the connectivity of the U.S. bank JPMorgan's share price to its five-year senior unsecured CDS spread shows a determination coefficient or R^2 of 0.74. The Merton model determines by how many standard deviations the call option is in-the-money; the smaller the value, the closer the firm's distance to default or the higher the likelihood of a default. The relationship between stock prices and debt risk premium takes the shape of a hockey stick for those firms where a significant decrease of the stock price reflects concerns regarding the sustainability of the business model.

Given the close relationship of debt and equity and concerns about negative feedback loops where rising CDS spreads were suspected of driving down stock prices of a firm and vice versa, as well as substantial losses of market value of financial institutions, has led to a ban of shorts on some bank stocks in the aftermath of the financial crisis. Since the CDS spread is of fundamental importance to any corporate, as it determines at least partly its funding costs, a reverse engineering of the Merton model reveals the recapitalization requirement needed to increase the distance to default for those names that trade at higher spread levels.

9.3.4 Conclusion

The hedge strategy based on equity indices or stocks appears to be a valid alternative and may also be cost efficient, since those options are more liquid and often trade at lower transaction costs than CDSs. However, macro hedges in general do not offer direct compensation for losses from a borrower's default. Therefore, any such strategy aims at covering potential losses from changes in the market valuation of the hedged item or spread risk rather than default risk. In case of higher basis risks or when the hedged item is not measured at fair value, significant profit and loss volatility can be introduced. Moreover, regulators do not accept macro hedges for capital relief purposes even though these strategies may be effective at mitigating risks within a credit portfolio and thus optimize economic capital.

References

Abberger, K and W. Nierhaus (2010), 'The Ifo Business Cycle Clock: Circular Correlation with the Real GDP', CESIFO Working Paper No. 3179.

Avdjiev, Stefan, Jacob Gyntelberg and Christian Upper (2009), 'Highlights of International Banking and Financial Market Activity'. *BIS Quarterly Review*, December.

Bain and Company (2012), *Managing Risk and Capital*. www.bain.com.

Banks, Erik, Morton Glantz, and Paul Siegel (2007), *Credit Derivatives. Techniques to Manage Credit Risk for Financial Professionals*. McGraw-Hill.

Banks, Erik and Paul Siegel (2007), *The Options Applications Handbook. Hedging and Speculating Techniques for Professional Investors*. McGraw-Hill.

Banks, Erik (2011), *See No Evil*. Palgrave MacMillan.

Basel Committee on Banking Supervision (BCBS) (1988), *International Convergence of Capital Measurement and Capital Standards*. www.bis.org.

Basel Committee on Banking Supervision (BCBS) (2000), *Principles for the Management of Credit Risk*. www.bis.org.

Basel Committee on Banking Supervision (BCBS) (2001), *The New Basel Capital Accord*. www.bis.org.

Basel Committee on Banking Supervision (BCBS) (2006a), *International Convergence of Capital Measurement and Capital Standards: A Revised Framework. Comprehensive Version*. www.bis.org.

Basel Committee on Banking Supervision (BCBS) (2006), *Studies on Credit Risk Concentration*. Working Paper No. 15. www.bis.org.

Basel Committee on Banking Supervision (BCBS) (2009), *Principles for Sound Stress Testing Practices and Supervision*. www.bis.org.

Basel Committee on Banking Supervision (BCBS) (2010), *Principles for Enhancing Corporate Governance*. www.bis.org.

Basel Committee on Banking Supervision (BCBS) (2011), *Basel III: A Global Regulatory Framework for More Resilient Banks and Banking Systems*. www.bis.org.

Basel Committee on Banking Supervision (BCBS) (2011b), *High Cost Credit Protection*. www.bis.org.

Becker, Axel (2008), *Kreditreporting und Kreditrisikostrategie*. Erich Schmidt Verlag GmbH & Co., Berlin.

Beinstein, Eric (2003), *Corporate Bonds and Credit Default Swaps. A Simple and Robust Method to Compare Bonds to CDS*. J.P. Morgan, Credit Derivatives Research.

Beinstein, Eric and Andrew Scott (2006), *Credit Derivatives Handbook. Detailing Credit Default Swap Products, Markets and Trading Strategies*. J.P. Morgan, Corporate Quantitative Research.

Black, Fischer and Myron S. Scholes (1973), 'The Pricing of Options and Corporate Liabilities'. *Journal of Political Economy*, 81.

Bohn, Jeffrey R. and Roger M. Stein (2009), *Active Credit Portfolio Management in Practice*. Wiley Finance.

Bohn, Jeffrey R. and Roger M. Stein (2011), 'Some Observations on Improving a Bank's Share Value with Credit Portfolio Management, Credit-Transfer Pricing and Stress Testing'. Draft.

Bonti, Gabriel, Michael Kalkbrener, Christopher Lotz, and Gerhard Stahl (2006), 'Credit Risk Concentrations under Stress'. *Journal of Credit Risk*, Volume 2, No. 3. 115–136.

Böve, Rolf, Klaus Düllmann, and Andreas Pfingsten (2010), 'Do Specialization Benefits Outweigh Concentration Risks in Credit Portfolios of German Banks?' Deutsche Bundesbank, Discussion Paper, Series 2: *Banking and Financial Studies*. No 10/2010.

Brigo, Damiano and Naoufel El-Bachir (2010), 'An Exact Formula for Default Swaptions' Pricing in the SSRJD Stochstic Intensity Model'. *Mathematical Finance*, Volume 20, No. 3. 365–382, July 2010.

Bruyere, Richard, Rama Cont, Régis Copinot, Fery Loic, Chrisophe Jaeck, and Thomas Spitz (2006), *Credit Derivatives and Structured Credit. A Guide for Investors*. Wiley Finance, Chichester, England.

Burmeister, Christian (2009), 'Credit Portfolio Management: Accounting Implications'. In *The Handbook of Credit Portfolio Management*, McGraw-Hill.

Cappiello, Lorenzo, Arjan Kadareja, Christoffer Kok Sorensen, and Marco Protopapa (2010), *Do bank loans and credit standards have an effect on output?*. European Central Bank, Working Paper Series No. 1150/ January 2010.

Committee of European Banking Supervisors (2006a), *Guidelines on the Application of the Supervisory Review Process under Pillar 2 (CP03 revised)*. http://www.eba.europa.eu

Committee of European Banking Supervisors (2006b), *Technical Aspects of the Management of Concentration Risk under the Supervisory Review Process – CP 11–2*nd *Part*. http://www.eba.europa.eu

Committee of European Banking Supervisors (2009), *Guidelines of the Implementation of the Revised Large Exposure Regime*. http://www.eba.europa.eu

Committee of European Banking Supervisors (2010a), *CEBS Guidelines on the Management of Concentration Risk under the Supervisory Review Process (GL31)*. http://www.eba.europa.eu

Committee of European Banking Supervisors (2010b), *CEBS Guidelines on Stress Testing (GL32)*. http://www.eba.europa.eu

DeYoung, Robert, Dennis Glennon, Dennis and Peter Nigro (2006) *Borrower-Lender Distance, Credit Scoring, and the Performance of Small Business Loans*, FDIC Center for Financial Research Working Paper No. 2006–04.

Doctor, Saul, Abel Elizalde, and Harpret Singh (2010), *CDS v2.0. The New Architecture of the CDS Market*. J.P.Morgan, Europe Credit Research.

Doctor, Saul, Abel Elizalde, Harpret Singh and Danny White (2011), *Restructuring Credit Events. Case Studies of Restructuring and the Impact on CDS*. J.P.Morgan, Europe Credit Research.

Domian, Dale L. and William Reichenstein (2008), 'Returns-Based Style Analysis of High-Yield Bonds'. *The Journal of Fixed Income* Volume 17, No. 4, Spring 2008.

Du, Songzi, Haoxiang Zhu (2011), 'Are CDS Auctions Biased?' Working paper, Stanford University GBS.

Duffie, D. and K. Singleton (2003), *Credit Risk: Pricing, Measurement, and Management*. Princeton University Press, Princeton, New Yersey.

European Central Bank (2009), *Credit Default Swaps and Counterparty Risk*. www.ecb.int.

European Commission (2011), Commission Staff Working Paper: *European Financial Stability and Integration Report 2010*, May 2011.

Felsenheimer, Jochen, and Philip Gisdakis(2008), *Credit Crises. From Tainted Loans to a Global Economic Meltdown*. Wiley Finance.

Financial Services Authority Board Report (FSA) (2011), *The Failure of the Royal Bank of Scotland*. www.fsa.gov.uk.

Foux, Mikhail and Ratul Roy (2008), *LCDS – A Step in the Right Direction*. Citi Corporate Bond Strategy, High Grade Strategy Notes.

Gann, Philipp and Bernd Hofmann (2005) 'Die Bedeutung des Kreditrisikohandels für spezialisierte Kreditinstitute'. In *Österreichisches Bankarchiv*, 53. Jg., Nr. 7, S. 473–482

Gann, Philipp (2008), *Der Internal Capital Adequacy Assessment Process als regulatorischer Treiber eines aktiven Kreditportfoliomanagements*. Münchener Wirtschaftswissenschaftliche Beiträge (BWL) 2008–2011.

Gann, Philipp (2009), *Liquidität, Risikoeinstellung des Kapitalmarktes und Konjunkturerwartung als Preisdeterminanten von Collateralized Debt Obligations (CDOs) – Eine simulationsgestützte Analyse*. Münchener Wirtschaftswissen schaftliche Beiträge (BWL) 2009–2018.

Gann, Philipp (2010), *Der marktphasenabhängige Einfluss der Liquidität auf die Credit Spreads von Corporate Bonds*. Münchener Wirtschaftswissenschaftliche Beiträge (BWL) 2010–2017.

Gürtler, Marc, Martin Hibbeln, and Clemens Vöhringer (2009), *Measuring Concentration Risk for Regulatory Purposes*.

Haworth, Helen (2011), *A Guide to Credit Events and Auctions*. Credit Suisse, Fixed Income Research.

IMF (2010), *IMF Staff Comments on EU Commission Consultation on Short Selling*. www.imf.org.

IMF (2013), 2013 Global Financial Stability Report. www.imf.org

Institute of International Finance (2009), *Risk Culture. Reform of the Financial Services Industry: Strengthening Practices for a More Stable System*. December 2009. www.iif.com.

International Association of Credit Portfolio Managers (2005), *Sound Practices of Credit Portfolio Management*.

Jersey, Ira, Alex Makedon, and David Lee, (2007), *Credit Derivatives Handbook*. Credit Suisse, Fixed Income Research.

Levy, Cindy, Eric Lamarre, and James Twining (2010), 'Taking Control of Organizational Risk Culture'. *McKinsey Working Papers on Risk*, No. 16. February.

Mahadevan, Sivan, Ashley Musfeldt, and Phanikirian Naraparaju (2012), *Credit Derivatives Insights. Handbook of Credit Derivatives and Structured Credit Strategies*. Sixth Edition. Morgan Stanley Research.

McKinsey and Company (2009), *Shaping the Future of CPM: A Workshop Discussion*. Discussion document for the IACPM 2009 Fall Annual Meeting.

Merton, Robert C. (1974), 'On the Pricing of Corporate Debt: The Risk Structure of Interest Rates'. *Journal of Finance*, 29.

Merton, Robert C. (1970), *A Dynamic General Equilibrium Model of the Asset Market and Its Application to the Pricing of the Capital Structure of the Firm*. Unpublished manuscript. Available in Merton, Robert C. (1990), Continuous-Time Finance.

Moody's Analytics (2011), *2011 Stress Testing Progress Survey*. Preliminary highlevel findings.

Musfeldt, Ashley, Sivan Mahadevan, Sivan, Vishwas Patkar, and Phanikirian Naraparaju (2012), *Credit Derivatives Insights. What Happens in a Default?* Morgan Stanley Research.

Oltmanns, E. (2009), *Das Bruttoinlandsprodukt im Konjunkturzyklus*, Wirtschaft und Statistik 10/2009, 963–969.

Oricchio, Gianluca (2011): *Credit Treasury. A Credit Pricing Guide in Liquid and Non-Liquid Markets*. Palgrave Macmillan.

Polleit, Thorsten and Jonathan Mariano (2011), 'Credit Default Swaps from the Viewpoint of Libertarian Property Rights and Contract Credit Default Swaps Theory.' *Libertarian Papers* 3, No. 32.

PricewaterhouseCoopers (1999), *Active Credit Portfolio Risk Management*.

Rudolph, Bernd (2009), *Die internationale Finanzkrise: Ursachen, Treiber, Veränderungsbedarf und Reformansätze*. Münchener Wirtschaftswissenschaftliche Beiträge (BWL) 2009–2010.

Rudolph, Bernd and Julia Scholz (2007), *Pooling und Tranching im Rahmen von ABS-Transaktionen*. Münchener Wirtschaftswissenschaftliche Beiträge (BWL) 2007–4.

Rutkowski, Marek and Anthony Armstrong (2009), 'Valuation of Credit Default Swaptions and Credit Default Index Swaptions'. *International Journal of Theoretical and Applied Finance*, 12.

Sachs, Angelika (2010), 'Completeness, Interconnectedness and Distribution of Interbank Exposures: A Parameterized Analysis of the Stability of Financial Networks'. Deutsche Bundesbank, Discussion Paper. Series 2: *Banking and Financial Studies* No 08/2010.

Schmidt, Wolfgang M. (2007), 'Default Swaps and Hedging Credit Baskets'. Working Paper.

Scholz, Julia (2009), 'Collateralized Debt Obligations: Anreizprobleme im Rahmen des Managements von CDOs'. *Münchener Wirtschaftswissenschaftliche Beiträge* (BWL) 2009–15.

Schubert, Dirk (2009), 'Credit Solution'. In *Risk Magazine*, February 2009.

Schubert, Dirk (2010), 'The Risks of Tailoring Credit Default Swaps'. In *Risk Magazine*, June 2010.

Schubert, Dirk (2011a), 'Die Gestaltung eines CDS-Vertrages als Finanzgarantie – Anforderungen der ISDA und des IASB'. In Die *Wirtschaftsprüfung*, May 2011.

Schubert, Dirk (2011b), *The Financial Economics of Hedge Accounting of Interest Rate Risk According to IAS 39*.

Schuh, Dirk Wilhelm (2009), *Finanzmarktkrise: Chancen für das Risikomanagement*. Präsentation im Rahmen des Arbeitskreises 'Strategieentwicklung und Controlling in Banken' der Schmalenbach-Gesellschaft am 20.

Schwarz, Christian, Tom Gibney, Tom, Helen Haworth, Somaia Chiraag and Ali Atif (2010), *European Credit Views: Crossing Barriers*. Credit Suisse, Fixed Income Research.

Standard and Poors (2011a), *Why Basel III and Solvency II Will Hurt Corporate Borrowing in Europe More Than in the U.S.* September 27, 2011.

Standard and Poors (2011b), *Banks: Rating Methodology and Assumptions*. November 9, 2011.

Tschirhart, John, James O'Brian, Michael Moise, Michael and Emily Yang (2007), *Bank Commercial Loan Fair Value Practices*. Finance and Economics Discussion Series, Federal Reserve Board, Washington, D.C. www.federalreserve.gov.

Tolk, Jeffrey S. (2001), *Understanding the Risks in Credit Default Swaps*. Moody's, Structured Finance Special Report.

Towers Perrin (2010), *Risk Appetite. The Foundation of Enterprise Risk Management*. www.towersperrin.com.

Vause, Nicolas (2011), *Enhanced BIS Statistics on Credit Risk Transfer*. www.bis.org.

Zhiyong, Chen and Paul Glasserman (2006), 'Fast Pricing of Basket Default Swaps'. Working paper.

Index

Printed and bound by CPI Group (UK) Ltd, Croydon, CR0 4YY